'*Sowing Seeds* is an invaluable blend of Sharon Moughtin's reflective practice and contemporary thinking about childhood spirituality. The result is an exceptional and inspiring resource for churches working with the very youngest children. A powerful case for seeing why the very young deserve the very best, and this is a well-tested method for doing that.'

*Dr Rebecca Nye, Godly Play ex*_____ *n's spirituality*

'I'm excited by *Sowing Seeds*! It's a celebration of Psalm 8.2 and all _____ ip. Movement, stories, actions and songs combine in carefully craftec _____ y of worshipping that will enrich everyone involved. I can't wait to star _____

*The Revd Mary Hawes, former N*_____ *ch of England*

'Sowing Seeds is being taken up enthusiastically by a growing number of parishes in the Diocese of Southwark. Helping young children grow into the fullness of Christ through creative, age-appropriate engagement is a wonderful journey of adventure and discovery; and this book, which I gladly commend, will be an essential resource for anyone starting out on that path.'

The Rt Revd Christopher Chessun, Bishop of Southwark

'We've loved using the Sowing Seeds material at St Albans Cathedral for our babies and young children as part of our worship on Sunday mornings. The modular format makes it easy to adapt for different ages or lengths of time, and the children really respond to the familiarity of the structure, the singing and interactive storytelling, and the repetition. We've seen steady growth in the number of families who come regularly on Sundays, and the parents are often less ready to move on from this resource than their children! Having such clear material has been great for our volunteer leaders, and we particularly love the fact that even our smallest babies and toddlers can participate in worship, rather than just being in a crèche.'

Beccy Baird, children's worship leader, St Albans Cathedral

'Our young children love joining in with the simple songs and actions, and before we know it they (and I) have a real understanding of the church liturgy. The resources give all types of children a chance to engage in a variety of activities: the chatty ones can sing, the active ones can move, the creative ones can get arty but the highlight of the week is always "What's in the Box?"

'I love preparing as it is all done for me – I just pick up the book and off I go. If I can't remember a tune, I either hum it and it comes back to me or one of the children sings it for me, as they all know the nursery-rhyme tunes. The crafts are all very basic and the children seem to like to be able to "make it their own". Before using this resource I used to spend hours preparing complicated crafts that took the children two minutes to complete, leaving them bored and me frazzled!!'

Charlotte Chappell, Christ Church Aughton, Liverpool

'The *Sowing Seeds* resource has become a crucial part of our worship at Sheffield Cathedral. The careful attention Sharon Moughtin has paid to immersing our very youngest members in the changing seasons and the liturgical rhythm of the Eucharist makes it the perfect resource for our context. Hearing the voices of children and encouraging them as they grow and develop as disciples is absolutely key for us, and it is a very great delight to hear them sing and praise using the Sowing Seeds materials with such joy. Seeing our very youngest members stride into the Cathedral, own the space and join in worship with so much confidence is in a very large part down to this thoughtful and imaginative resource.'

The Very Revd Abi Thompson, Dean of Sheffield Cathedral

'*Sowing Seeds* is an invaluable resource that we use in school to support our collective worship and Religious Education curriculum with the youngest of pupils. It helpfully provides some background knowledge of theological concepts and Bible stories to support the staff leading the sessions. I would highly recommend this to schools as it is unlike any other resource we have found.'

Kate Penfold-Attride, Headteacher, St Matthew's Church of England Primary School, Redhill

'*Sowing Seeds* is a gift to the church. Sharon Moughtin manages to combine sharp biblical insight, creative use of the liturgy, the immersive experience of storytelling, and a great deal of fun in a single resource. What you have here is a way to engage the children in your church, school or home with robust biblical scholarship, the lessons liturgy teaches without words, and an experience of worshipping God in community. Just be warned: you'll be humming the Sowing Seeds songs all week long.'

The Revd Dr Casey Strine, Theological Adviser to the House of Bishops and Secretary for Theology

'I warmly commend *Sowing Seeds*. A church which uses *Sowing Seeds* consistently over time will see its work with children, young people and families transformed. Everything you need is in the book. Commit your hopes to God and let the Lord work with you in sowing seeds.'

The Rt Revd Jane Steen, Bishop of Lynn

'*Sowing Seeds* is a game changer for any church wanting to engage with younger children. This is seriously impressive biblical theology presented in an engaging, fun and accessible way. My own children love it.'

The Revd Michael Robinson, Rector, Holy Trinity, Sloane Square

'Wonderful! We have here a handling of Christian worship and the Bible that embodies a rich and creative imaginative seriousness, a sure understanding of theology and an experienced appreciation of the practicalities of working with young children. I haven't come across anything else nearly as good as this.'

The Revd Professor Walter Moberly, Durham University

'We all think we know that biblical scholarship and Sunday School teaching belong in different worlds. *Sowing Seeds* shows that we are wrong. Sharon Moughtin brings the wisdom of a professional biblical scholar to the task of communicating the essence of the Bible to very young children, unveiling the depths of biblical stories for young disciples. Very user-friendly material from which adults can learn too.'

The Revd John Barton, Emeritus Professor, University of Oxford

'When Jesus taught, he often used a language that was unafraid to hover rather than land. Through imaginative and playful provocation, he was opening up spaces for his listeners to move into. This is exactly what *Diddy Disciples* (now *Sowing Seeds*) does. It takes for granted the fact that young children are intelligent and perceptive, and it therefore doesn't look down on them. Neither does it pretend that Christian faith is anything but a rich, complex and teasing migration towards the love and mystery of God, where questions can be as vital as insights. This is a liberating combination for everyone involved.'

The Very Revd Dr Mark Oakley, Dean of Southwark Cathedral

'This resource approaches worship and storytelling with reverence and joy! Children and leaders alike will learn from the liturgical intelligence, sensitivity and natural language of Sharon Moughtin's approach. An inspirational resource for all on the way of discipleship, including special attention to the new texts for baptism.'

Dr Matthew Salisbury, National Liturgy and Worship, Church of England

'This is a flexible resource that acknowledges the importance and significance of enabling the youngest at church to engage in worship and begin a faith journey. The book not only offers ideas for a range of different settings and of personality and learning styles, but is also clearly built upon a theological and developmental understanding of children and faith. This is a resource that we will be using within our church setting, as we seek to engage and empower children from the youngest age in their understanding of God, faith, themselves and the world.'

Steve Chalke, founder and leader, Oasis Global

'Even though Jesus makes it clear that entering the kingdom of God requires us to become like children, real children are often neglected in the catechetical and formational life of the Church. *Diddy Disciples* (now *Sowing Seeds*) puts that right! Here is a resource to help the children come to Jesus and grow as his disciples.'

The Most Revd and Rt Hon. Stephen Cottrell, Archbishop of York

'This resource is aimed at pedagogy for children, but the author is mindful of Jesus' words, and what she has written is just as relevant for adult education and pedagogy as well. Sharon Moughtin's book stresses that education is "not words alone", and that doesn't just apply to children. What she has produced gives due attention to what it is one is wanting to communicate. What she has given us is based on the importance of movement, repetition, attending to children's own voices and emotions, nurturing what's already there and offering children a space in church that is dedicated to their needs and gifts. We are all in her debt for this insightful mixture of information and method.'

The Revd Professor Christopher Rowland, Emeritus Professor of Exegesis of Holy Scripture, University of Oxford

'Sharon Moughtin has accomplished something marvellously fresh, profound and practical with *Diddy Disciples* (now *Sowing Seeds*). There is a depth of biblical and liturgical understanding here which sets this resource apart, yet that understanding consistently serves the most kinetic and straight-out joyful set of Christian materials for children that one could hope to encounter. The rich array of options on offer within each unit and section means that it is all superbly flexible and adaptable for churches of different sizes, shapes and settings. I cannot recommend it highly enough.'

The Revd Dr David Hilborn, Principal, St John's College, Nottingham

The Revd Dr Sharon Moughtin is the author of Sowing Seeds, which began when her own wriggly and chatty children were 3, 3 and 2, and going to church with them felt impossible! She is now Vicar of St Mary in the Wilderness, created by Lambeth Palace and the Diocese of Southwark (Church of England) to respond to the challenges of climate change and the biodiversity crisis. Sharon is a professional Bible scholar, previously teaching Old Testament at Ripon College Cuddesdon and now Visiting Research Fellow at King's College London. She is passionate about the Bible, the environment, education, creativity and learning how to 'be like a child' from the youngest of children.

Sowing Seeds

Book 2: Bible storytelling and worship with children

Includes Lent and Easter

Second edition

Sharon Moughtin

First published in Great Britain in 2017

SPCK Publishing
Part of the SPCK Group, Studio 101, The Record Hall, 16–16A Baldwin's Gardens, London EC1N 7RJ
https://spckpublishing.co.uk

Second edition published 2025

Text copyright © Sharon Moughtin 2017, 2025
This edition copyright © Society for Promoting Christian Knowledge 2025

Sharon Moughtin has asserted her right under the Copyright, Designs and Patents Act, 1988, to be identified as Author of this work.

All rights reserved. No part of this book may be reproduced or transmitted in any form or by any means, electronic or mechanical, including photocopying, recording, or by any information storage and retrieval system, without permission in writing from the publisher.

SPCK does not necessarily endorse the individual views contained in its publications.

The author and publisher have made every effort to ensure that the external website and email addresses included in this book are correct and up to date at the time of going to press. The author and publisher are not responsible for the content, quality or continuing accessibility of the sites.

Unless otherwise noted, Scripture quotations are taken from the New Revised Standard Version of the Bible, Anglicized Edition, copyright © 1989, 1995 by the Division of Christian Education of the National Council of the Churches of Christ in the USA. Used by permission. All rights reserved.

Quotations marked NIV are taken from The Holy Bible, New International Version (Anglicized edition). Copyright © 1979, 1984, 2011 by Biblica. Used by permission of Hodder & Stoughton Ltd, an Hachette UK company. All rights reserved.'NIV' is a registered trademark of Biblica. UK trademark number 1448790.

Every effort has been made to seek permission to use copyright material reproduced in this book. The publisher apologizes for those cases where permission might not have been sought and, if notified, will formally seek permission at the earliest opportunity.

Permission is given to photocopy the following, provided that they are for use by the purchaser's organization only and are not for resale: the Bible Storytelling material and Building Blocks, and the music resources and craft templates.

There are supporting web resources at <**www.sowingseeds-online.org**>. The password for the website is **mustard252**

EU GPSR Authorised Representative
LOGOS EUROPE, 9 rue Nicolas Poussin, 17000, La Rochelle, France
Email: Contact@logoseurope.eu

British Library Cataloguing-in-Publication Data
A catalogue record for this book is available from the British Library

ISBN 978–0–281–09091–4
eBook ISBN 978–0–281–09092–1

10 9 8 7 6 5 4 3 2 1

Designed by Melissa Brunelli
Typeset by Fakenham Prepress Solutions, Fakenham, Norfolk NR21 8NL
Printed and bound in Great Britain by Clays Ltd, Elcograf S.p.A.

eBook by Fakenham Prepress Solutions, Fakenham, Norfolk NR21 8NL

Produced on paper from sustainable sources

For Zoe, with thanks for all she brings to the world.

CONTENTS

Acknowledgements   xiii

Introduction   1

Part 1: Interactive Bible storytelling

Introduction   7

The Journey to the Cross unit (Lent)   10

The Journey to the Cross storybox   10
Jesus Gives Up Everything for Us (the Week before Lent)   11
Jesus Is Tested in the Wilderness (Matthew 4.1–11; Luke 4.1–13)   16
Jesus Enters Jerusalem (Matthew 21.1–11; Mark 11.1–10; Luke 19.28–40)   19
Jesus Cleans the Temple (Matthew 21.12–13; Luke 19.45–46)   23
    Option 1: The people in the Temple, they pray   23
    Option 2: In Jerusalem   27
Jesus Is Like a Mother Hen (Mothering Sunday, Luke 13.34–35; Matthew 23.37–39)   31
Mary Anoints Jesus (John 12.1–8)   35
Jesus Washes the Disciples' Feet (John 13.1–17)   39
    Option 1: Servant King   40
    Option 2: Washing feet   45
Jesus' Last Meal (The Last Supper, Luke 22.14–23)   50
The Story of Love: The Story of the Cross (Good Friday)   53

Jesus Is Alive! Alleluia! unit (Easter)   60

Jesus Is Alive! Alleluia! storybox   60
Jesus Is Risen! Alleluia! (John 19.40—20.1a)   61
The Women's Story (John 20.1–10)   64
The Walk to Emmaus (Luke 24.13–35)   68
The Good Shepherd   71
    Option 1: 'There was a once a flock of sheep' (John 10.11–15)   71
    Option 2: David the shepherd king (1 Samuel 17.34–36)   74
    Option 3: God's my shepherd (1 Samuel 17.34–36; Psalm 23)   77
Thomas's Story (John 20.19–29)   80
The Catch of Fishes (John 21.1–14)   85
Peter's Story (John 18.15–27; 21.15–19)   88
The Ascension   91
    Option 1: Jesus goes up! (Luke 24.42–53)   91
    Option 2: You will tell the world about me! (Acts 1.8–14)   94
Come, Holy Spirit! (The Day of Pentecost, Acts 2.1–4)   97
1, 2, 3, the Trinity! (Trinity Sunday)   102

Part 2: Bible storytelling for baby and toddler groups

Introduction   109

Basic Structure   110

The Journey to the Cross unit (Lent)   113

The Journey to the Cross songbox   113
    'I am going to follow Jesus'   113

'Jesus came riding on a donkey'	114
'Love is stronger'	114
'When the king says . . .'	115
The Sowing Seeds footwashing song	116
'Do this to remember me'	117

Jesus Is Alive! Alleluia! unit (Easter) — 118

Jesus Is Alive! Alleluia! songbox	118
'He is risen, risen, risen!'	118
'On Easter Day in the morning'	119
'Back in Galilee'	120
'The Good Shepherd'	121
'Go! And wait for the Holy Spirit!'	122
'Holy Spirit, come!'	123

Part 3: Creative Response starter ideas

Introduction — 127

The Journey to the Cross unit (Lent) — 127

Story Starter Ideas	128
Sensory Starter Ideas (including for babies and toddlers)	132
Unit Starter Ideas	133

Jesus Is Alive! Alleluia! unit (Easter) — 135

Story Starter Ideas	135
Sensory Starter Ideas (including for babies and toddlers)	140
Unit Starter Ideas	141

Part 4: The Building Blocks

Introduction — 145

The Sowing Seeds Website	145

The Building Blocks — 146

Welcome	146
Getting Ready to Worship	147
Introducing the Unit	148
Gathering Song	151
Getting Ready for Bible Storytelling	156
Interactive Bible Storytelling	157
Saying Sorry to God	157
Saying Sorry Action	160
God Gives Us a New Start	168
Prayers for Other People	170
Prayer Actions	173
Thank You, God	176
Creative Response	179
Sharing God's Peace	179
The Peace	181
Around a Table	181
Taking God's Love into the World	182
Go in Peace to Love and Serve!	183

Sowing Seeds resources

Introduction	187
Imaginative aids	187
Peace cloth	187
Focal table	188
Creative Response resources	188
Collage materials	188
Interesting media	189
Recipes	190
Photocopiable templates	191
Notes	220

ACKNOWLEDGEMENTS

Sowing Seeds would never have happened without the children who have been part of creating it along the way. Many of the words, phrases, actions, symbols and ideas in this book came from them, as well as all the illustrations for the book cover, icons and templates. Thank you, little sisters and brothers, for your energy, insights, playfulness and willingness to share your gifts.

With special thanks to the amazing illustrators: Abigail, Amelia, Anastasia, Bella, Christian, Connie, Daijuan, Darcey, Ebba, Eden, Elijah, Gavin, Grace, Harry, Isabella, Isla, Jessica, Joy, Julia, Kayleigh, Marlon, Michael, Mitchell, Mya, Nancy, Ottie, Pearl, Philip, Rita, Samson, Samuel, Susan, Susannah, Zoe and Zoe.

Thank you also to all who have walked alongside me, advised me, and contributed to Diddy Disciples and Sowing Seeds in other ways over the years. Particular thanks go to Bishop Christopher Chessun, Bishop Jane Steen, Bishop Martin Gainsborough, Betsy Blatchley, Bill McGarvey, Brother Sam SSF, Dan Trott, Eve Bradshaw, Gene Doughlin, Henrietta Hastings, John Barton, Kate Penfold-Attride, Karen Wilson, Kev Smart, Mary Hawes, Michael Robinson, Mike Smith, Niall Sloane, Odette Penwarden, Renate Tulloh, Robert Harris, Rosy Fairhurst, Ruth Martin, Sarah Dawson, Sarah Fielding, Sheridan James, Simon Gates, Sarah Smith, Sister Judi CSF, Tom Hassan, Tracey Messenger and Will Cookson.

Thank you to the children and adults of St Mary in the Wilderness and all the placement students who have passed through there.

Thank you to the team at SPCK for their guidance and experience, especially Deborah Lock and Rima Devereaux.

Thank you to my mum and dad, my sisters, Debs, Beth and Jen, and the wider Moughtin clan.

Most of all, thank you to my daughters, Joy, Ana and Zoe, for your inspiration, love and energy – without you this would never have been written.

INTRODUCTION

Sowing Seeds is a collection of Bible storytelling, prayer and worship materials especially designed for groups of children ranging from babies and toddlers to 8–9 years old. The materials aim to create a space for children to encounter God for themselves. Through movement, imagination, faces and bodies, symbols, creative activities, music and song, Sowing Seeds encourages and enables children to participate fully. Older children and young people also have the opportunity to become leaders with the easy-to-access material.

Parts 1 and 2 contain interactive Bible Storytelling materials. Part 3 has a wealth of creative responses to the storytelling, including art, craft and sensory play. Part 4 has the Building Blocks of worship resources in the form of prayers and songs.

Sowing Seeds is flexible enough to be used in a variety of settings and Christian traditions. Some groups will create a session entirely from the books. Others will find a song or story or creative idea within its pages which will contribute to an established pattern. There's no single 'right way' to use the materials! Instead, explore the books and discover the materials that most resonate with your church setting, and that will support your time with God alongside children.

As Sowing Seeds was developed, seven principles emerged which underpin the resources. It might be helpful to familiarise yourself with these as you explore the materials. It will help you understand the decisions made in their creation (and re-creation) as we learned through trial and error.

Sowing Seeds: seven principles

1 Sowing Seeds celebrates movement

Sowing Seeds celebrates body language as our first language, which we can all share. This includes babies, children who are non-verbal, and those who speak English as an additional language. The materials encourage full body actions so that everyone can join in.

Children are naturally wriggly and chatty, so Sowing Seeds celebrates that. It scoops up children's desire to move and be heard and incorporates it in worship, growing a people of God who are active, vocal and expect to be included from the very beginning.

2 Sowing Seeds celebrates our voices

In Sowing Seeds, almost everything is sung. That's because we've found that singing when worshipping with children helps in all sorts of ways.

- Singing is something we do together. It gives everyone the opportunity to feel what it's like to be part of God's family, whatever their age.

- Singing means the words of the story are not said just once, they're repeated again and again. This can help children whose attention may wander, as well as babies and toddlers, and those who speak English as an additional language. Alongside this, the song's shape, tune, rhythm, pitch and volume provide additional clues to the story's meaning.

- With singing there is no need for shushing! Wriggly and chatty children can make it difficult for others to hear if there's only one voice telling the story. But if the whole room is telling the story together and singing, a chatty child is much less likely to become a distraction and far more likely to actually join in! Singing tends to attract and keep children's attention far more easily than words alone.

- Songs and tunes tend to stay with us much longer than words alone (thanks to Mary Hawes for this insight and all her other contributions).

Through listening and swaying, moving and dancing, and joining in actions and even some of the words, even the youngest present can join in worshipping God through song. Perhaps most importantly, singing allows the Bible stories to become 'our story and our song' for the children. This is fundamental in Sowing Seeds. It's why everything is sung or said 'my turn', 'your turn'.

> ### Tip: Our story: our song
>
> In Deuteronomy 5.3–4 (NIV), Moses speaks about God's covenant to the people gathered before him. He says:
>
> It was not with **our ancestors** that the Lord made this covenant, but with **US**, with all of us who are **alive here** TODAY. The Lord spoke to YOU **face to face** out of the fire on the mountain.
>
> The words are emphatic. The point is clear. The people that Moses is talking to were there at the mountain when God made the covenant.
>
> The unexpected thing is that a closer look at the story reveals that most of the people present were not there at all. This is the next generation; it **was** their parents who were at the mountain.
>
> Moses hasn't made a mistake here. He's making a vital point about storytelling in God's family. These stories are not just their parents' stories, which happened long ago to be passed on and remembered. These stories are to become **their** story, and – as children adopted into God's family – **our** story too.
>
> Sowing Seeds takes this seriously. When we tell these stories together with children, we're not simply remembering a story that happened to someone else. It's **our** story. We **ourselves** are becoming part of the story. We find ourselves in it in all sorts of different places. And as we tell the story together, it is to **us** that God is speaking.

> ### Tip: Leading Sowing Seeds
>
> Christian philosopher Søren Kierkegaard wrote:
>
> 'People have an idea that the preacher is an actor on a stage and they are the critics, blaming or praising the preacher.'
>
> Leading worship and telling Bible stories to groups can feel like this sometimes! Thankfully, Kierkegaard continues:
>
> 'What they **don't** know is that **they** are the actors on the stage; the preacher is merely the prompter standing in the wings, reminding them of their lost lines.'[1]
>
> The good news for leaders is that this takes the pressure off. When we tell these stories with the children, the attention is not on us. The quality of our singing voice is not the point.
>
> The **children** and their adults are the actors on the stage, we leaders are simply the prompter, standing in the wings, reminding them of their lost lines – or often, in this case, the lines they haven't even been told yet. And how are they to know if no one tells them?

3 Sowing Seeds celebrates repetition: 'Again! Again!'

Finding a pattern and rhythm is key to Sowing Seeds. Choose the material that resonates best with your context, then keep to that pattern at least for a unit (4–7 sessions). This repetition gives children and their adults confidence. They know what's coming next and are therefore more likely to take part fully and maybe even take a lead, rather than having to wait or watch because they're not sure what's happening.

Sowing Seeds moves between periods of movement and (very short) periods of quieter calm. As the children become familiar with this, it becomes much easier for them to remain quiet for a short time when appropriate. A familiar pattern also takes the pressure off the person leading worship. Once you're in the rhythm, it can be liberating to know that almost all the next week's worship will be familiar to you as well as to others in the group.

4 Sowing Seeds celebrates children's spirituality

Dr Rebecca Nye's work on children's spirituality has been a very important influence on Sowing Seeds.[2] Her research (and that of many others) shows that children possess an innate sense of wonder and an innate sense of God. We do not need to introduce this sense of spirituality to children – it's already there! The challenge is how we make connections so that a child's spirituality resonates with what they see and experience when they enter a church. Sowing Seeds aims to create safe spaces, building what Rebecca Nye calls 'two-way bridges', between children's spirituality and the worship they will experience in church.

5 Sowing Seeds celebrates being part of the Church

Babies and children are full members of the worshipping community and Sowing Seeds celebrates this. By choosing from worship materials laid out in 'Building Blocks' in Part 4, alongside Bible storytelling, your group can create a service that reflects the main Sunday service of your church as closely as possible. This can help to build bridges between Sowing Seeds sessions and the other worship that takes place in your church.

The Building Blocks include plenty of opportunities for children to lead, enabling them to discover their own ministries and what they can offer. Sowing Seeds also recognizes that adults will be present during the sessions – as leaders, parents and carers – and that it's important that these adults are also fed and nourished by your time together, with opportunities to grow too.

> **Tip**
>
> If your church holds all-age or whole church services, encourage the leaders to borrow elements from Sowing Seeds which will already be familiar to the children. The Sorry Song (p. 158) and Prayers for Other People (p. 170) are among the worship elements in Building Blocks which can be incorporated into other worship services.

6 Sowing Seeds celebrates learning

Sowing Seeds seeks to grow a people of God who naturally bring their relationship with God into their home life and work, and their home life and work into their relationship with God. For this reason, the material makes multiple links with the learning that babies, toddlers and children are experiencing at home, school and nursery. There's lots of counting out loud on fingers, naming colours, noticing different kinds of weather, learning how plants grow and exploring different kinds of emotions. Well-known nursery-rhyme tunes also bring a sense of familiarity to the Bible storytelling and worship.

> **Tip: Everyday connections matter**
>
> Throughout the Bible, everyday objects and experiences are used to make connections between our daily lives and God. Jesus used the everyday of Galilee: wildflowers, bread, water, wine, wheat, sparrows, sheep, goats, vineyards. The apostle Paul focussed on the everyday experiences of people living in the Roman empire: architecture, discoveries about the human body, war, Olympic games, trading. Following their examples, Sowing Seeds helps young children make two-way connections between their everyday life and the stories of God's people.

7 Sowing Seeds celebrates our feelings and emotions

God created humans with a wide range of emotions and feelings. All human emotions are explored openly in the Bible: jealousy, rage, anger and fear are acknowledged, as well as joy, peace, love and so on. In countless passages, negative emotions are brought before God and transformed. Moses' deep anger – expressed in murderous rage – is seen by God, transformed and used to set God's people free. Peter's fear and his denial of even knowing Jesus are brought into the open and lead to a new start for Peter not only as a follower of Jesus but as a leader.

Sowing Seeds can help to create safe spaces where human emotions and feelings are named and explored together. Early childhood is a time of big emotions, that can sometimes startle young children (and their parents and carers!). Together, God's people can learn to bring all sorts of feelings before God, growing in hope and trust that even negative emotions can be transformed by God into something beautiful, holy and life-giving. Early childhood is a wonderful place to begin this way of life.

Part 1
Interactive Bible storytelling

Introduction

Sowing Seeds was originally created for babies, toddlers and young children aged around 0–7. As the children in our group grew older, however, we found that most of the material worked with children up to the age of around 9. For the few stories that didn't work, we've created a separate option. Each story now begins with an indication of the age range it has been designed for: either 0–7 or 0–9. When choosing which stories to use for your group it may be helpful to think of the age range currently represented there.

Groups that include no children above the age of two and a half may find the material in Part 2 more appropriate.

Tip: Including babies in mixed groups

For babies, Sowing Seeds represents an immersive approach to worship. They're not expected to follow and understand every word, but they're drawn into the experience that is taking place around them, encouraged to participate and lead in their own ways (which usually involves using their bodies). Being actively included from the very beginning is important in itself. As part of God's family, these babies take part in the family's activities, just as at home they spend some time in the melee of family life. By being immersed in activities that are especially designed for the first years of life – alongside children only a little older than they are – these babies are also given the opportunity to gradually develop skills that will deepen their experience over time.

Including babies can also be beneficial for parents and carers, meaning they no longer have to spend the adult sermon either 'shushing' their children or segregated into a crèche area where it can be difficult for them to feel an active part of the church. We've found that many adults themselves find Sowing Seeds worship and Bible storytelling meaningful, and are often moved by the experience of worshipping alongside – and being led by – the youngest of children.

The Building Blocks

Sowing Seeds isn't just Bible storytelling. The Building Blocks in Part 4 provide a wide range of prayer, worship and creative materials to resource and nurture your group's time with God. Once you've chosen your stories from the storyboxes in this section, take a look to see what those Building Blocks might have to offer your group. Find out more in the introduction to the Building Blocks on p. 143.

On the website there is an introduction to teaching songs for the first time, which might also sometimes come in useful for the storytelling below.

What's in the Box?

'What's in the Box?' is one of the Building Blocks that is often referred to in the storytelling material below. This option is especially helpful for groups that include babies and toddlers who might need support with some of the vocabulary in the story. Simply find a box for your group that looks inviting. Place within it the items suggested at the beginning of each story and open it with the children each time you meet to discover what's inside, asking 'What's in the box?' and inviting a child to lead the group in responding.

The 'I'm Sorry' and 'New Start' signs

The 'I'm Sorry' and 'New Start' signs that appear throughout the storytelling material are among the very few Sowing Seeds signs and actions that are fixed. Usually, the children are trusted with the responsibility for creating the actions for the songs and storytelling as the hope is that this will become *their* story and *their* song (p. 2). However, the 'I'm Sorry' and 'New Start' signs have been chosen for the resonances they create through the material. Videos of the movement for both signs can be found on the website next to the Sorry Song Building Block in any of the units.

The 'I'm Sorry' sign

The 'I'm Sorry' sign not only conveys sadness. It calls to mind the waters of baptism being splashed over us. The echoes of an 'X' shape not only show that we know that we've got something wrong, but can also call to mind at the same time the cross of Jesus in the background. Start with your hands lightly crossed in front of your forehead, then move them in opposing arcs downwards towards your chest and round in opposing circles, and back just in front of your forehead. This opposing circular motion is the 'I'm Sorry' sign.

The 'New Start' sign

The 'New Start' sign can best be described as the 'winding' action from the nursery rhyme 'Wind the bobbin up'. Repeatedly rotate your arms around each other in front of your body. It shows that we want a chance to 'start again' but it has been chosen to point us also to the rolling away of the stone on Easter Day that brings about that great 'new start' for the whole world. The 'New Start' sign appears and reappears in so many of the stories throughout the Sowing Seeds units. It's the sign for:

- Mary's song about the 'topsy turvy God who turns things upside down' (which is sung in response to John's prophetic somersault).
- 'The first will be last and the last will be first' in God's revolutionary, 'topsy turvy' kingdom.
- Jesus turning the tables 'topsy turvy' in the Temple – 'Look! Jesus is giving the Temple a new start!'.
- Jesus washing the disciples' feet, as the longed for king turns everything upside down to become the servant.
- The prayer 'Holy Spirit, come!' as Jesus' friends wait for the Spirit who will turn their lives (and the world) topsy turvy at Pentecost.
- Paul falling 'topsy turvy' off his horse when he meets Jesus and is given his 'new start'.

And more. Keep an eye out for the 'New Start' sign in the storytelling. It creates a golden thread of forgiveness and can appear in the most surprising of places!

Tip: Creative Responses

There are a wealth of suggestions for Creative Responses to the storytelling through art and sensory resources in Part 3. See p. 125 for more information and options.

Tip: Presentation folders

Presentation folders can really help when leading Sowing Seeds. They're much easier to manage than loose sheets, especially when doing actions! We've found that A5 folders are best, and the Bible storytelling has been formatted to slip easily into A5 folders.

Tip: Continuity

Sowing Seeds assumes that children won't be present every week and that new people may join or visit at any time! Units that involve an ongoing story that unfolds over a few weeks therefore tell the whole story from the beginning each week in abbreviated form, as if it hasn't been told before (a little like a recap sequence at the beginning of some TV series). This allows those who weren't there for a previous session to take full part in the storytelling, while giving those who were there the opportunity to strengthen and deepen their knowledge of the story.

Tip: Sowing Seeds and the Lectionary

Some churches use the Lectionary (a set pattern of reading followed each week in worship). It's not exactly child-friendly so, rather than follow it precisely, Sowing Seeds works in units which match the church's seasons and broader themes. This allows for the rhythm of the liturgical year to be approached in a way specially formed and shaped for young children.

The Journey to the Cross unit (Lent)

The focus of this unit is the Bible stories from the last week of Jesus' life, offering groups the opportunity to explore stories that are central to our Christian faith and relationship with Jesus. The Gospels themselves give the stories of Jesus' last week considerable importance.

For groups that follow the church seasons, it may feel strange to tell the story of Palm Sunday so close to the beginning of Lent, but the stories of Jesus' last week are so important and there are a lot of them! Palm Sunday is the day that Jesus enters Jerusalem and starts off the chain reaction of events that will inevitably lead to the cross. So it makes sense to start with Palm Sunday towards the beginning of the unit so that the group can begin to see the connections. In practice, we've found that familiarizing the children with these stories – as well as introducing them to waving palm branches and footwashing in meaningful ways through the course of Lent – gives children confidence to join in with these moments during Holy Week itself and a deeper understanding of the story unfolding around them.

The Journey to the Cross storybox

Choose from the stories according to your own context. It will be most helpful for the children if you keep them in chronological order represented here where possible.

The free resource page on the website includes a special service for Ash Wednesday for groups that would like to invite even the youngest children to join in one of the most visual and sensory moments of the church year. Note: this isn't your average Sowing Seeds material! Whether with adults or with children, it requires more preparation than usual!

Jesus Gives Up Everything for Us 11
Appropriate for mixed groups of 0–9 years
Designed for the days close to Shrove Tuesday for groups that would like to explore giving things up for Lent

Jesus Is Tested in the Wilderness (Matthew 4.1–11; Luke 4.1–13) 16
Appropriate for mixed groups of 0–9 years

Jesus Enters Jerusalem (Matthew 21.1–11; Mark 11.1–10; Luke 19.28–40) 19
Appropriate for mixed groups of 0–9 years

Jesus Cleans the Temple (Matthew 21.12–13; Luke 19.45–46) 23
Option 1: The people in the Temple, they pray, pray, pray, pray
Appropriate for mixed groups of 0–7 years
Option 2: In Jerusalem 27
Appropriate for mixed groups of 0–9 years

Jesus Is Like a Mother Hen (Luke 13.34–35; Matthew 23.37–39) 31
Appropriate for mixed groups of 0–7 years
Mothering Sunday

Mary Anoints Jesus (John 12.1–8) 35
Appropriate for mixed groups of 0–9 years
Includes options for Mothering Sunday but is also relevant for other weeks

Jesus Washes the Disciples' Feet (John 13.1–17)

Option 1: Washing feet — 40
Appropriate for mixed groups of 0–7 years

Option 2: Servant King — 45
Appropriate for mixed groups of 0–9 years

Jesus' Last Meal (The Last Supper, Luke 22.14–23) — 50
Appropriate for mixed groups of 0–9 years

The Story of Love: The Story of the Cross (Good Friday) — 53
Appropriate for mixed groups of 0–9 years

Tip

Even if you don't use the other Building Blocks, you may find it helpful to use one of the Gathering Songs ('I am going to follow Jesus' or 'Take up your cross') just before the storytelling in every session of this unit as these songs gather together the themes of the unit as a whole. See pp. 151–4.

Jesus Gives Up Everything for Us (the Week before Lent)

→ Luke 4.1–2; Matthew 4.1–2
→ Song: 'I am going to follow Jesus'. Words: © Sharon Moughtin.
→ Tune: 'Bobby Shaftoe' (traditional).

This session is designed for groups who would like to explore the giving up of chocolate, food, alleluias or other things for Lent. This material opens up lots of opportunities for children to make connections between your time together with God and the things they see taking place in the world around them such as pancake parties, Easter eggs, mini eggs in the shops and people talking about 'giving things up for Lent'.

For the storytelling (optional)

- a wilderness tray to support the children in imagining the wilderness. This is a tray filled with sand (or brown sugar) with a few rocks and stones placed around so that it looks desolate;
- a Jesus figure: for instance, the Joseph figure from a Nativity set. If you have no appropriate figures, you could print a picture of Jesus to lay on the sand.

Especially with young children (optional):

- a pancake or a picture of a pancake;
- an egg and a bowl to break the egg into or a picture of an egg.

If your group would like to experience giving something up for Lent (optional):

- one hollow chocolate Easter egg (taken out of its box) that can be shared by the group at Easter. It needs to be hollow as it will represent the empty tomb during the Easter unit.
- a box to put the egg in and tape/ribbon to fasten it shut.
- a small chocolate egg for each child and adult. Check if any children have allergies (e.g. dairy/nuts). You may prefer

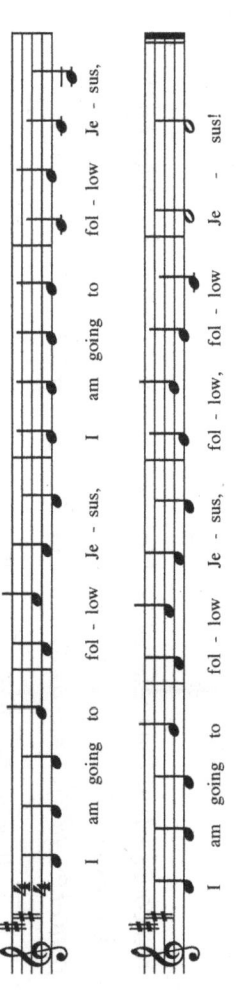

Appropriate for mixed groups of babies, toddlers and children up to the age of 9.

to use pieces of chocolate if there are younger children present for whom chocolate eggs could prove a choking hazard.

You could adapt the material to share pancakes with the children (or hold a pancake party!) but in our experience some young children don't like pancakes, which takes away some of the significance of the experience.

If your church gives up alleluias during Lent, you may find the following helpful:

This is the last time we're going to say 'Alleluia!' for a very long time!
We'll find out why later.
That's why today we're going to be saying 'Alleluia!' as much as we can!

···
Tip
If your group will be using the 'Praise the Lord! **Alleluia!**' call-and-response for the first time, you may find it helpful to say, for example:

Now it's 'my turn'. *Point to self*, 'your turn' *Leader's hands out.*
When I say, 'Praise the Lord', *Both hands to self*
you say, 'Alleluia!' *Both arms upwards in 'V' shape*

Praise the Lord!
Alleluia! *Both arms upwards in 'V' shape*
···

It's time to get ready!
Lent starts *this Wednesday*!
Can you say 'Lent'?

Lent

In 'Lent' we go to the 'wilderness' with Jesus.

Optional: a wilderness tray (see p. 11).

Place the wilderness tray in the centre of the circle. If your group usually uses the What's in the Box? option (p. 7), this can act as the object for the story. You may like to cover it with fabric and change the question to 'What's under the cloth?' Invite a child to uncover the wilderness.

What can you see?
Accept the child's response.

This is the 'wilderness':
sand, rocks and sky and nothing else.
Jesus went to the wilderness!
Place Jesus figure in the wilderness.

Let's imagine we're going to the 'wilderness' with Jesus.
Let's get up and march on the spot:
1, 2, 3, 4! 1, 2, 3, 4!
Let's sing 'I am going to follow Jesus'.

This song is one of the options for the Gathering Song for Lent. The words are so repetitive that it won't need teaching. Start singing and the children will gradually join in.

**I am going to follow Jesus,
I am going to follow Jesus,
I am going to follow Jesus,
follow, follow Jesus!**

We're in the 'wilderness' with Jesus.

12

If your church is giving up alleluias:
Praise the Lord!
Alleluia! *Both arms upwards in 'V' shape*

Jesus looked one way . . . .
Let's look this way . . . .
Lead the children in looking to one side.
And there was sand and rocks and sky.

And Jesus looked the other way . . . .
Lead the children in looking to the other side.
And there was sand and rocks and sky.

Jesus looked behind him . . . .
Lead the children in looking behind.
And there was . . . *Encourage the children to join in*
sand and rocks and sky.

If your church is giving up alleluias say:
Praise the Lord!
Alleluia! *Both arms upwards in 'V' shape*

In the wilderness there's no food! *Shake head*
Jesus was very, very hungry! *Rub tummy*
Can you show me hungry? *Rub tummy*
Can you show me thirsty? *Pant with thirst*

Jesus was hungry and thirsty in the wilderness:
not just for one minute, *Shake head and wag finger from side to side*
not just for one day, *Shake head and wag finger*
but for *Show ten fingers four times as you say* FORTY whole days!

In Lent some people give up one kind of food or drink for forty days
so they can feel how Jesus felt,
hungry and thirsty in the wilderness.

Let's imagine we're giving up a kind of food for Lent.
Let's sing again and rub our tummy
to show we're feeling hungry the way Jesus felt hungry.

Rubbing tummy throughout:
**I am going to follow Jesus,
I am going to follow Jesus,
I am going to follow Jesus,
follow, follow Jesus!**

Let's sit down for a moment.
When the group is ready:

If you're using an egg or picture of an egg, show it to the children.
Can anyone tell me what this is?
Eggs are amazing!
We can make lots of treats with eggs like cakes! Mmmm!

A long time ago, people started giving up EGGS for Lent.
They wanted to be like Jesus, hungry, in the wilderness.
Let's go back in time 200 years ago . . . .
Let's put our hands over our eyes and count to 3 . . . .
1, 2, 3! *If appropriate, you could count backwards.*
We've done it! We've gone back in time!
Let's open our eyes!

If your church is giving up alleluias say:
Praise the Lord!
Alleluia! *Both arms upwards in 'V' shape*

We're going to give up eggs for Lent!
Quick! Lent starts tomorrow!
We need to use up all our eggs!
We're going to make pancakes! Mmmmm!

If you're using a pancake or picture of a pancake, show it to the children.
If your group has a real egg, you could ask a child or one of the helpers to demonstrate breaking the egg into a bowl. Make sure you have washing facilities handy. It's best not to do this yourself due to the need to wash hands immediately.

Let's all break our eggs.
Lead the children in imagining picking up an egg.
1, 2, 3 . . . Crack! *Mime tapping your egg on the bowl*
Put your thumbs inside and open it up!
We've got two more eggs! Let's break them.

1, 2, 3 . . . Crack!
Put your thumbs inside and open it up!
Repeat.

If your church is giving up alleluias say:
Praise the Lord!
Alleluia! *Both arms upwards in 'V' shape*

Now let's add some flour . . . *Mime tipping in flour*
and milk. *Tip in milk*
Let's stir and stir and stir.
We're ready to cook our pancake.

Let's pour our mixture into the pan *Pour action*
And cook it . . . *Mime holding pan over stove*
Now let's toss our pancake. *Demonstrate*
After 3, let's toss our pancake . . .
1, 2, 3 . . . *Lead the children in tossing their pancake high*
Make sure you catch it again!
Lead the children in catching their pancake in the pan.
Did you catch it?
I hope there's none on the ceiling!

If your church is giving up alleluias say:
Praise the Lord!
Alleluia! *Both arms upwards in 'V' shape*

People used to eat pancakes to use up all their eggs.
Then they wouldn't eat eggs for the whole of Lent
so they could feel hungry like Jesus.
Let's toss our pancakes and imagine we're giving up eggs for Lent.
Lead the children in tossing and catching pancakes as you sing:

I am going to follow Jesus,
I am going to follow Jesus,
I am going to follow Jesus,
follow, follow Jesus!

It's time to come back in time to nowadays.
Let's put our hands over our eyes and count to 3 . . .
1, 2, 3 . . . We're back! Phew!

If your church is giving up alleluias say:
Praise the Lord!
Alleluia! *Both arms upwards in 'V' shape*

Let's open our eyes.
We still eat pancakes on the day before Lent
on 'Shrove Tuesday'.

> If your group is not giving up a chocolate egg or sharing mini eggs or chocolate, skip the next section and continue from the box like this below.

Show the hollow chocolate egg to the children.
But can anyone tell me what this is?
Accept responses.

Chocolate is a wonderful treat!
Lots of people give up chocolate for Lent too.
They want to be like Jesus, hungry in the wilderness.
We're going to give up this chocolate egg for Lent
so we can be like Jesus.

Shall we have a last taste of chocolate before Lent starts?
Show chocolate mini eggs or chocolate.
I have some *mini chocolate eggs* here,
enough for everyone.

> *If your church is giving up alleluias say:*
> Praise the Lord!
> **Alleluia!** *Both arms upwards in 'V' shape*

Name and *Name* are going to bring the *eggs* around.
If you'd like one, hold your hands out like this.
Model putting both your hands out in a cupped shape.
Don't eat it straight away!
Keep it on your hand and wait till everyone has an *egg*.
Make sure you keep your hand open so *the egg* doesn't melt!
Ask a responsible child to show everyone how to hold their egg or chocolate on their hand. Don't worry too much if the very young children eat theirs straight away.

**I am going to follow Jesus,
I am going to follow Jesus,
I am going to follow Jesus,
follow, follow Jesus!**

Let's smell our *chocolate egg* . . . Mmmmm!
Now let's taste our *chocolate egg!*
Let's really enjoy it!

As the children eat . . .

Now we're going to give up our big chocolate egg!
We're going to wrap it up and put it in this box.
Wrap up the egg.
We're going to keep it _____ *Name the place it will be kept*
until Lent is finished and it's Easter.
Then we can eat our Easter egg!

> *If your church gives up alleluias in Lent say:*
> So we've given up our chocolate egg.
> We're also going to give up singing our special alleluia!
> Let's get ready to give our alleluias up now
> by making our alleluia action *Hands up in a 'V' shape*
> for the last time as we sing.

Lead them in repeatedly making the alleluia action as you sing.
**I am going to follow Jesus,
I am going to follow Jesus,
I am going to follow Jesus,
follow, follow Jesus!**

As appropriate:
So we've been very busy getting ready for Lent!
We've used up all our eggs and made pancakes!
Toss pancake.
We've eaten our chocolate eggs. Mmm!
Rub tummy.
We've given up our big egg.
Show Easter egg.
And we've given up our, ssshhh! *Whisper* alleluia.

But we need to remember to get ready INside for Lent, too.
Trace a circle around your heart.

15

If your group is not giving up a chocolate egg or sharing mini eggs or chocolate, continue from this box.

Giving up eggs and eating pancakes
[and giving up alleluias]
help people get ready for Lent.
But we need to remember to get ready for Lent INside, too.

Let's put our hands on our heart
Model placing hands like a cross on your heart,
and close our eyes for a moment.
Let's ask Jesus to help us get ready for Lent INside.

Let's sing our song one last time very gently.
Let's make it into a prayer to Jesus.
Let's ask Jesus to help us get ready INside.

**I am going to follow Jesus,
I am going to follow Jesus,
I am going to follow Jesus,
follow, follow Jesus!**

Jesus Is Tested in the Wilderness

→ Matthew 4.1–11; Luke 4.1–13
→ Song/poem: 'God's way of love I'll go'. Words: © Sharon Moughtin.
→ Tune: 'Zoom, zoom, zoom! We're going to the moon!' (traditional).

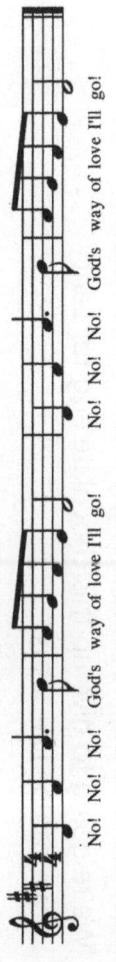

No! No! God's way of love I'll go! No! No! No! God's way of love I'll go!

Appropriate for mixed groups of babies, toddlers and children up to the age of 9.

For today's session, you may like to use:

- *a wilderness tray to support the children in imagining the wilderness. This is a tray filled with sand (or brown sugar) with a few rocks and stones placed around so that it looks desolate. See the website for images;*
- *a Jesus figure: for instance, the Joseph figure from a Nativity set. If you have no appropriate figures, you could print a picture of Jesus to lay on the sand.*

If your group is not using the 'I am going to follow Jesus' Gathering Song (p. 151), begin by imagining going to the wilderness together, for example:

It's time to go to the 'wilderness'!
If you're using a wilderness tray place this in the centre of the circle.

This is the 'wilderness':
sand, rocks and sky and nothing else.
Jesus went to the wilderness!

Place Jesus figure in the wilderness.
In Lent we go to the wilderness with Jesus.
Let's get up and march on the spot:
1, 2, 3, 4 . . . 1, 2, 3, 4 . . .

All groups:
We're here! We're in the wilderness with Jesus.
Look over here! *Point one way*
All we can see is sand and rocks and sky!

Look over there! *Point opposite way*
Encourage the children to join in after the dots.
All we can see is sand and rocks . . . **and sky!**

And look behind us! *Point behind*
Encourage the children to join in after the dots.
All we can see is . . . **sand and rocks and sky!**

We're going to tell the story of Jesus in the wilderness.
But, first, we need to learn a song.
Start off by saying the words without any tune.
Let's say the words 'my turn' *Point to self,* 'your turn' *Leader's hands out.*

No! No! No! *Wag finger from side to side*
God's way of love I'll go! *Cross arms before chest*
No! No! No! *Wag finger from side to side*
God's way of love I'll go! *Cross arms before chest*

Now let's add the tune:
'my turn' *Point to self,* 'your turn' *Leader's hands out to group.*
No! No! No! *Wag finger from side to side*
God's way of love I'll go! *Cross arms before chest*
No! No! No! *Wag finger from side to side*
God's way of love I'll go! *Cross arms before chest*
Repeat until the children are confident.

   Optional: What's in the Box? (see p. 7)
   Invite a child to open the box.
   Inside are: stones, a globe (or picture of the world) and
   a picture of an angel).

   What's in the box?
   Accept the child's response.

In the wilderness, Jesus is given three tricky choices about:
stones, the world and an angel!
We need three actions!

If you're using the What's in the Box? option, show each item as you
ask for the action.

Number 1: *Show one finger*
Who can show us an action for stones?
Choose one of the children's actions.

Number 2: *Show two fingers*
Who can show us an action for EVERYTHING in the world?
Choose one of the children's actions.

And number 3: *Show three fingers*
Who can show us an action for an angel?

We're ready to tell our story!
Jesus was in the wilderness, all by himself.
All he could see anywhere was . . .
Encourage the children to join in:
. . . **sand and rocks and sky!**

Jesus was very hungry and very thirsty.
Can you show me hungry?
Can you show me thirsty?
Lead the children in looking very hungry and thirsty.

Then at the point that Jesus was MOST hungry
And MOST thirsty, a tester came!
The tester wanted to see if Jesus was ready
to follow God's way of love. *Cross arms on chest*

The tester asked THREE tricky questions.
Show three fingers.
And Jesus had to make THREE tricky choices:
1, 2, 3. *Count on fingers*

17

Will Jesus follow God's way of love?! *Rhetorical question*
Let's find out!

Choice number 1: let's hold up one finger.
Lead the children in holding up one finger.

The tester showed Jesus some stones.

If you're using the What's in the Box? option, show the stones.

What's our action for stones?
Encourage the children to show their 'stone action'.

The tester said, 'Jesus, you're very hungry!
You don't have to follow God! *Shake head*
Why don't you just make these stones *Stone action* into bread?'

Mmmmm! Imagine how much Jesus wanted to eat bread!
Can you show me again how hungry Jesus was?
Lead the group in rubbing tummy and looking hungry.

But Jesus knew the tester was trying to trick him!
THAT's not God's way of love! *Shake head and cross arms on chest*
So Jesus said . . .
Aside: Let's see if you can join in . . .

No! No! No! *Wag finger side to side*
God's way of love I'll go! *Cross arms*
If the children don't join in naturally, encourage them to join in now.
No! No! No! *Wag finger side to side*
God's way of love I'll go! *Cross arms*

Choice number 2: let's hold up two fingers.
Lead the children in showing two fingers.

If you're using the What's in the Box? option, show the globe.

Can you show me our action for EVERYTHING in the world!?
Ask a child to lead the group in the 'everything' action.

The tester showed Jesus the whole world! *Everything action*
The tester said, 'Why don't you follow me and not God?!
I'll give you the whole world and EVERYTHING in it!'
Can you imagine being given EVERYTHING as a present?!

But Jesus knew the tester was trying to trick him!
THAT's not God's way of love! *Shake head and cross arms on chest*
So Jesus said:

Lead the children in singing:
No! No! No! *Wag finger side to side*
God's way of love I'll go! *Cross arms*
No! No! No! *Wag finger*
God's way of love I'll go! *Cross arms*

Choice number 3: let's hold up three fingers.
Lead the children in showing three fingers.

If you're using the What's in the Box? option, show the angel.
If appropriate: Can anyone remember our third action?
Accept responses.

Let's show our angel action.
The tester took Jesus up to the top of a tall, tall tower.
Reach up high.

The tester said: 'Why don't you throw yourself off?!
Angels will catch you!
Then everyone will see how special you are!'

It's nice to feel special, isn't it!
But Jesus knew the tester was trying to trick him!

18

THAT's not God's way of love! *Shake head and cross arms on chest*
So Jesus said:

No! No! No! *Wag finger side to side*
God's way of love I'll go! *Cross arms*
No! No! No! *Wag finger*
God's way of love I'll go! *Cross arms*

Jesus chose God's way of love!
Let's all cross our arms to show love.
Lead the children in crossing arms on your chest.

The way of love is also called the way of the cross.
Look at our arms! We've made the sign of the cross.
Show the children how their arms look like a cross.

Let's close our eyes for a moment.
When the group is ready:
Sometimes we have to make tricky choices.
There are things we really, really want to do,
but we know they're wrong.
We know they don't show love. *Shake head and cross arms on chest*
Hold silence for a few seconds.

Let's open our eyes again.
When we follow Jesus, we choose to say, 'No!' *Wag finger side to side*
to things we know are wrong.
We choose to follow God's way of love. *Cross arms*

If we like, we can make Jesus' words into OUR words. *Point to self*
Let's sing/say them as a prayer and a promise to Jesus [this Lent].

Lead the children in singing/saying:

No! No! No! *Wag finger side to side*
God's way of love I'll go! *Cross arms*
No! No! No! *Wag finger*
God's way of love I'll go! *Cross arms*

Jesus Enters Jerusalem

→ The story behind Palm Sunday
→ Matthew 21.1–11; Mark 11.1–10; Luke 19.28–40
→ Song: 'Jesus came riding on a donkey'. Words: © Sharon Moughtin.
→ Tune: 'Sing hosanna' (traditional).

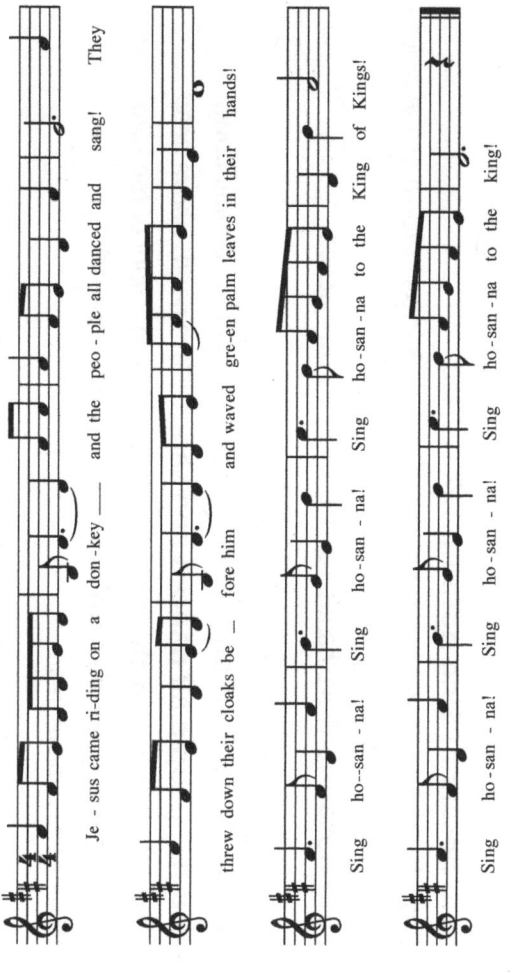

Appropriate for mixed groups of babies, toddlers and children up to the age of 9.

It may feel strange to tell the story of Palm Sunday here so close to the beginning of Lent, but the stories of Jesus' last week are so important and there are so many of them! Palm Sunday is the day that Jesus enters Jerusalem and starts off the chain reaction of events that will inevitably lead to the cross. It makes sense to start here so that the group can begin to see the connections.

Optional: What's in the Box? (see p. 7)
Invite a child to open the box.
Inside is a palm leaf (real or a picture).

What's in the box?
Accept the child's response.

This is a 'palm leaf'
Today we're going to tell the story
of when all the people waved palm leaves for Jesus.

To tell our story today, we're going to learn a song.
Let's sing the words
'my turn' *Point to self,* 'your turn' *Leader's hands out to group.*
Jesus came riding on a donkey. *Hold reins and jig up and down*
Jesus came riding on a donkey. *Hold reins and jig up and down*

And the people all danced and sang! *Wave hands above head*
And the people all danced and sang! *Wave hands above head*

They threw down their cloaks before him.
Lift two hands above head and then bring them down to show throwing cloaks on the floor. If your group is familiar with 'You are welcome in the name of the Lord!' (Welcome Song: Option 2), use the action from 'I can see all over you the glory of the Lord!' (p. 147).
They threw down their cloaks before him *Wave hands*

and waved gree-een palm leaves in their hands! *Wave hands*
and waved gree-een palm leaves in their hands! *Wave hands above head.*

That song has lots of words!
Let's try and sing it all together.
If you can't remember all the words,
can you help with the actions?

Jesus came riding on a donkey *Hold reins and jig up and down*
and the people all danced and sang! *Wave hands above head*
They threw down their cloaks before him *'Glory of the Lord' sign*
and waved gree-een palm leaves in their hands!
Wave hands above head.

Then we're going to sing the song that the people sang!
If appropriate: You might recognize it.
I'm going to sing it: see if you can join in!

Lead the children in singing while waving hands above head:

Sing hosanna! Sing hosanna! *Wave hands*
Sing hosanna *Wave hands* **to the King of Kings!** *Crown action twice*
Sing hosanna! Sing hosanna!
Sing hosanna *Wave hands* **to the king!** *Crown action*

Let's try that all together:

Jesus came riding on a donkey *Hold reins and jig up and down*
and the people all danced and sang! *Wave hands above head*
They threw down their cloaks before him *'Glory of the Lord' sign*
and waved gree-een palm leaves in their hands!
Wave hands above head.

Sing hosanna! Sing hosanna! *Wave hands above head*
Sing hosanna *Wave hands* **to the King of Kings!** *Crown action twice*
Sing hosanna! Sing hosanna!
Sing hosanna *Wave hands above head* **to the king!** *Crown action*

We're ready to tell our story.
Jesus and his friends, the disciples, were going to the big city.

Let's stand up and show a big shape with our body.
Lead the children in stretching out your body into the biggest shape.

Bigger! Even bigger!
Jerusalem was the biggest city in the whole land!

The disciples were feeling excited.
Can you show me excited?
Lead the children in looking excited.
And the disciples were feeling scared.
Can you show me scared?
Lead the children in looking scared.

The big city was busy and full of people.
What if no one liked them there?
Let's be the disciples and look:
excited . . . *Excited*
and scared . . . *Scared*

Then Jesus said:
'Look! *Point* There's a donkey over there.
Go and get the donkey for me!' *Point*

If very young children are present for whom this will be helpful, say:

Can you hear the donkey? *Hand behind ear*
If the children don't naturally make the sound:
What sound does a donkey make?
Eeyore! Eeyore!

Let's take the donkey for Jesus.
Lead the children in holding an imaginary rope.
Let's stroke our donkey's nose
so it knows we'll be gentle. *Stroke imaginary donkey's nose.*
Now let's take our donkey to Jesus.
Listen to this and see if you can do the same!

Tongue click to make a 'clip clop' sound and walk on the spot in time with the rhythm, miming holding the donkey's reins. Encourage the children to join in.

The disciples gave the donkey to Jesus.
Lead the children in miming passing the donkey's rope over.
Then Jesus got on the donkey.
Let's be Jesus and get on our donkey.
Lead the children in being Jesus getting on the donkey.
Bob up and down on the spot holding reins as if you're riding a donkey.
Let's ride our donkey to the big city.

Lead the group in trotting on the spot: tongue click to make a 'clip clop' sound and walk on the spot in time with the rhythm, miming holding the donkey's reins. Encourage the children to join in.

And freeze!
In Jerusalem, the people heard Jesus coming!
Let's be the people together.
Sssssh! Listen! *Hand behind ear* Can you hear?
What can we hear?

Lead the children in very quietly making a 'clip clop' sound with tongue as if from a distance, with hand to ear.
Interrupt Who's that?
Let's stand on our tiptoes and try to see . . .
Lead the children in tiptoeing up with hand shading eyes.
Look! Can you see Jesus? *Point*

The people saw Jesus coming on the donkey!
They thought Jesus was going to be the new king!
They whispered to each other.
After 3, let's whisper, 'Jesus is the new king!' *Sound excited and amazed*

21

Lead the children in whispering louder and louder, turning to one another.
1, 2, 3 . . . Jesus is the new king!
Jesus is the new king!
Jesus is the new king!

Everyone was so excited!
They pulled their cloaks off.
Lead the children in miming ripping a cloak off.
They threw them in front of Jesus.
Lift two hands above head and then bring them down to show throwing cloaks on the floor.

If your group is familiar with 'You are welcome in the name of the Lord!' (Welcome Song: Option 2 p. 147), say:
Look, the people can see the 'glory of the Lord' all over Jesus!

Lead the children in shouting 'Hosanna', getting louder and louder. They will almost certainly instinctively copy you. If not, encourage them to.
Hosanna! *Raise hands above head*
Hosanna! *Raise hands above head*
Hosanna! *Raise hands above head*
Hosanna! *Raise hands above head*
Hosanna! *Raise hands above head*

Then they began to pull branches off the palm trees!
Let's climb up the tree . . . .
Lead the children in miming shimmying up a tree.
Let's pull branches off to wave for Jesus.
Lead the children in reaching up and pulling down branches.
Not little leaves. *Show little with your fingers*
But huge green branches with long green leaves.

Lead the children in reaching up tall to show a tall long branch.
Branches taller than me.

They waved their palm branches in the air!
Mime being the branch, swaying with your whole body with your hands raised above your head.
Let's wave our whole body, like a branch, in the air.
Lead the children in shouting 'hosanna', getting louder and louder.

If they don't instinctively copy you, encourage them to:
Hosanna! *Raise hands above head*
Hosanna! *Raise hands above head*
Hosanna! *Raise hands above head*
Hosanna! *Raise hands above head*
Hosanna! *Raise hands above head*
Jesus is HERE!

That was exciting, wasn't it?
That's the story of Palm Sunday!

Let's tell our story again with our song.

If appropriate, you could distribute branches, leaves, green imaginative aids (see p. 187) (or a mixture).
You might like to try singing the song while moving around the room or even leaving the room and going outside if appropriate.

When the group is ready:
What do we need to get on to start our song?
If the children need a clue: What did Jesus ride into Jerusalem on?
Accept the children's responses.

Let's get on our donkey!

Jesus Cleans the Temple

Option 1: The people in the Temple, they pray

→ Aka: 'Jesus makes a mess!'
→ Matthew 21.12–13; Luke 19.45–46
→ Song: 'The people in the Temple'. Words: © Sharon Moughtin.
→ Tune: 'The wheels on the bus' (traditional).

Appropriate for mixed groups of babies, toddlers and children up to the age of 7. Groups that include children up to the age of 9 may prefer to use Option 2. The storytelling is almost identical, but a different tune is used that is more appropriate when including older children, who might find singing 'The wheels on the bus' a little young for them. Choose which version works best in your setting.

Optional: What's in the Box? (see p. 7)
Invite a child to open the box.
Inside are cows and/or sheep (toys or a picture).

What's in the box?
Accept the child's response.

We're going to tell the story of when Jesus CHASED the cows and sheep out of God's House.

Lead the group in trotting on the spot: tongue click to make a 'clip clop' sound and walk on the spot in time with the rhythm, miming holding the donkey's reins. Encourage the children to join in.

Jesus came riding on a donkey *Hold reins and jig up and down*
and the people all danced and sang! *Wave hands above head*
They threw down their cloaks before him *'Glory of the Lord' sign*
and waved gre-en palm leaves in their hands!
Wave hands above head.

Sing hosanna! Sing hosanna! *Wave hands above head*
Sing hosanna *Wave hands* **to the King of Kings!** *Crown action twice*
Sing hosanna! Sing hosanna!
Sing hosanna *Wave hands above head* **to the king!** *Crown action*

Repeat.

Continue singing as you collect any imaginative aids, leaves or branches.
When the group is ready:

Hosanna! *Raise hands above head*
Hosanna! *Raise hands above head*
Hosanna! *Raise hands above head*
Hosanna! *Raise hands above head*
Hosanna! *Raise hands above head*
Hosanna! *Raise hands above head*
Hosanna! *Raise hands above head*
Hosanna! *Raise hands above head*

If appropriate:
Come back next time to find out
what happens to Jesus in the big city.

Today's story starts with a BIG house.
Let's stand up and make a big shape with our bodies.
Lead the children in reaching out big with their arms.
Bigger! Bigger!
This house is God's House, the Temple.
It's huge!
It's the biggest house in the biggest city in the whole land.
Can you show me big again?
And freeze!
That's big!

People went to the Temple to pray,
a bit like our church.

Let's sit down quietly and PRAYERfully.
When the children are seated say slowly and clearly:
'The people in the Temple, they pray, pray, pray.'
Let's sing that – ssssshhhh! – ever so peacefully.
Either hold your hands upwards or put them together in prayer.

Lead the children in singing. The words are so repetitive they won't need teaching: the children will naturally begin to join in as you sing.

**The people in the Temple
they pray, pray, pray,** *Prayer action*
pray, pray, pray, *Prayer action*
pray, pray, pray . . . *Prayer action*
**The people in the Temple
they pray, pray, pray,** *Prayer action*
all day long!

Very peaceful . . .
But the problem was
there were other people in the Temple!

There were people trying to sell things!
First of all they were selling cows!
What noise do cows make?
Accept the children's responses.
And what action could we use for cows?
Choose one or more of the actions suggested by one of the children and invite the others to follow their lead.

**The cows in the Temple
go 'Moo, moo, moo, moo,** *Cow action*
moo, moo, moo, *Cow action*
moo, moo, moo!' *Cow action*
**The cows in the Temple
go 'Moo, moo, moo',** *Cow action*
all day long!

Hmm. It's getting a bit noisy.
This feels more like a cow shop than God's House.

And that wasn't the only animal in the Temple.
The sellers were also selling sheep!
What noise do sheep make?
Accept the children's responses.
And what action could we use for sheep?
Choose one or more of the actions suggested by one of the children and invite the others to follow their lead.

**The sheep in the Temple
go 'Baa, baa, baa,** *Sheep action*
baa, baa, baa, *Sheep action*
baa, baa, baa!' *Sheep action*
**The sheep in the Temple
go 'Baa, baa, baa',** *Sheep action*
all day long!

Hold reins and move hands up and down as if on a donkey.

If appropriate, you could recap the story of Palm Sunday from last time. Lead the group in trotting on the spot: tongue click to make a 'clip clop' sound and walk on the spot in time with the rhythm, miming holding the donkey's reins. Encourage the children to join in.

And/or repeat the Palm Sunday song:
Jesus came riding on a donkey
Hold reins and jig up and down.
and the people all danced and sang!
Wave hands above head.
They threw down their cloaks before him
Wave hands above head.
and waved green palm leaves in their hands!
Wave hands above head.
Sing hosanna! Sing hosanna!
Wave hands above head.
Sing hosanna *Wave hands* **to the King of Kings!**
Crown action twice.
Sing hosanna! Sing hosanna!
Sing hosanna *Wave hands above head* **to the king!**
Crown action.

Jesus came riding on a donkey!
And Jesus went straight to the Temple.
He wanted to pray in God's House.

Let's be Jesus and walk on the spot into the Temple.
Lead the children in walking on the spot.
And freeze!

We're here! We're in the Temple!
Let's pray.
Hang on a minute!

25

The sellers in the Temple were making lots of money
selling cows and sheep.
The sellers were taking money from poor people!

Let's be the poor people and hold our empty hands out.
Lead the children in holding empty hands out.
No more money! *Shake head and look sad*

Let's be the sellers and hold our bags of money in our hands.
Lead the children in holding imaginary money.
Let's jingle our money to show ALL the money!
Jingle, jingle, jingle! *Shake money*
Listen to all that money:
all the money we're taking from the poor people.

The sellers in the Temple
go 'Jingle, jingle, jingle, jingle, *Shake money*
jingle, jingle, jingle, jingle, *Shake money*
jingle, jingle, jingle!' *Shake money*
The sellers in the Temple
go 'Jingle, jingle, jingle', *Shake money*
all day long!

What a lot of noise! *Hold hands on ears*
Encourage the children to fill in the gaps.
We have cows going . . . .
Sheep going . . .
Sellers and their money going . . . .
What a lot of noise! *Hold hands on ears*
I can't pray!
I can't even hear myself think!

Then one day Jesus came riding on a donkey.

What can Jesus hear? *Hand behind ear*
Encourage the children to fill in the gaps.
We have cows going . . . .
Sheep going . . . .
Sellers and their money going . . . .
And the poor people with no more money.
Shake head and hold hands out and look sad.

Jesus was CROSS!
Can you show me cross like Jesus?
Lead the children in looking cross.

Jesus was ANGRY!
Can you show me angry?
Lead the children in looking furious.
Even MORE angry!

And Jesus shouted . . . .
Can you shout after me:
'my turn' *Point to self*, 'your turn' *Leader's hands out to group.*

Loudly and authoritatively in outrage:
This is GOD's House! *Two hands pointing down*
This is GOD's House!
You've turned it into a SHOP! *Arms folded*
You've turned it into a SHOP!
Raise voice and sound even more angry.
And now you're taking money from POOR people! *Hands on hips*
And now you're taking money from POOR people!

Then Jesus THREW OVER all the shop tables! *Pushing action*
He turned the tables upside down! Topsy turvy! *'New Start' sign (p. 8)*
And all the money fell on the floor! *Throw arms outwards*

Let's show Jesus turning the tables topsy turvy!
Lead the children in the 'New Start' sign.

If appropriate: Look! Jesus is giving the Temple a new start!

Jesus in the Temple said, 'This is God's House.'
Let's sing and show Jesus turning over the tables
with our arms. *'New Start' sign*

If appropriate:
But for the rest of our song
we won't sing 'all day long' at the end.
We'll sing 'on that day!'
Let's practise that:
Lead the children in singing 'on that day!'
Don't worry too much if this last change of words is too much for your group when you come to singing the rest of the song.

And remember, Jesus is CROSS! *Show cross face*
Let's sound cross as we sing!

Jesus in the Temple said, 'This is God's House!' *'New Start' sign*
'This is God's House!' *'New Start' sign*
'This is God's House!' *'New Start' sign*
Jesus in the Temple said, 'This is God's House!' *'New Start' sign*
on that day!

Then Jesus chased all the cows and sheep out!
Let's be the cows for the first half of the song.
Then let's be the sheep!

Lead the children in sounding unsettled as you 'moo' and 'baa'.
The cows in the Temple
went 'Moo, moo, moo, *Cow action*

moo, moo, moo, moo! *Cow action*
moo, moo, moo! *Cow action*
Interrupt: And now the sheep!
**The sheep in the Temple
went 'Baa, baa, baa',** *Sheep action*
on that day!

Now the leaders in the Temple saw this.
Let's be the leaders in the Temple and look important.
Lead the children in looking important.

How do you think the leaders felt
when Jesus turned the tables topsy turvy? *'New Start' sign*
Can you show me with your face?
Accept all suggestions.

In our story, some of the leaders were cross!
Can you show me cross?
Lead the children in looking cross.
Now angry! Really angry!
Lead the children in looking furious.

The leaders wanted Jesus OUT of the Temple! *Point outwards in anger*
OUT of the big city! *Point outwards in anger*
The leaders wanted NO MORE JESUS! *Shake head and point finger*
Let's be the angry leaders and sing
Speak in the rhythm of the last line of the song:
'NO MORE JESUS!' on . . . that . . . day. *Point finger in anger in time*

**The leaders in the Temple
said, 'No more Jesus!'** *Point finger in anger three times*
'No more Jesus!' *Point finger in anger three times*
'No more Jesus!' *Point finger in anger three times*
**The leaders in the Temple
said, 'No more Jesus!'** *Point finger in anger three times*
on that day.

That was when the leaders decided to put Jesus on the cross.
Hold arms out in a cross shape.
Come back next time to find out what happens next.

Option 2: In Jerusalem

- Aka: 'Jesus makes a mess!'
- Matthew 21.12–13; Luke 19.45–46
- Song: 'The people in the Temple'. Words: © Sharon Moughtin.
- Tune: 'The big ship sails on the Ally, Ally-O' (traditional).

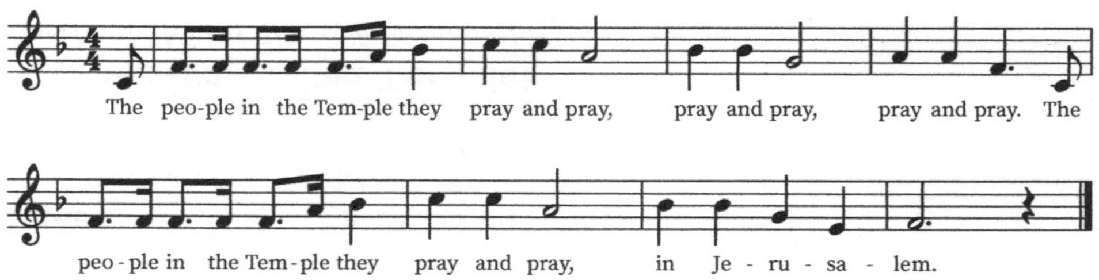

The people in the Temple they pray and pray, pray and pray, pray and pray.
The people in the Temple they pray and pray, in Je-ru-sa-lem.

Appropriate for mixed groups of babies, toddlers and children up to the age of 9. Groups that only include children up to the age of 7 may prefer to use Option 1.

Optional: What's in the Box? (see p. 7)
Invite a child to open the box.
Inside are cows and/or sheep (toys or a picture).

What's in the box?
Accept the child's response.

We're going to tell the story of when Jesus
CHASED the cows and sheep out of God's House.

Today's story starts with a BIG house.
Let's stand up and make a big shape with our bodies.
Lead the children in reaching out big with their arms.

Bigger! Bigger!
This house is God's House, the Temple.
It's huge!
It's the biggest house in the biggest city in the whole land.
Can you show me big again?
And freeze! That's big!

People went to the Temple to pray,
a bit like our church.

Let's sit down quietly and PRAYERfully.
When the children are seated say slowly and clearly:
'The people in the Temple, they pray, pray, pray.'
Let's sing that – sssshhhh! – ever so peacefully.
Either hold your hands upwards or put them together in prayer.

Lead the children in singing. The words are so repetitive they won't need teaching: the children will naturally begin to join in as you sing.

The people in the Temple
they pray and pray, *Prayer action*
they pray and pray, *Prayer action*
The people in the Temple
they pray and pray, *Prayer action*

Interrupt singing: and where was the Temple?
The Temple was in Jerusalem.
The BIG city.
Let's sing 'in Jerusalem' and show 'big' as we sing!
'My turn', 'your turn':
in Jerusalem *Big shape*
in Jerusalem *Big shape*

Very peaceful . . .
But the problem was
there were other people in the Temple!
There were people trying to sell things!

The sellers in the Temple were selling cows and sheep.
What noise do cows make?
Accept the children's responses.
And what about sheep?
Accept the children's responses.
And can you show me an action for cows?
Choose action. This will become the 'cow action'.
And sheep!
Choose action. This will become the 'sheep action'
Let's show the noise in the Temple!
We're going to sing:
Spoken:
And the cows went 'Mooo!' *Cow action*
And the sheep went 'Baaa!' *Sheep action*
And the **sellers called 'For sale!'**
Beckon with arm. This will become the 'come action'.
Twice! Are you ready!

And the cows went 'Mooo!' *Cow action*
And the sheep went 'Baaa!' *Sheep action*
The sellers called 'For sale!' *Come action*
The sellers called 'For sale!' *Come action*
And the cows went 'Mooo!' *Cow action*
And the sheep went 'Baaa!' *Sheep action*
in Jerusalem. *Big shape*

Repeat if appropriate.

The sellers in the Temple were making lots of money selling cows and sheep . . .
The sellers were taking money from poor people!

Let's be the poor people and hold our empty hands out.
Lead the children in holding empty hands out.
No more money! *Shake head and look sad*

Let's be the sellers and hold our hands filled with money.
Lead the children in holding imaginary money.
Let's jingle our money to show ALL the money!
Jingle, jingle, jingle! *Shake money*

What a lot of noise! *Hold hands on ears*

Then one day Jesus came riding on a donkey.
Hold reins and move hands up and down as if on a donkey.

If appropriate, you could recap the story of Palm Sunday here by leading the group in making a clip clop sound

And/or repeat the Palm Sunday song:
Jesus came riding on a donkey
Hold reins and jig up and down.
and the people all danced and sang!
Wave hands above head.
They threw down their cloaks before him
'Glory of the Lord' sign.
and waved green palm leaves in their hands!
Wave hands above head.
Sing hosanna! Sing hosanna!
Wave hands above head.
Sing hosanna *Wave hands* **to the King of Kings!**
Crown action twice.
Sing hosanna! Sing hosanna!

Sing hosanna *Wave hands above head* **to the king!**
Crown action.

Jesus came riding on a donkey!
And Jesus went straight to the Temple.
He wanted to pray in God's House.

Let's be Jesus and walk on the spot into the Temple.
Lead the children in walking on the spot.
And freeze!

We're here! We're in the Temple!
Look at all the people praying!

**The people in the Temple they
pray and pray,** *Prayer action*
pray and pray, *Prayer action*
pray and pray, *Prayer action*
**The people in the Temple they
pray and pray,** *Prayer action*
in Jerusalem. *Big shape*

But hang on a minute!
What can Jesus hear? *Hand behind ear*
Lead the group in singing:
And the cows went 'Mooo!' *Cow action*
And the sheep went 'Baaa!' *Sheep action*
The sellers called 'For sale!' *Come action*
The sellers called 'For sale!' *Come action*
And the cows went 'Mooo!' *Cow action*
And the sheep went 'Baaa!' *Sheep action*
in Jerusalem. *Big shape*

29

Jesus was CROSS!
Can you show me cross like Jesus?
Lead the children in looking cross.

Jesus was ANGRY!
Can you show me angry?
Lead the children in looking furious.
Even MORE angry!
Can you show me angry like Jesus?!

And Jesus shouted . . . . .
Can you shout after me:
'my turn' *Point to self*, 'your turn'? *Leader' hands out to group.*

Loudly and authoritatively in outrage:
This is GOD's House! *Two hands pointing down*
This is GOD's House!
You've turned it into a SHOP! *Arms folded*
You've turned it into a SHOP!
Raise voice and sound even more angry.
And now you're taking money from POOR people! *Hands on hips*
And now you're taking money from POOR people!

Then Jesus THREW OVER all the shop tables! *Pushing action*
He turned the tables upside down! Topsy turvy!
'New Start' sign (p. 8).
And all the money fell on the floor! *Throw arms outwards*

Let's show Jesus turning the tables topsy turvy!
Lead the children in the 'New Start' sign.

If appropriate: Look! Jesus is giving the Temple a new start!
Jesus in the Temple said, 'This is God's House.'
Let's sing and show Jesus turning over the tables
with our arms. *'New Start' sign*
And remember, Jesus is ANGRY! *Show cross face*
Let's sound angry as we sing!

**Jesus in the Temple said,
'This is God's House!** *'New Start' sign*
'This is God's House! *'New Start' sign*
'This is God's House! *'New Start' sign*
**Jesus in the Temple said,
'This is God's House!** *'New Start' sign*
in Jerusalem.

Then Jesus chased all the cows and sheep out!
And the sellers too!
The sellers aren't going to shout 'For Sale!' anymore.
They're going to shout 'Help!'
And the cows and sheep are going to sound scared too!

Lead the group in singing:

And the cows went 'Mooo!' *Cow action*
And the sheep went 'Baaa!' *Sheep action*
The sellers called "Help!" *Raise hands*
the sellers called "Help!" *Raise hands*
And the cows went 'Mooo!' *Cow action*
And the sheep went 'Baaa!' *Sheep action*
in Jerusalem. *Big shape*

Now the leaders in the Temple saw this.
Let's be the leaders in the Temple and look important.
Lead the children in looking important.

How do you think the leaders felt
when Jesus turned the tables topsy turvy? *'New Start' sign*
Can you show me with your face?

30

Jesus Is Like a Mother Hen (Mothering Sunday)

→ Luke 13: 34–35; Matthew 23.37–39
→ Song: 'I am so important! Look, look, look at me!' Words: © Sharon Moughtin.
→ Tune: 'Chick, chick, chick, chick, chicken! (Lay a little egg for me!)' (traditional).

I am so imp-ort-ant! — Look, look, look at me!

I am so imp-ort-ant! — Look, look, look at me!

Appropriate for mixed groups of babies, toddlers and children up to the age of 7. Groups that include children up to the age of 9 may prefer to tell the 'Mary anoints Jesus' story (p. 35), as they may find acting out being little chicks a little young for them. Choose which version works best in your setting.

The following material is designed to enable groups to celebrate the themes of Mothering Sunday while continuing the unit's exploration of Jesus' journey to Jerusalem and the cross.

Optional: What's in the Box? (see p. 7)
Invite a child to open the box.
Inside is a chick (either a toy or a picture).

What's in the box?
Accept the child's response.

Today's story is all about little chicks!
Can you show me what a little chick looks like?
What does a little chick sound like?
Lead the children in pretending to be a chick.

Accept all suggestions.

In our story, some of the leaders were cross!
Can you show me cross?
Lead the children in looking cross.
Now angry! Can you show me really angry!
Lead the children in looking angry.

The leaders wanted Jesus OUT of the Temple! *Point outwards in anger*
OUT of the big city! *Point outwards in anger*
The leaders wanted NO MORE JESUS! *Shake head and point finger*
Let's be the angry leaders and sing
Speak in the rhythm of the last line of the song:
'NO MORE JESUS!' in Jerusalem. *Point finger in anger in time*

The leaders in the Temple
said, 'No more Jesus!' *Point finger in anger three times*
'No more Jesus!' *Point finger in anger three times*
'No more Jesus!' *Point finger in anger three times*
The leaders in the Temple
said, 'No more Jesus!' *Point finger in anger three times*
in Jerusalem *Big shape*

That was when the leaders decided to put Jesus on the cross.
Hold arms out in a cross shape.
Come back next time to find out what happens next.

31

Freeze!
We're going to sing a chicken song!
Let's learn it *'my turn' Point to self, 'your turn' Leader's hands out to group.*

Sing it with the tune straight away.
Chick, chick, chick, chick, chicken!
Cheep, cheep, cheep, cheep, cheep!
Chick, chick, chick, chick, chicken!
Cheep, cheep, cheep, cheep, cheep!

Chicks don't know what they're doing or where they're going.
They wander this way and that and get lost.
Then they cheep for their mummy hen.
Let's turn around on the spot and look lost while we sing our song.
Lead the children in pretending to be a lost chick.

Chick, chick, chick, chick, chicken! *Flap wings*
Cheep, cheep, cheep, cheep, cheep!
Chick, chick, chick, chick, chicken! *Flap wings*
Cheep, cheep, cheep, cheep, cheep!

Freeze!
Chicks also spend a lot of time hiding and resting under their mummy's wing.
Let's sit down and pretend we're hiding under our mummy's wing, while she keeps us safe and warm.
Lead the children in sitting down. Make your arm into a wing and pretend it's your mummy hen's wing to hide behind.
Sssssh! Let's sing our song ever so quietly.
Chick, chick, chick, chick, chicken!
Cheep, cheep, cheep, cheep, cheep!

Chick, chick, chick, chick, chicken!
Cheep, cheep, cheep, cheep, cheep!

I wonder how the little chicks feel when they're with their mummy hen?
Accept responses.

We're ready to tell our story.
Jesus went to the big city Jerusalem.
Let's make a big shape with our body to show the big city!
Lead the children in making a big shape.
Bigger! Even bigger!

Lots of people in the big city saw themselves as ever so important.
Can you show me how you look when you're being important?
Lead the children in looking important and a little snooty.

We're going to sing a song for the important people.
It goes like this:
'my turn' *Point to self,* 'your turn' *Leader's hands out to group.*

To the same tune as 'Chick, chick, chick, chicken':
I am so important! *Puff chest up and stand tall*
Look, look, look at me! *Point at yourself with both hands*
I am so important! *Puff chest up and stand tall*
Look, look, look at me! *Point at yourself with both hands*

The people in the big city saw themselves as always right.
Can you show me what you look like when you think you're completely right?
Let's sing our song again.

I am so important! *Puff chest up and stand tall*
Look, look, look at me! *Point at yourself with both hands*
I am so important! *Puff chest up and stand tall*
Look, look, look at me! *Point at yourself with both hands*

But when JESUS looked at the people of the big city.
They didn't look important or right at all! *Shake head*
They looked like little lost chicks,
running around getting lost
and cheeping for their mummy.

Can you show me little chicks again?
Lead the children in being little chicks.
Chick, chick, chick, chick, chicken!
Cheep, cheep, cheep, cheep, cheep!

So the people in the big city
thought they looked important and always right.
Lead the children in singing:
I am so important! *Puff chest up and stand tall*
Look, look, look at me! *Point at yourself with both hands*

But when Jesus saw them they looked like little chicks.
Lead the children in singing:
Chick, chick, chick, chick, chicken! *Flap wings*
Cheep, cheep, cheep, cheep, cheep!

Let's sit down for a moment.
When the group is ready:
Jesus wanted to keep the people of the big city safe,
to love them, to cuddle them under his wing
like a mummy hen.

And so Jesus did a very surprising thing.
Jesus cried. *Run fingers down cheeks to show tears*

Can you make your fingers run down your cheeks
to show Jesus crying?
Lead the children in the crying action.

And Jesus said a beautiful thing to Jerusalem.
Let's say Jesus' words together,
'my turn' *Point to self*, 'your turn' *Leader's hands out to group.*

Jesus said . . . .
Like a mummy hen *Flap wings gently*
Like a mummy hen *Flap wings gently*
Keeps her chicks safe and warm *Cross arms on chest*
Keeps her chicks safe and warm *Cross arms on chest*
I want to take care of you! *Hands outwards, palms up*
I want to take care of you! *Hands outwards, palms up*

Let's close our eyes for a moment.
When the group is ready:
Sometimes we feel very small.
Sometimes we feel lost.
And everyone else around us can look so big and important
and always right.

When we feel like that, let's imagine Jesus saying those words to us.
Let's say them after Jesus
and take them deep in our heart.
Jesus said . . . .

Like a mummy hen *Flap wings gently*
Like a mummy hen *Flap wings gently*
Keeps her chicks safe and warm *Cross arms on chest*
Keeps her chicks safe and warm *Cross arms on chest*
I want to take care of you! *Hands outwards, palms up*
I want to take care of you! *Hands outwards, palms up*

Let's imagine we're with Jesus, our mummy hen, right now.
Let's imagine hiding safe under our mummy's wing.
After a moment.
Let's open our eyes.
How did that feel to be safe with Jesus?
Can you show me with your face?

If appropriate:

Today/this week is Mothering Sunday when we celebrate mummies.
We celebrate mummies in three ways.

If your church also celebrates Mary as Jesus' mother, adapt the material to read four.

Let's count to 3.
Lead the children in counting to three on fingers.

1, 2, 3.

1: *Lead the children in showing one finger.*
We remember
how Jesus wants to be like a mummy hen to us.
2: *Lead the children in showing two fingers.*
We remember how the Church can be like a mummy to us.

If your church also celebrates Mary as Jesus' mother, add:
3: *Lead the children in showing three fingers.*
We remember Mary, Jesus' mummy.

And, what's next?
3 or 4: *Lead the children in showing three (or four) fingers.*
We remember
all the people who have been like mummies to us like Jesus.

I wonder who's been like a mummy to you?
At this point, you can:

Either: end this time of storytelling;
Or: lead into the Prayers for Other People (p. 170), using the material below as the Prayer Action;
Or: move straight into the following material that gives thanks for and prays for everyone who has been like a mother to us.

Mothering Sunday thank you prayers

Either: placing flowers as prayers on a 'garden' (a tray with brown cloth/paper folded on it). The flowers could be real flowers, silk flowers, paper flowers, 'flowers' made from tissue/crepe paper, or pictures of flowers, etc.
Or: placing little chicks onto a mother hen template (p. 207 or website);
Or: placing paper hearts on a cross (continuing the theme of Lent).

Let's close our eyes for a moment.
Let's remember someone who's been like a mummy to us.
Let's say thank you to God for all our mummies!

Let's open our eyes again.
Show the children the symbols you have chosen in one or more baskets or trays.
Name and Name are going to bring around these flowers/hearts/chicks.
If you like, you can take a flower/heart/chick and hold it up.
Let's ask God to see these flowers/hearts/chicks as a thank you prayer for someone who's been like a mummy to us.

As the symbols are taken around, lead the group in:

Either: humming the refrain of your Prayer Song together, with the words 'Jesus, hear our prayer' as a refrain as usual;

34

Mary Anoints Jesus

→ John 12.1–8
→ Song: 'Look! Look! This is my special thing!' Words: © Sharon Moughtin.
→ Tune: 'Oh dear! What can the matter be?' (traditional).

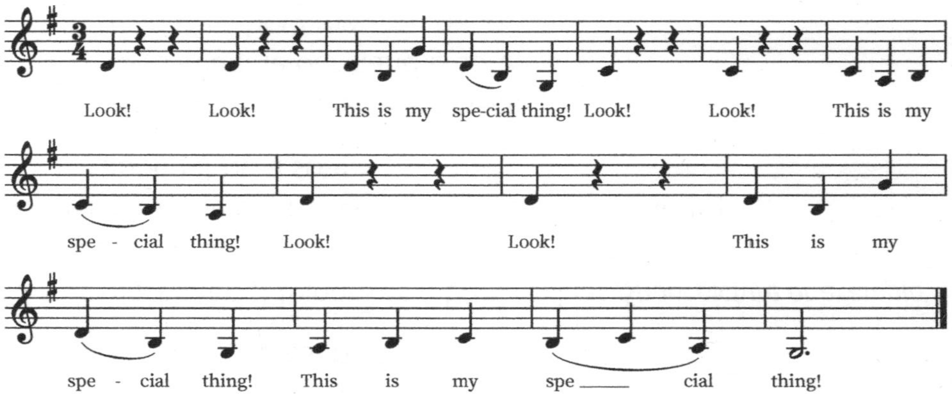

Appropriate for mixed groups of babies, toddlers and children up to the age of 9.

This story includes options to make it relevant for Mothering Sunday. Groups that only include children up to the age of 7 may prefer to tell the story of 'Jesus Is Like a Mother Hen' (p. 31) on Mothering Sunday.

For today's session, you will need a 'special thing' or photograph of it to show to the group: choose something that is important to you.

Our story today is all about someone's most special thing.
Show the special thing you have chosen to share.
If your group usually uses the What's in the Box? option (p. 7), this can become this story's object.

What do you see? *Invite a child to respond*

This is MY special thing.
It's a picture of my three lovely daughters.
When I look at it, it makes me feel happy inside.

Or: singing new words to the tune of 'Chick, chick, chick, chick, chicken'.

Let's sing our song again. This time let's sing:
'Thank you for our mummies!
Thank you, thank you God!'

Thank you for our mummies!
Thank you, thank you God!

Repeat as appropriate.

When the group is ready, place your 'garden'/cross/mother hen in the centre of the circle.

Either:
If you like,
you can place your flower in our 'garden' as a prayer.
Let's say thank you for everyone who's like a mummy and makes the world beautiful.

Or:
If you like, you can place your heart on this cross as a prayer.
Let's say thank you for everyone who's like a mummy and shows us how to love as Jesus loves.

Or:
If you like,
you can place your chick on this mummy hen as a prayer.
Let's say thank you for everyone who's like a mummy and shows us how to love as Jesus loves.

Hum or sing together again while the children place their symbols. Some groups may like to invite two children to carry the 'garden'/cross/hen around the group to collect the symbols. These can then be placed in the centre.

End by singing the final verse of your Prayer Song, or by singing the 'Thank you for our mummies' song one last time.

Put object to one side.
We're going to learn a song.
It goes like this:
Let's learn it 'my turn', 'your turn'.

Look! Look! This is my special thing!
Look! Look! This is my special thing!
Look! Look! This is my special thing!
Look! Look! This is my special thing!

Look! Look! This is my special thing!
This is my special thing!
Look! Look! This is my special thing!
This is my special thing!

Let's sing that all together:

Look! Look! This is my special thing!
This is my special thing!
Look! Look! This is my special thing!
This is my special thing!

We all have special things.
If you could only keep one thing, *Show one finger* what would it be?
Let's close our eyes for a moment.
When the group is ready:
Think for a moment: what's YOUR most special thing?
It might be in your home, or at school, or outside . . .

Let's open our eyes again.
Who'd like to tell us what their special thing is?
Invite one or two children to share what their special thing is, then ask them for an action for their special thing.

For example:
Child: 'My teddy'; Leader: 'What do you like to do with your teddy?
Can you show us an action with your body?'
Child: 'My ___ game'; Leader: 'Can you show us an action for playing your game?'
Child: 'My swing'; Leader: 'Can you show us what you look like when you're swinging?'

Let's all be *Name* and show their action as we sing:
Continue the action suggested by the child as you sing.

Look! Look! This is my special thing!
Look! Look! This is my special thing!
Look! Look! This is my special thing!
This is my special thing!
Repeat if appropriate.

Today's story is about someone's most special thing.
Mary's special thing.
Not Mary, Jesus' mummy.
But Mary, one of Jesus' best friends.

Mary's most special thing was a beautiful jar. *Show picture or example*
It was filled with oil:
special medicine oil that could stop you from hurting if you rubbed it on a sore.

If very young children are present:
Let's imagine our hand is sore.
Can you show me your hand?!
Let's rub the oil on our sore hand.

It smelled amazing! Let's smell it.
Lead the children: Sniff Mmmm!
And it was in a beautiful bottle!

Most people saved it until someone had died.
It could make people who had died smell beautiful like flowers!
Let's be Mary and sniff our special oil.
Sniff. Mmmm!

Then one day, Mary heard that Jesus was coming to visit!
Jesus is one of our best friends and is coming to visit.
How are we feeling.
Mary's sister, Martha, got busy, busy, busy, busy!
Let's be busy Martha and tidy up!
Super fast!
Let's sing 'Quick! Quick! Jesus is coming here!' as we tidy.

Lead the group in miming tidying up very quickly, for instance, miming gathering things left on the floor into a box.

Quick! Quick! Jesus is coming here!
Quick! Quick! Jesus is coming here!
Quick! Quick! Jesus is coming here!
Jesus is coming here!

Mary's brother, Lazarus, went and sat close to Jesus.
He went to have 'special time'.
Can you show me how you feel
when you get to be close to your best friend?
Accept responses.

But Mary did something different.
Mary brought out her most special thing.
Not just to **show** to Jesus.
But to **give** to him.
Mary opened her special jar.
Let's open our special jar.
Mime opening the jar.

Someone had given it to Mary.
And Mary loved it.
Let's be Mary.
Let's hold our special jar of oil high.
Let's show it to our friends.
And let's look really, really proud!
Can you show me proud!
Let's sing 'Look! Look! Look! This is my special OIL!'

Lead the children in singing and holding the oil high, swaying.

Look! Look! This is my special oil!
Look! Look! This is my special oil!
Look! Look! This is my special oil!
This is my special oil!

But this jar of oil wasn't just special to Mary.
EVERYONE knew it was special!
To buy this oil, someone would have to work hard.
Not just for 1 day . . . Or for 1 week . . . Or for 1 month!
They would have to work hard for ONE WHOLE YEAR!
Let's imagine we're a farmer.
We're digging and getting the field ready for the seeds.
Let's dig and sing 'Dig! Dig! Work for the special oil!'

Let's go!
Lead the group in digging and singing.

Dig! Dig! Work for the special oil!
Dig! Dig! Work for the special oil!
Dig! Dig! Work for the special oil!
Work for the special oil!

So this oil was very special.
So special that most people didn't even use oil like this!

And poured ALL the oil over Jesus' feet.
Let's be Mary. Let's pour and sing:
'Here! Here! You have my special oil!'
Lead the group in pouring and singing:
Here! Here! You have my special oil!
Here! Here! You have my special oil!
Here! Here! You have my special oil!
You have my special oil!

How much does Mary love Jesus?
Can you show me with your body?
Lead the children in making a big shape.
Bigger! Bigger!
Mary gave all her special oil to Jesus
So the smell of the special oil filled the whole house!
Can you imagine?

Then Mary dried Jesus' feet with her hair!
She wanted to be close to him.
She wanted to take care of him and show how special he was.
Let's sing: 'Here! Here! Let me take care of you!'
Let's be Mary drying Jesus' feet with her long hair as we sing.

Lead the group in drying feet and singing:
Here! Here! Let me take care of you.
Here! Here! Let me take care of you.
Here! Here! Let me take care of you.
Let me take care of you.

One of Jesus' friends, Judas was cross.
Can you show me cross?
Lead the children in looking cross.
And not just cross. . . Judas was angry!

Can you show me angry?
Lead the children in looking angry.

Then Judas said to Jesus: 'my turn', 'your turn':
That oil took ONE WHOLE YEAR to work for! *Show index finger*
That oil took ONE WHOLE YEAR to work for! *Show index finger*
You could have sold it! *Hands on hips*
You could have sold it! *Hands on hips*
You could have given money to poor people! *Hands out*
You could have given money to poor people! *Hands out*

Let's be angry Judas and wag our finger at Mary and sing:
'Stop! Stop! Stop! *Wag finger*
What a waste! What a waste!
Shake head with hands on hips

Lead the group in wagging finger then shake head with hands on hips as you sing.

Stop! Stop! What a waste! What a waste!
Stop! Stop! What a waste! What a waste!
Stop! Stop! What a waste! What a waste!
What a waste! What a waste!

But Mary didn't think it was a waste! *Shake head*
Jesus was special!
Special oil for a very special friend!

Jesus didn't think it was a waste either.
Jesus said: "Leave her alone!" *Hand outstretched*
And then Jesus said something that made the whole room go quiet.
Sssssssh!
Whisper: Listen! *Hand behind ear*

Jesus said:

In the rhythm of the song: **Soon! Soon! Soon I will need this oil.**
Jesus was talking about the cross!

Soon Jesus would have sore nails
in his feet with the special oil on. *Point to feet*
Soon Jesus would die on the cross. *Stretch arms out on the cross*
Jesus' friends would take Jesus down from the cross.
Mime taking Jesus body down.
They would put his body in the Dark Cave. *Mime placing Jesus' body*
They would roll the stone of the cave shut.
Mime rolling the stone across.
Jesus' body would need the special oil for then.

Let's make the shape of the cross with our body. *Make cross shape*
Then show tears on our face. *Tears on face*
Let's sing to each other 'Soon! Soon! Soon! Jesus will need this oil!'

Soon! Soon! *Cross shape* **Jesus will need this oil!** *Tears on face*
Soon! Soon! *Cross shape* **Jesus will need this oil!** *Tears on face*
Soon! Soon! *Cross shape* **Jesus will need this oil!** *Tears on face*
Jesus will need this oil! *Tears on face*

Jesus' friends don't understand!
They're confused!
Can you show me confused?
Lead the group in looking confused.
Can you show me sad?
Lead the group in looking sad and show tears on face.

Mary and Jesus' friends didn't know how many days to the cross.
But Jesus knew it was soon! Very soon!
If you want to hear what happens next, come back next time.

If you're telling this story on Mothering Sunday:
In our story, Mary shows us how to follow Jesus
Today is Mothering Sunday
And we're remembering people, like Mary
who show us how to be with Jesus.
Jesus said: 'Whenever people tell the Good News about ME
they'll tell this story to remember her.'

Mary helps us remember people who don't just give a bit.
They give a lot!
They give everything they have!
Today on Mothering Sunday,
let's remember people who give a lot!

If there is time, you might like to lead the group in the prayers from the other option for Mothering Sunday on p. 34. You could hum the tune of 'Look! Look! This is my special oil' on p. 35 as you place flowers of thanks for people who have taken care of us.

Jesus Washes the Disciples' Feet

There are two versions of this story. Option 1 is appropriate for mixed groups of babies, toddlers and children up to the age of 7. Groups that include children up to the age of 9 may prefer to use Option 2. The storytelling is almost identical, but a different tune is used that is more appropriate for older children. Choose which version works best in your setting.

Both options offer the opportunity to include real footwashing. If your group takes part in this, it's important to think through the logistics beforehand and it may make sense to have extra helpers available. You may find it helpful to think through:

39

- Where will the footwashing take place? If you need to use the space where you would normally have a Creative Response following the storytelling, are you going to skip the Creative Response this time (you may not have time), or do it differently (for instance, in the part of the room where you normally sit for the storytelling)? We've found it works as a one-off to give children clipboards and a simple pencil so they can draw their experience of footwashing afterwards while kneeling on the floor in the part of the room that is dry.

- If everyone is going to take part, you will need a chair, a bowl of water and a towel for each pair of children. The chairs could be placed in a row or in a circle. It can be helpful to set the chairs and towels out beforehand. We've found it works best to put one towel under (not on) each chair so they don't get sat on!

- We've found it works best for the bowls of water to be taken to each pair once the children who will have their feet washed are already seated, to prevent spillages. This is where extra helpers can come in handy. It also means that the water can still be warm.

- If there are a range of ages in your group, it might be helpful to pair up younger children with older children for the footwashing where possible. Where there are parents/carers with babies and toddlers, the baby/toddler can sit on their knee on the chairs.

- We've found that it can help to ask the children to take their shoes and socks off at the beginning of the session as they enter the room to keep the flow of the session (making sure they place their socks inside their shoes!)

- If there are children wearing tights who need help to remove them, make sure that the child does want to take her/his tights off, then **make sure that this is done by their adult or that you check the safeguarding procedures for your church/group for helping children change clothes.** You could make an announcement in the weeks prior to the session asking children and adults to make sure that tights aren't worn to that session. However, it inevitably happens!

- If it emerges at any point that any of the children do not want to have their feet washed, simply swap them over to become the 'footwasher'. It's very important that your group and church respects their choices about what happens to their body and to model this clearly. If they also don't want to wash other people's feet, then simply let them watch and help the group sing. They may like to take part in the drying of feet later.

Option 1: Servant King

→ John 13.1–17
→ Song: 'I am going to follow Jesus'. Words: © Sharon Moughtin.
→ Tune: 'Bobby Shaftoe' (traditional).

I am going to fol-low Je-sus, I am going to fol-low Je-sus,
I am going to fol-low Je-sus, fol-low, fol-low Je-sus!

Appropriate for mixed groups of babies, toddlers and children up to the age of 7. Groups that include children up to the age of 9 may prefer to tell the version of the story in Option 2. Choose which version works best in your setting.

This story uses the 'New Start' sign as the action for 'servant' and 'washing'. This is deliberate. The 'New Start' sign looks like the action of washing but it also reminds us that Jesus is the one who turns things 'topsy turvy', upside down: the king who will take the action of the servant. And it reminds us that in the footwashing we are also being given a new start: learning to be church in a different way. See p. 8 for a description and explanation of the 'New Start' sign.

Optional: What's in the Box? (see p. 7)
Invite a child to open the box.
Inside is a crown.

What's in the box?
Accept the child's response.

Today we're going to tell a story about a king.
King Jesus, the Servant King.

The king-and-servant game:
When Jesus was alive, it was different being a king!
You got to tell everyone what to do . . . And they obeyed!
Imagine that!
To get ready for today's story,
we're going to practise being servants and kings!

Invite a child to be 'king'.
Name is going to be our king!
Here's your crown! *Place an imaginary crown on the king's head*
Can you show us your crown on your head?
If necessary help the king in making a crown action with her/his hands.
The rest of us are going to be servants! *Point around the group*

Name, we're your servants.
What would you like us to do?
If necessary, aside to the king:
Say, 'Mop the floor!' or 'Cook some food!'
King: 'Mop the floor!'
We're King *Name*'s servants, we have to do as the king says!
Let's mop the floor! Lead the children in miming mopping the floor

Choose another child to be king.
Now *Name* is going to be our king!
Here's your crown! *Place an imaginary crown on king's head*
Can you show us your crown on your head?
If necessary help the king in making a crown action with her/his hands.

Name, we're your servants.
What would you like us to do?
If necessary, aside to the king:
Say, 'Wash my clothes!' or 'Run on the spot!'
King: 'Run over there!'
We're King *Name*'s servants, so let's run on the spot.
Lead the group in running on the spot.
Repeat as appropriate.

Let's sit down.
When the group is ready:
We're ready to tell our story about Jesus the king.

Tip
It's best to use the language of 'king' for both girls and boys as it will be the 'Servant KING', Jesus, that we're talking about later.

Jesus' friends, the disciples, were excited!
Can you show me excited?
Lead the children in looking excited.
Really excited!
Jesus had invited them to a special party!
If appropriate: the Passover!

And . . . ssssh! *Look around*
Listen! *Hand behind ear*
Whispering: 'Jesus is going to tell us he's the king!'
Let's turn to each other and whisper, 'Jesus is the king!'
Lead the group in whispering to each other.
Jesus is the king!
Jesus is the king!
Jesus is the king!

So the disciples were sitting down ready to eat.
Let's look ready for our special meal.
Let's sit up!
Lead the children in sitting up and looking expectant.
Then Jesus the king did something very surprising!

Let's all be Jesus.
Jesus stood up.
Let's stand up! *Lead the children in standing.*
He tied a towel around his waist like an apron.
Let's put our apron on . . . *Lead the children in tying apron on*
Then Jesus poured water into a bowl.
Lead the children in miming pouring water.
Jesus knelt on the floor. *Lead the children in kneeling*
and washed the feet of one of his disciples.
'New Start' sign (p. 8).

The words to this song are so straightforward, if you start singing the children will gradually join in.
Washing, washing, washing feet, *'New Start' sign*
washing, washing, washing feet, *'New Start' sign*
washing, washing, washing feet, *'New Start' sign*
washing, washing, washing feet. *'New Start' sign*

The room went silent!
This is the hard bit of the story!
Let's try one second of complete silence after 3!
Let's put our hands over our mouth to show silent!
1, 2, 3 . . .
Lead the children in clamping hands on mouth.

Leave a second or as long as you think the group can, then:
Silence!
The room went silent!

The disciples looked at each other shocked.
Let's be the disciples again.
Can you show me your shocked face?
Lead the group in look at each other shocked.
Nobody spoke.

Kings don't wash feet! *Crown action and shake head*
Kings don't kneel on the floor! *Crown on head and shake head*
Servants wash feet! *'New Start' sign*
Not kings!
The disciples were shocked!
Can you show me shocked? *Lead the group in looking shocked*

Then it was Peter's turn.
Let's be Peter.

Let's put our feet in front of us and wiggle them.
Lead the children in wiggling feet.
Wiggle, wiggle, wiggle!

Jesus came to wash Peter's feet. *Keep wiggling feet*
But Peter said, 'NO! *Wag finger*
Not MY feet! No!' *Wag finger*
Let's be Peter and say, 'No! No! *Wag finger*
No!' *Wag finger*

Peter wanted Jesus to act like a REAL king. *Crown on head*
Not like a servant. *'New Start' sign and shake head*

But Jesus said, 'Yes!'
Jesus washed Peter's feet!
Let's be Peter. *Wiggle feet*
Let's close our eyes and imagine Jesus
Kneeling down before us and washing our feet.

Singing gently and making the 'New Start' sign throughout:
**Washing, washing, washing feet,
washing, washing, washing feet,
washing, washing, washing feet,
washing, washing feet.**

I wonder how Peter felt when Jesus washed his feet?
Can you show me with your face?

That was when the disciples knew:
Jesus wasn't just the king! *Crown action*
Jesus was the SERVANT *'New Start' sign* KING! *Crown action*

Let's say that
'my turn' *Point to self,* 'your turn' *Leader's hands out to group.*
Slowly: Jesus is the SERVANT *'New Start' sign* KING! *Crown action*
Jesus is the SERVANT *'New Start' sign* **KING!** *Crown action*

And again:
Jesus is the SERVANT *'New Start' sign* **KING!** *Crown action*

Optional footwashing:
Then Jesus said something surprising.

Let's be Jesus.
Let's say these words
'my turn' *Point to self,* 'your turn' *Leader's hands out to group.*

YOU must wash each other's feet! *Point to children then feet*
YOU must wash each other's feet! *Point to children then feet*
YOU must be like a servant! *Point to children then 'New Start' sign*
YOU must be like a servant! *Point to children then 'New Start' sign*

When we wash each other's feet.
We're showing we're ready to be a servant like Jesus.
We're following Jesus!

If your group is taking part in the act of footwashing:
We're going to wash each other's feet this morning/afternoon.
We're going to follow Jesus.

Be very clear about what you would like the children to do, according to your resources and space. This is especially important if you have a large group. If it emerges at any point that any of the children do not want to have their feet washed, simply swap them over to become the 'footwasher'. It's very important that your group and church respect their choices about what happens to their body and to model this clearly. If they also don't want to wash other people's feet, then simply let them watch and help the group sing. They may like to take part in the drying of feet later.

For example:
Either (in groups of the same age):
Can this half of the room go and sit on the chairs?

Or (in mixed-age groups):
Can everyone who doesn't go to school sit on the chairs?
These children may need some help to identify themselves.
Now everyone in nursery. Now everyone in reception.
Until half the group is sitting.

As they find their places, let's sing:
I am going to follow Jesus,
I am going to follow Jesus,
I am going to follow Jesus,
follow, follow Jesus!

When the children are sitting ready, ask helpers to move the bowls of water in front of each seated child. Continue singing as this takes place. When the bowls are in place, to the remaining children (which should be half the group):
Can you go and kneel next to one of the children sitting on a chair?
In large groups, you may find it helpful to send the children over one by one, telling them the name of the child they should kneel in front of.

Continue singing as this takes place.
I am going to follow Jesus,
I am going to follow Jesus,
I am going to follow Jesus,
follow, follow Jesus!

When the group is ready:
It's time for our footwashing.

If you're sitting on a chair,
you're going to have your feet washed!
If you're kneeling on the floor,
you're going to be washing feet!
Let's sing as we wash.

Lead the children in singing as they wash feet.
Washing, washing, washing feet,
washing, washing, washing feet,
washing, washing, washing feet,
washing, washing feet.

I am going to serve like Jesus,
I am going to serve like Jesus,
I am going to serve like Jesus,
serve like, serve like Jesus.

I am going to follow Jesus,
I am going to follow Jesus,
I am going to follow Jesus,
follow, follow Jesus!
Repeat as appropriate.

When the group is ready:
Now if you're kneeling,
it's time to dry your friend's feet.
Let's take our towel . . .
If appropriate: it's under the chair!

Let's dry our friend's feet.
Lead the children in singing as they wash feet.
Drying, drying, drying feet,
drying, drying, drying feet,
drying, drying, drying feet,
drying, drying feet.

I am going to serve like Jesus,
I am going to serve like Jesus,
I am going to serve like Jesus,
serve like, serve like Jesus.

Option 2: Washing feet

→ John 13.1–17
→ Song: 'Servant King'. Words: © Sharon Moughtin.
→ Tune: 'Sur le Pont d'Avignon' (traditional).

Ser - vant King, Ser - vant King, Kneel - ing serv - ing, kneel - ing, serv - ing.

Ser - vant King, Ser - vant King, Je - sus is the Ser - vant King.

Appropriate for mixed groups of babies, toddlers and children up to the age of 9. Groups that only include children up to the age of 7 may prefer to use Option 1.

> This story uses the 'New Start' sign (p. 8) as the action for 'servant' and 'washing'. This is deliberate. The 'New Start' sign looks like the action of washing but it also reminds us that Jesus is the one who turns things 'topsy turvy', upside down: the king who will take the action of the servant. And it reminds us that in the footwashing we are also being given a new start: learning to be church in a different way. See p. 8 or the website for a description and explanation of the 'New Start' sign.

For today's story, we need to learn a song.

Let's sing it 'my turn', 'your turn'!

Servant King! Servant King! *'New Start' sign followed by crown action*
Kneeling, serving! *'New Start' sign*

I am going to follow Jesus,
I am going to follow Jesus,
I am going to follow Jesus,
follow, follow Jesus!

Repeat as appropriate.

If there's time, you could invite the children to swap and repeat the material. If there are pairs where this doesn't work, the helpers could join that pair to have their feet washed by both children at this point, now the children know what they're doing. Or groups of two to three children could wash one child's feet.

When the footwashing is over:

When we wash each other's feet
We're showing we're ready to serve people like Jesus.
We're following Jesus, the SERVANT *'New Start' sign* KING! *Crown action.*

Let's say that
'my turn' *Point to self,* 'your turn' *Leader's hands out to group.*
We follow the SERVANT *'New Start' sign* KING! *Crown action*
We follow the SERVANT *'New Start' sign* KING! *Crown action*
We follow the SERVANT *'New Start' sign* **KING!** *Crown action*
Let's say that three times!

Lead the children in saying:
We follow the SERVANT *'New Start' sign* **KING!** *Crown action*
Louder!
We follow the SERVANT *'New Start' sign* **KING!** *Crown action*
Even louder!
We follow the SERVANT *'New Start' sign* **KING!** *Crown action*

Encourage the children to find their shoes and put them on again.

If appropriate:
The Passover is a feast with special food.
Everyone remembers the story of God sending Moses
to rescue God's People from Egypt.

The Passover is a big party!
Can you show me big for the big party in the big city?
Lead the group in stretching out arms wider and wider.
Even bigger!
At the party, Jesus' friends, the disciples sat down to eat . . .
Let's be the disciples and sit down.
The disciples are excited! Can you show me excited?
Because . . . ssssssh! *Look around*
Listen!
Whispering: Jesus is going to tell us he's the king!
Let's turn to each other and whisper:
'Jesus is the king! Jesus is the king!'

Then Jesus, the king, did something very surprising!
Jesus stood up. Let's stand up . . .
Jesus took off his cloak. Let's take off our cloak . . .
Jesus tied a towel around his waist like an apron.
Let's put our towel apron on . . .
Jesus poured water into a bowl . . . Let's pour water . . .
Sound shocked: And Jesus started to wash his disciples' feet!

Servant King! Servant King! *'New Start' sign followed by crown action*
Kneeling, serving! *'New Start' sign*
Kneeling, serving! *'New Start' sign*
Servant King! Servant King! *'New Start' sign followed by crown action*
Jesus is the Servant King! *'New Start' sign followed by crown action*

Kneeling, serving! *'New Start' sign*
Servant King! Servant King! *'New Start' sign followed by crown action*
Kneeling, serving! *'New Start' sign*
Kneeling, serving! *'New Start' sign*
Servant King! Servant King! *'New Start' sign followed by crown action*
Jesus is the Servant King! *'New Start' sign followed by crown action*

Let's sing that all together:
Servant King! Servant King! *'New Start' sign followed by crown action*
Kneeling, serving! *'New Start' sign*
Kneeling, serving! *'New Start' sign*
Servant King! Servant King! *'New Start' sign followed by crown action*
Jesus is the Servant King! *'New Start' sign followed by crown action*

If appropriate:
We're in a countdown to the cross!
Today's story is the night before Jesus will die!
But no one knows it yet. *Shake head*
Except Jesus.
Jesus knows. How do you think Jesus was feeling?
Can you show me?

If there are babies, toddlers or children present who will not understand the concepts 'servant' and 'king' you may like to include the king-and-servant game from Option 1 above (p. 41).

We're ready to tell our story.
Jesus and his friends are in the big city, Jerusalem!
Can you show me big with your body?
Lead the group in stretching out arms wide
It's time for a party: the Passover!

The room went silent!
Everyone was shocked! Can you show me shocked?
Lead the group in looking shocked!

Jesus is meant to be king!
Kings don't kneel on the floor! *Shake head*
Kings don't wash feet! *Shake head*
Servants wash feet! Not kings!

But Jesus is the . . .
Encourage group to join in:
Servant King.

Let's sing our song again and show Jesus washing:
Servant King! Servant King! *'New Start' sign followed by crown action*
Kneeling, serving! *'New Start' sign*
Kneeling, serving! *'New Start' sign*
Servant King! Servant King! *'New Start' sign followed by crown action*
Jesus is the Servant King! *'New Start' sign followed by crown action*

Then it was Peter's turn.
Jesus knelt in front of Peter.
That was too much for Peter!
Peter said . . . 'my turn', 'your turn' . . . .

'No!' *Hold our hand in a stop sign*
'No!' *Hold our hand in a stop sign*
Not MY feet! *Wave hands to show 'never' in front of body*
Not MY feet! *Wave hands to show 'never' in front of body*

Jesus said, 'If I don't wash you, you're not part of me!' *Shake head*
Then Peter was even more shocked!
Can you show me even more shocked?

So Jesus washed Peter's feet.

Let's be Jesus washing Peter's feet.

Servant King! Servant King! *'New Start' sign followed by crown action*
Kneeling, serving! *'New Start' sign*
Kneeling, serving! *'New Start' sign*
Servant King! Servant King! *'New Start' sign followed by crown action*
Jesus is the Servant King! *'New Start' sign followed by crown action*

Then Jesus said something surprising.
Let's say Jesus' words 'my turn', 'your turn':

You must wash each other's feet! *Point around the group*
You must wash each other's feet! *Point around the group*
You must do the same as me! *Point to group then self*
You must do the same as me! *Point to group then self*

Let's imagine we're washing each other's feet now.
Let's sing our song again, but this time let's sing 'Servant Church'.
Who can show us an action for 'church'?
Choose one of the actions and this will become the 'church action'.

Servant Church! Servant Church!
'New Start' sign followed by church action.
Kneeling, serving! *'New Start' sign*
Kneeling, serving! *'New Start' sign*
Servant Church! Servant Church . . .
'New Start' sign followed by church action.
Interrupt the singing:
Wait a minute: who's the Servant Church?
We are! Everyone here!
Let's sing:
We are all the Servant Church!
'New Start' sign followed by church action.

47

We are all the Servant Church!
'New Start' sign followed by church action.

When we wash each other's feet.
We're showing we're ready to be a servant like Jesus.
We're following Jesus!

If your group is taking part in the act of footwashing:
We're going to wash each other's feet this morning.
We're going to follow Jesus.

Be very clear about what you would like the children to do, according to your resources and space. This is especially important if you have a large group. If it emerges at any point that any of the children do not want to have their feet washed, simply swap them over to become the 'footwasher'. It's very important that your group and church respect their choices about what happens to their body and to model this clearly. If they also don't want to wash other people's feet, then simply let them watch and help the group sing. They may like to take part in the drying of feet later.

For example:
Either (in groups of the same age):
Can this half of the room go and sit on the chairs?
Or (in mixed age groups):
Can everyone who doesn't go to school sit on the chairs?
These children may need some help to identify themselves.
Now everyone in nursery. Now everyone in reception.
Until half the group is sitting.

Groups that are not familiar with the 'I am going to follow Jesus' song could sing the 'Servant Church' song instead as they find their places.

As they find their places, let's sing:
**I am going to follow Jesus,
I am going to follow Jesus,
I am going to follow Jesus,
follow, follow Jesus!**

When the children are sitting ready, ask helpers to move the bowls of water in front of each seated child. Continue singing as this takes place.

When the bowls are in place, to the remaining children (which should be half the group):
Can you go and kneel next to one of the children sitting on a chair?
In large groups, you may find it helpful to send the children over one by one, telling them the name of the child they should kneel in front of.

As they find their places, let's sing:
**I am going to follow Jesus,
I am going to follow Jesus,
I am going to follow Jesus,
follow, follow Jesus!**

Continue singing as this takes place.
**I am going to follow Jesus,
I am going to follow Jesus,
I am going to follow Jesus,
follow, follow Jesus!**

When the group is ready:
It's time for our footwashing.

If you're sitting on a chair,
you're going to have your feet washed!
If you're kneeling on the floor,
you're going to be washing feet!
Let's sing as we wash.

As the footwashing takes place, lead the group in singing alternate verses:
I am going to follow Jesus,

48

Servant King! Servant King! *'New Start' sign followed by crown action*
Kneeling, serving! *'New Start' sign*
Kneeling, serving! *'New Start' sign*
Servant King! Servant King! *'New Start' sign followed by crown action*
Jesus is the Servant King! *'New Start' sign followed by crown action*

Servant Church! Servant Church!
'New Start' sign followed by church action.
Kneeling, serving! *'New Start' sign*
Kneeling, serving! *'New Start' sign*
Servant Church! Servant Church!...
'New Start' sign followed by church action.
We are all the Servant Church!
'New Start' sign followed by church action.

When the group is ready:
Now if you're kneeling,
it's time to dry your friend's feet.
Let's take our towel . . .

If appropriate: it's under the chair!

Let's dry our friend's feet.
Lead the children in singing as they wash feet.

Servant King! Servant King! *'New Start' sign followed by crown action*
Kneeling, serving! *'New Start' sign*
Kneeling, serving! *'New Start' sign*
Servant King! Servant King! *'New Start' sign followed by crown action*
Jesus is the Servant King! *'New Start' sign followed by crown action*

Servant Church! Servant Church!
'New Start' sign followed by church action.
Kneeling, serving! *'New Start' sign*
Kneeling, serving! *'New Start' sign*

Servant Church! Servant Church!...
'New Start' sign followed by church action.
We are all the Servant Church!
'New Start' sign followed by church action.
Repeat as appropriate.

If there's time, you could invite the children to swap and repeat the material. If there are pairs where this doesn't work, the helpers could join that pair to have their feet washed by both children at this point, now the children know what they're doing. Or groups of two to three children could wash one child's feet.

When the footwashing is over, invite the children to carefully move into the dry part of the room. It may be best to do this in small groups.

When the group is ready:
So in the Church we tell the story of Jesus washing feet.
We wash each other's feet.
But that's not the only way to serve
and do what Jesus did.

There are lots of ways of serving:
Who can think of different ways
we can be like servants to each other,
and to all the people living around us?
Who can think of ways we can love and serve?
Accept responses.

If appropriate: those are some of the ways we can show we're following Jesus' 'way of love'

Let's sing our song again. Let's sing 'loving, serving'. This time, let's cross our arms on our chest to show 'love' then our washing action.

Servant Church! Servant Church!
Cross arms on chest followed by church action.
Loving, serving! *Cross arms followed by 'New Start' sign*
Loving, serving! *Cross arms followed by 'New Start' sign*
Servant Church! Servant Church!
Cross arms on chest followed by church action.
We are all the Servant Church!
Cross arms on chest followed by church action.

Jesus' Last Meal

↑ The Last Supper
↑ Luke 22.14–23
↑ Poem: 'Do this to remember me' © Sharon Moughtin (p. 117).

Appropriate for mixed groups of babies, toddlers and children up to the age of 9.

Tip

You could use everyday bread or pitta bread for this story. Try to have a gluten free option also available. We cut the bread into small squares beforehand with scissors.

There are benefits in making connections both with the kind of bread that you use in your church's communion service and with the kind that your children will be familiar with from home, school or nursery. As this story is told at Easter time as well, you could move between the different kinds of bread to support the children in making these connections.

If you prefer, you could tell the story with cups and plates (or wooden egg cups and wooden coasters acting as chalices and patens) for the children and simply imagine the bread and wine on them. Or you could even mime the actions without any props.

To tell the story of Jesus' Last Supper, you'll need to have ready two or more trays: one set holding a piece of bread for each child and adult; the other set holding a cup with a small amount of grape juice at the bottom for each child and adult.

Optional: What's in the Box? (see p. 7)
Invite one of the children to open the box. Inside will be bread and a cup or chalice.

What's in the box? *Ask the child to respond*
We're going to tell the story of when Jesus shared bread and wine.
Show cup and bread.

Jesus' friends, the disciples, were excited!
Can you show me excited?
Lead the children in looking excited.
Really excited!
They were in the big city, Jerusalem!

If you're telling this story on Palm Sunday before or after a procession:
Jesus had ridden into the city on a donkey!
Everyone had waved palm leaves and shouted:
Lead the children in shouting 'Hosanna', getting louder and louder.
If necessary: Let's shout 'my turn' *Point to self,* 'your turn' *Leader's hands out to group.*

Hosanna! *Raise hands above head*
Hosanna! *Raise hands above head*
Hosanna! *Raise hands above head*
Hosanna! *Raise hands above head*
Hosanna! *Raise hands above head*
Hosanna! *Raise hands above head*

Now Jesus had invited them to a special party!
If appropriate: The Passover!
and . . . ssssh! *Look around*
Listen! *Hand behind ear*
Whispering with finger near lips: 'Jesus is going to tell us he's the king!'

Let's turn to each other and whisper, 'Jesus is the king!'
Lead the group in whispering to each other.
Jesus is the king!
Jesus is the king!
Jesus is the king!

The sun had gone down . . . .
Let's show the sun going down with our arms.
Lead the children in raising your arms then lowering them to your sides to show the sun setting.
It was dark!
It was time!
Then after dinner, Jesus did something new.

If your church has a communion service every week:
We tell this story every week in church.
It's one of our most important stories!

Invite two children to take around small pieces of bread in two baskets for everyone who wants to receive them.

Name and *Name* are going to bring around some bread now.
If you'd like some bread, can you hold your hands out like this?
Model to the children holding out cupped hands.
Name and *Name* will give you a piece.
Keep the bread in your hands till everyone has some.

Don't eat it yet!

If your group is using 'I am going to follow Jesus' as a Gathering Song, you may like to sing this as you wait for your bread. Or you could sing another appropriate song that the group is familiar with.

When the group is ready:
After dinner, Jesus did something new.

Can you say these words after me and copy my actions,
'my turn' *Point to self*, 'your turn' *Leader's hands out to group?*

Jesus took the bread.   *Take bread in one hand*
Jesus took the bread.   *Take bread in one hand*
He said, 'Thank you, God!'   *Hold bread up if this is in your tradition*
He said, 'Thank you, God!'   *Hold bread up if this is in your tradition*
Jesus broke the bread.   *Break bread*
Jesus broke the bread.   *Break bread*
Then he shared it.   *Mime handing bread out in a circle*
Then he shared it.   *Mime handing bread out in a circle*

This is my body,   *Hold bread or point to it*
This is my body,   *Hold bread or point to it*
broken for you.   *Hold bread together then separate again*
broken for you.   *Hold bread together then separate again*
Do this to remember me!   *Hold bread up if this is in your tradition*
Do this to remember me!   *Hold bread up if this is in your tradition*

Invite the children to eat their bread slowly, really tasting and enjoying it. Once the children's hands are empty, distribute cups with just 1–2 cm of grape juice at the bottom. These cups are best distributed by adults or responsible older children.

51

While you finish eating,
we're going to bring around cups.
If you'd like a cup,
can you hold your hands out like this? *Model to the children*
Keep the cup in your hands till everyone has one.
Don't drink from it yet!

If your group is using 'I am going to follow Jesus' as a Gathering Song, you may like to sing this as you wait for your cup. Or you could sing another appropriate song that the group is familiar with. Once all the children and adults who wish to receive a cup have done so:

When they'd finished eating,
Jesus took the cup.

Can you say these words after me and copy my actions,
'my turn' *Point to self*, 'your turn' *Leader's hands out to group?*

Jesus took the cup.	*Take cup in both hands*
Jesus took the cup.	*Take cup in both hands*
He said, 'Thank you, God!'	*Hold cup up if this is in your tradition*
He said, 'Thank you, God!'	*Hold cup up if this is in your tradition*
Jesus poured the wine.	*Mime pouring wine*
Jesus poured the wine.	*Mime pouring wine*
Then he shared it.	*Mime handing cup out in a circle*
Then he shared it.	*Mime handing cup out in a circle*
This is my blood,	*Lift cup or point to it*
This is my blood,	*Lift cup or point to it*
poured out for you.	*Mime pouring wine*
poured out for you.	*Mime pouring wine*
Do this to remember me!	*Hold cup up if this is in your tradition*
Do this to remember me!	*Hold cup up if this is in your tradition*

Invite the children to drink the grape juice slowly and to really taste and enjoy it. When they've finished, ask for a moment of quiet.
I wonder how you feel when you eat the bread
and drink from your cup?
Can you show me?

The children may respond silently, inside themselves, or they may offer a facial expression, or a single word or more. Accept all of their responses.

Then Jesus said to his friends:
'Tonight, all of you will run away!
You'll leave me all alone!'
I wonder how the disciples felt now?
Can you show me with your face?

Peter said, 'No!' *Shake head, looking cross*
Can you shake your head and say, 'No!'
No! *Shake head*
'I will never leave you!' Peter said.
'I *Point to self* will stay with you!'

And all the other disciples said the same thing.
Let's all shake our heads and say,
'We will never leave you!' *Shake head*
'We will never leave you! *Shake head*
We will never leave you!' *Shake head*

Then Jesus went with his friends to a quiet garden to pray.

If appropriate:
Come back on *Good Friday* to hear what happens next.

The Story of Love: The Story of the Cross (Good Friday)

→ Song: 'Love is stronger!' Words: © Sharon Moughtin.
→ Tune: 'She'll be coming round the mountain' (traditional).

Love is strong-er than ev - 'ry thing! Love is strong-er! Love is strong-er than ev - 'ry thing! Love is strong-er! – Love is strong-er! Love is strong-er than ev - 'ry thing! Love is strong-er than ev - 'ry thing!

Appropriate for mixed groups of babies, toddlers and children up to the age of 9.

> This story is designed to be told on Good Friday itself, but can be told at any time during the year. Adapt the material accordingly.

You will need . . .

- a thick red ribbon;
- a figure of Jesus (a simple version is provided in the appendix);
- a cup/chalice and bread;
- a plant (e.g. rosemary) or small leafy branch (olive or other) to represent the Garden of Gethsemane;
- a piece of rope or string;
- a crown of thorns (this can be made from twisting wire);
- a cross or crucifix;
- a white piece of cloth;
- a box with a lid (e.g. a shoebox) that the figure of Jesus can fit inside when wrapped in the cloth.

You might like to give each child a mini version of the storytelling box to take home, along with a simple version of the story for children to read and sing themselves. You could offer them the option to personalize during the session at one of the tables, where felt tips/pencils/crayons and scissors are provided. See the Creative Response starter ideas for Good Friday for more information (p. 131). For photographs of a mini storytelling box laid out for the storytelling see the Sowing Seeds website.

If you're telling the story on Good Friday:
All through Lent, we've been getting ready
to follow Jesus to the cross.
Today it's Good Friday.
It's time.

All groups:
It's time to tell the story of the cross.
It's the story of love.
Lay the red ribbon along the floor and place the Jesus figure at one end.
(If you find it easier, you may like to lay all the objects on the ribbon at this point, so it is clear what the path facing Jesus is from the beginning.)
The way of the cross is the way of love: red for love.
Let's show our sign for love with our arms.
Lead the children in crossing arms on chest.

Move your arms slightly away from your chest to show them, or indicate how the crossed arms of a neighbour make the shape of a cross.
Look! Our sign for love is a cross!

To tell our story, we need to learn a song called 'Love is stronger'.
'Love Cross arms is stronger *Clench fists gently but firmly* than everything!' *Arms out*

For each time you sing 'Love is stronger' throughout this storytelling, cross your arms for 'love' and clench fists gently but firmly for 'stronger'. This is then followed with the action for each verse, as indicated.

Let's sing the song
'my turn' *Point to self*, 'your turn' *Arms out to the group.*

Singing:
Love *Cross arms* is stronger *Clench fists*
than everything! *Arms out*
Love *Cross arms* **is stronger** *Clench fists*
than everything! *Arms out*

Then a bit higher:
Love *Cross arms* is stronger *Clench fists*
than everything! *Arms out*
Love *Cross arms* **is stronger** *Clench fists*
than everything! *Arms out*

Then:
Love *Cross arms* is stronger! *Clench fists*
Love *Cross arms* is stronger *Clench fists*
Love *Cross arms* **is stronger!** *Clench fists*
Love *Cross arms* **is stronger!** *Clench fists*
than everything! *Throw arms out wide*
Love *Cross arms* is stronger! *Clench fists*
than everything! *Throw arms out wide*

Let's sing that all together.

Love *Cross arms* **is stronger** *Clench fists*
than everything! *Throw arms out wide*
Love *Cross arms* **is stronger** *Clench fists*
than everything! *Throw arms out wide*
Love *Cross arms* **is stronger!** *Clench fists*

Love *Cross arms* **is stronger!** *Clench fists*
Love *Cross arms* **is stronger** *Clench fists*
than everything! *Throw arms out wide*
Repeat until the group is sounding confident.

We're ready to tell our story.

The Last Supper

Place a bread roll and a cup or chalice at the end of the ribbon next to Jesus.
It's the night before Jesus will die.
Jesus shares bread and wine with his friends.

The Garden of Gethsemane

Place a plant or small leafy branch to represent a tree on the ribbon, next to the cup. Move the figure of Jesus along the ribbon so it's next to the plant.

Jesus goes with his friends to a garden.
Jesus is scared about what's going to happen.
Jesus cries.
Run your fingers down your face to show tears (this is the tears action)
Let's show Jesus crying. *Tears action*
Even when Jesus cries, *Tears action*
Jesus keeps on loving.
Slowly:
Love *Cross arms* is stronger *Clench fists*
than tears *Tears action*

Lead the group in singing:
Love *Cross arms* **is stronger** *Clench fists*
than tears! *Tears action*
Love *Cross arms* **is stronger** *Clench fists*
than tears! *Tears action*
Love *Cross arms* **is stronger** *Clench fists*

Love *Cross arms* **is stronger!** *Clench fists*
Love *Cross arms* **is stronger** *Clench fists*
than tears! *Tears action*

The Arrest

Place a piece of rope on the ribbon.
Move the Jesus figure along the ribbon so that it is next to the rope.

Soldiers come to the garden.
They tie Jesus up. *Tie the Jesus figure gently with the rope or string*
They take Jesus away!
Move the Jesus figure off the ribbon and towards you.
Jesus' friends are scared! They hide!
Let's hide behind our hands like the disciples.
Lead the group in hiding behind hands. This will become the hiding action.

But Jesus keeps on loving. *Crossed arms on chest*
Slowly:
Love *Cross arms* is stronger *Clench fists*
than 'fear'! *Hiding action*

> *If appropriate:* 'Fear' is when we're frightened!

Lead the group in singing:
Love *Cross arms* **is stronger!** *Clench fists*
than fear. *Hiding action*
Love *Cross arms* **is stronger!** *Clench fists*
than fear! *Hiding action*
Love *Cross arms* **is stronger!** *Clench fists*
Love *Cross arms* **is stronger!** *Clench fists*
than fear! *Hiding action*

The Trial

Place the lid of the box that will become Jesus' tomb on the ribbon.
Stand the Jesus figure on this 'platform'

The soldiers drag Jesus to the leaders.
People tell lies about Jesus.
Let's point at Jesus to show we're telling lies.
Lead the children in pointing.

The leaders want to put Jesus on the cross,
even though it's not fair. *Shake heads*
The people lie about Jesus
but Jesus keeps on loving. *Cross arms*
Slowly:
Love *Cross arms* is stronger *Clench fists*
than lies. *Point*

Lead the group in singing:
Love *Cross arms* **is stronger!** *Clench fists*
than lies. *Point*
Love *Cross arms* **is stronger!** *Clench fists*
than lies. *Point*
Love *Cross arms* **is stronger!** *Clench fists*
Love *Cross arms* **is stronger!** *Clench fists*
Love *Cross arms* **is stronger!** *Clench fists*
than lies! *Point*

The Bullying

Place a crown of thorns on or next to the Jesus figure.

The soldiers bully Jesus.
They put a crown of thorns on his head.

They hit Jesus and laugh at him.
But Jesus keeps on loving.
Love *Cross arms is stronger Clench fists
than* **hate.** *Fist in hand*
Slowly: Love *Cross arms is stronger Clench fists
than* hate. *Fist in hand*

Lead the group in singing:
Love *Cross arms* **is stronger** *Clench fists*
than hate. *Fist in hand*
Love *Cross arms* **is stronger** *Clench fists*
than hate. *Fist in hand*
Love *Cross arms* **is stronger!** *Clench fists*
Love *Cross arms* **is stronger!** *Clench fists*
Love *Cross arms* **is stronger** *Clench fists*
than hate. *Fist in hand*

The Crucifixion

Place a cross on the ribbon next to the platform.
When indicated, hang the Jesus figure from the cross or change the Jesus figure to a crucifix.

On a hill, they nail Jesus to a cross.
Hang the Jesus figure on the cross.
They wait for him to die.
Even on the cross, hurting, Jesus never stops loving.
Jesus says, 'Give them a new start!'

Slowly:
Love *Cross arms* is stronger *Clench fists*
than 'pain'. *Touch wounds*
If appropriate: 'Pain' is hurting.

Let's touch the marks on our hands
where Jesus is nailed to the cross.
Lead the children in touching palms: one then the other.
Slowly: Love *Cross arms is stronger Clench fists*
than pain. *Touch wounds*

Lead the group in singing:
Love *Cross arms* **is stronger** *Clench fists*
than pain. *Touch wounds*
Love *Cross arms* **is stronger** *Clench fists*
than pain. *Touch wounds*
Love *Cross arms* **is stronger!** *Clench fists*
Love *Cross arms* **is stronger!** *Clench fists*
Love *Cross arms* **is stronger** *Clench fists*
than pain. *Touch wounds*

The Sun Stops Shining

Stay with the cross.

Jesus is hanging on the cross.
Suddenly the sun stops shining.
The land is as dark as night.
Let's close our eyes and feel the dark.
Lead the children in covering your eyes.

Everything is dark.
Jesus is completely alone.
Even God isn't there.
Jesus shouts: 'My God, My God, why have you left me?'

Slowly:
But Love *Cross arms is stronger Clench fists*
than darkness. *Cover eyes*

Lead the group in singing:
Love *Cross arms* **is stronger** *Clench fists*
than darkness. *Cover eyes*
Love *Cross arms* **is stronger** *Clench fists*
than darkness. *Cover eyes*
Love *Cross arms* **is stronger!** *Clench fists*
Love *Cross arms* **is stronger!** *Clench fists*
than darkness. *Cover eyes*

Jesus Is Buried

Place the open box on the ribbon on its side next to the cross to represent the tomb.
Have a white cloth ready.

Jesus dies. It's finished.
Jesus' friends take Jesus' body.
Take the figure of Jesus from the cross, or take the crucifix.

They wrap Jesus in a cloth.
Wrap the Jesus figure or crucifix in the cloth.
They take him to a garden
and put his body in a Dark Cave.
Place the Jesus figure or crucifix in the cave, with the box still on its side.
They roll a stone across the cave shut.
Place the lid on the box.

This isn't the end of the story,
even though it feels like it.
Because let me tell you a secret.
Whisper: Sssssssh! Listen!

Slowly with a loud whisper,
Love *Cross arms* is stronger *Clench fists*
than Death. *Finger to lips.* Ssssssss!

Can you whisper that?
Love *Cross arms* **is stronger** *Clench fists*
than Death. *Finger to lips.* **Ssssssss!**

Lead the group in singing in a whisper:
Love *Cross arms* **is stronger** *Clench fists*
than Death. *Finger to lips.* **Ssssssss!**
Love *Cross arms* **is stronger!** *Clench fists*
Love *Cross arms* **is stronger!** *Clench fists*
than Death. *Finger to lips.* **Ssssssss!**

Love *Cross arms* is stronger
than EVERYTHING. *Throw arms out wide*
Let's sing that!

Love *Cross arms* **is stronger** *Clench fists*
than EVERYTHING! *Throw arms out wide*
Love *Cross arms* **is stronger** *Clench fists*
than EVERYTHING! *Throw arms out wide*
Love *Cross arms* **is stronger!** *Clench fists*
Love *Cross arms* **is stronger!** *Clench fists*
than EVERYTHING! *Throw arms out wide*

Either:
It's time for us to go.
But remember, this isn't the end of the story.

egg will help to convey the surprise and awe of the women more visibly than a chocolate egg.

For this next part of the story,
we need an egg.
Show the group the egg that currently looks normal (it's still whole even though it's empty).
It's the story of Easter Day
and Easter is all about eggs!
Eggs remind us of new life:
with a little chick growing inside.
They also remind us of the Dark Cave that Jesus was shut in.

After Jesus died on the cross,
nothing happened for one day and two nights.
A long, long time.
Then on the third day
something amazing happened.

This egg helps us tell the story.
Show the group the egg again.

Jesus' friends, the women, went to the Dark Cave, the tomb.
They looked! And the Dark Cave had been broken open!
It's time to break open our egg: like the Dark Cave.
Crack the egg open visibly.
Show the empty two halves.

It's empty!
The Dark Cave is empty!
Because Love is stronger than the Dark Cave!
Slowly:
Love *Cross arms* is stronger *Clench fists* than Death. *Open arms wide to show the cross*

Come on Easter Day
to find out just how strong *Clench fists gently* Love is!

And remember:
you should never keep a secret from your important adult.
Make sure you whisper our secret in their ear today!
And maybe you can whisper it to other people, too!

Let's finish by singing our secret one more time.
I wonder who you could whisper our secret to today?

Lead the group in singing in a whisper. End each line as indicated with a spoken 'Ssssssh!'

Love *Cross arms* **is stronger** *Clench fists* **than Death.** *Finger to lips.* **Ssssssh!**
Love *Cross arms* **is stronger** *Clench fists* **than Death.** *Finger to lips.* **Ssssssh!**
Love *Cross arms* **is stronger!** *Clench fists*
Love *Cross arms* **is stronger!** *Clench fists*
Love *Cross arms* **is stronger** *Clench fists* **than Death.** *Finger to lips.* **Ssssssh!**

Or:

The storytelling above assumes that the story of the Risen Jesus will be told on or before Good Friday. It can be very helpful for children (and their adults) to understand that hard situations are not always resolved immediately. If it is not possible to tell the story of Jesus bursting from the Dark Cave with the group at another point, and you would like to include it here, however, you may find this material helpful.

For the egg, you could either use a chocolate egg or (preferably) a real chicken egg that's been 'blown' in the traditional way, and therefore empty (see the Sowing Seeds website for a guide to blowing eggs). A real chicken

58

Lead the group in singing triumphantly:
Love *Cross arms* **is stronger** *Clench fists*
than Death. *Cross shape*
Love *Cross arms* **is stronger** *Clench fists*
than Death. *Cross shape*
Love *Cross arms* **is stronger!** *Clench fists*
Love *Cross arms* **is stronger!** *Clench fists*
Love *Cross arms* **is stronger!** *Clench fists*
than Death. *Cross shape*

Love *Cross arms* is stronger *Clench fists*
than EVERYTHING! *Throw arms out wide*

Love *Cross arms* **is stronger** *Clench fists*
than EVERYTHING! *Throw arms out wide*
Love *Cross arms* **is stronger** *Clench fists*
than EVERYTHING! *Throw arms out wide*
Love *Cross arms* **is stronger!** *Clench fists*
Love *Cross arms* **is stronger!** *Clench fists*
Love *Cross arms* **is stronger!** *Clench fists*
than EVERYTHING! *Throw arms out wide*

Jesus Is Alive! Alleluia! unit (Easter)

The 'Jesus Is Alive! Alleluia!' unit gathers together some of the most famous Bible stories about the Risen Jesus. Many of these stories are from John's Gospel and include some of the most beautiful storytelling in the New Testament.

Optional: Throughout this unit, you might like to have an Easter Garden visible on a focal table. This Easter Garden could be as simple as an empty plant pot laid on its side with a large stone next to it. It could be an Easter Garden created by the children (see p. 136). Or you might like to plant a larger garden together. Choose what's right for your group.

Jesus Is Alive! Alleluia! storybox

Choose from the stories according to your own context.

Jesus Is Risen! Alleluia! (John 19.40—20.1a) 61
Appropriate for mixed groups of 0–7 years

The Women's Story (John 20.1–10) 64
Appropriate for mixed groups of 0–9 years

The Walk to Emmaus (Luke 24.13–35) 68
Appropriate for mixed groups of 0–9 years

The Good Shepherd 60

Option 1: 'There was a once a flock of sheep' (John 10.11–15) 71
Appropriate for mixed groups of 0–7 years

Option 2: David the shepherd king (1 Samuel 17.34–36) 74
Appropriate for mixed groups of 0–9 years

Option 3: God's my shepherd (1 Samuel 17.34–36; Psalm 23) 77
Appropriate for mixed groups of 0–9 years

Thomas's Story (John 20.19–29) 80
Appropriate for mixed groups of 0–9 years

The Catch of Fishes (John 21.1–14) 85
Appropriate for mixed groups of 0–9 years

Peter's Story (John 18.15–27; 21.15–19) 88
Appropriate for mixed groups of 0–9 years

The Ascension

Option 1: Jesus goes up! (Luke 24.42–53) 91
Appropriate for mixed groups of 0–7 years

Option 2: You will tell the world about me! (Acts 1.8–14) 94
Appropriate for mixed groups of 0–9 years

Come, Holy Spirit! (The Day of Pentecost, Acts 2.1–4) 97
Appropriate for mixed groups of 0–9 years

1, 2, 3, the Trinity! (Trinity Sunday) 102
Appropriate for mixed groups of 0–9 years

Tip

Even if you don't use the other Building Blocks, you may find it helpful to use one of the Gathering Songs ('When all the world was sleeping' or 'Let's praise the Lord! Alleluia!') just before the storytelling in every session of this unit as they gather together the themes of the unit as a whole. See pp. 154–6.

Jesus Is Risen! Alleluia!

→ John 19.40—20.1a
→ Song: 'When all the world was sleeping'. Words: © Sharon Moughtin.
→ Tune: 'Wide awake' © Mollie Russell-Smith and Geoffrey Russell-Smith, also known as 'The dingle, dangle scarecrow'. It is now published by EMI Harmonies Ltd.

The music for 'Wide awake' is under copyright so can't be reproduced here but can be found online by searching for 'Dingle dangle scarecrow'. A sung version of 'When all the world was sleeping' can be found on the Sowing Seeds website.

Appropriate for mixed groups of babies, toddlers and children up to the age of 7. Groups that include children up to the age of 9 may prefer to tell 'The Women's Story' (p. 64) as the first story of Easter.

This story introduces the Gathering Song, 'When all the world was sleeping', which is one of the options that can then be used throughout the unit (see p. 154).

This story uses the 'New Start' sign from the Sowing Seeds Sorry Song. This is deliberate. The 'New Start' sign is created to echo the rolling away of the stone from the tomb, which won a new start for all of us. See p. 8 or the website for a description and explanation of the 'New Start' sign.

Optional: an Easter Garden (see p. 60), place it in the middle of the circle.

If your group usually uses the What's in the Box? option (p. 7), this can be the object for this story. You may like to place a cloth over it and invite one of the children to remove the cloth.

Can anyone tell me what this is?
Accept children's responses and ways of naming the garden.

This is our Easter Garden with the tomb, the Dark Cave, in the middle.

On Good Friday, Jesus died on the cross.
Let's hold our hands out in love like Jesus on the cross.
Lead the children in stretching arms out to the side.

His friends took Jesus' body down from the cross.
Let's be Jesus' friends.
Lead the children in miming holding Jesus' body gently.

61

They put it gently into the Dark Cave.
Lead the children in miming placing Jesus' body in the tomb.
And rolled the stone across.
Lead the children in miming rolling a large stone across.
They went home feeling very, very, very sad.

Nothing happened for one whole night and day after that.
But then the night after, something very, very, very special,
something amazing happened.
Let's tell the story together with a song.

To tell our story, we need to imagine we're in a Dark Cave.
Let's curl up in a ball on the floor and shut our eyes.
Let's feel the dark.

Now we're ready to learn the words of our song.
Let's say them
'my turn' *Point to self,* 'your turn' *Leader's hands out to group.*

For the first time, say the words rather than sing them so the children can understand that they are different from the usual words to this very recognizable (and excitable) tune.
Still curled up on the floor or crouching down
When all the world was sleeping
When all the world was sleeping
and the sun had gone to bed
and the sun had gone to bed
Jump up with hands in the air.
Up jumped Lord Jesus!
Up jumped Lord Jesus!

And this is what he said . . . *Hands out, palms up*
And this is what he said . . . *Hands out, palms up*

'I am risen, risen, risen!'
Wave hands victoriously high in the air.
'I am risen, risen, risen!'
Wave hands victoriously high in the air.

'I have won us a new start!' *'New Start' sign (p. 8)*
'I have won us a new start!' *'New Start' sign*

'I am risen, risen, risen!' *Wave hands high in the air*
'I have won us a new start!' *'New Start' sign over head*
'I am risen, risen, risen!' *Wave hands high in the air*
'I have won us a new start!' *'New Start' sign over head*

Now we're ready to sing our song together.
Let's see if you recognize the tune.
Listen carefully for our new words!
Let's start off by curling up on the floor . . .

Lead the children in curling up on the floor or crouching.
When all the world was sleeping
and the sun had gone to bed . . .
up jumped Lord Jesus *Jump up with hands in the air*
and this is what he said: *Hands out, palms up*

'I am risen, risen, risen, *Wave hands high in the air*
I have won us a new start! *'New Start' sign over head*
I am risen, risen, risen, *Wave hands high in the air*
I have won us a new start! *'New Start' sign over head*
Repeat until the children are confident.

Let's sit down!

Optional: What's in the Box? (see p. 7)

Invite one of the children to open the box. Inside will be an Easter egg.
What's in the box? *Ask the child to respond*
Today is Easter Day! [*Or:* It's Easter!]
Who's been given an Easter egg?

Today we're going to tell the story
of why we give Easter eggs at Easter.

Show the children a hollow chocolate Easter egg.
At Easter, we celebrate Jesus bursting from the Dark Cave.
Can anyone tell me what this is?
Accept the children's responses.

Easter eggs help to show us what Jesus did.
They remind us of the Dark Cave,
the tomb, that Jesus was put in.
They're round and dark inside.
Show the group how the egg is round.

In this country, we use CHOCOLATE eggs,
because Easter is a time of joy and happiness.
Chocolate is a very happy, joyful thing!
Put your hand up if you like chocolate!

But what's inside real eggs when they are left to grow?
Accept responses from the children.
A tiny chick: new life!
Chicks burst out of their egg
when they're ready to be born.
Jesus burst from the Dark Cave
like a little chick
bursting out of an egg into new life!

If your group includes toddlers and babies, you may find the following helpful. If there are also children over the age of five present it might be helpful to start it off with the words:
To help the littlest here understand
Let's all imagine that we're a tiny chick
curled inside an egg in the dark.
Lead the children in curling up into a ball as if you're inside an egg.

Ssssh! Now let's tap on the egg three times.
After three taps,
we're going to burst out of the egg and shout, 'New life!'
Lead the children in tapping the imaginary egg that you are inside.
Tap one! Tap two! Tap three!
Lead the children in jumping up.
New life!

So at Easter we break open eggs.
We remember Jesus bursting from the Dark Cave
and giving us new life and a new start.

If your group wrapped an egg up at the beginning of Lent (p. 15):
Some of us wrapped up a chocolate egg
at the beginning of Lent.
Now Lent's finished! The time for giving things up is gone!
It's time to celebrate
because Jesus has burst from the Dark Cave!
Use the egg that you left wrapped up through Lent.

All groups: show the children a hollow chocolate Easter egg.
We're going to use this chocolate egg to celebrate Easter together.
In a moment, we're going to count to 3 and break open this egg.

Either: Then I'm going to say, 'Alleluia! Christ is risen!'
You can shout, **'He is risen indeed! Alleluia!'**

Taste and see that God is good!

Let's taste our chocolate egg together now.
Lead the children in eating the egg.
Mmmm! That tastes really, really good!
'Taste and see that God is good!'

Either: Alleluia! Jesus is risen!
He is risen indeed! Alleluia!
Or: Praise the Lord!
Alleluia!

The Women's Story

→ John 20.1–10
→ Song: 'On Easter Day in the morning'. Words: © Sharon Moughtin.
→ Tune: 'I saw three ships come sailing in' (traditional).

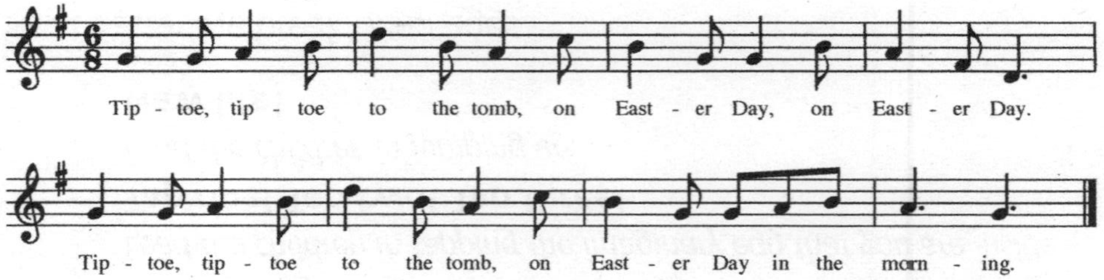

Tip - toe, tip - toe to the tomb, on East - er Day, on East - er Day.

Tip - toe, tip - toe to the tomb, on East - er Day in the morn - ing.

Appropriate for mixed groups of babies, toddlers and children up to the age of 9. Groups that only include children up to the age of 7 may like to start Easter with the 'Jesus Is Risen! Alleluia!' story (p. 61), which also introduces the Gathering Song for the unit. 'The Women's Story' here can then be told as the second story of Easter.

1, 2, 3 . . . *Break open the egg*
Alleluia! Christ is risen!
He is risen indeed! Alleluia!

Or: I'm going say, 'Praise the Lord!' and you can shout,
'**Alleluia!**'
1, 2, 3 . . . *Break open the egg*
Praise the Lord!
Alleluia!

You could say that with every Easter egg you break open this Easter!
Break the chocolate egg up into little pieces and place in one or two bowls or baskets.

Name and *Name* are going to bring around this egg now.
If you'd like a piece, hold your hands out like this.
Model putting both your hands out in a cupped shape.

Don't eat it straight away!
Keep it on your hand and wait till everyone has a piece.
Make sure you keep your hand open so the chocolate doesn't melt!

Ask a responsible child to show everyone how to hold their egg on their hand. Don't worry too much if the very young children eat theirs straight away.

Sing the 'He is risen, risen, risen!' chorus from the Gathering Song, an 'Alleluia!' song or another Easter song familiar to the children as the chocolate egg is taken around.

When the group is ready:
There's a Bible verse that says
'Taste and see that God is good!'
Let's say that:
'my turn' *Point to self,* 'your turn' *Leader's hands out to group.*
Taste and see that God is good!

This story uses the 'New Start' sign (the winding action from 'Wind the bobbin up'), which is among the very few Sowing Seeds signs and actions that are fixed. This is deliberate. The 'New Start' sign is created to echo the rolling away of the stone from the tomb, which won a new start for all of us. See p. 8 or the website for a description and explanation.

Let's sit down!
At Easter, Jesus burst from the tomb, the Dark Cave!

> *Optional: What's in the Box? (see p. 7)*
>
> *Invite one of the children to open the box. Inside will be NOTHING!*
> What's in the box? *Ask the child to respond*
> There's nothing in the box! It's empty!

Today we're going to tell the women's story.
They're the ones who found the Dark Cave empty!

To tell our story, we need to learn a song.
Let's say the words:
'my turn' *Point to self, 'your turn' Leader's hands out to group.*
Lead the children in saying the words to the rhythm that will be used in the song.

Tiptoe, tiptoe to the tomb
Tiptoe, tiptoe to the tomb
On Easter Day, on Easter Day.
On Easter Day, on Easter Day.
Tiptoe, tiptoe to the tomb
Tiptoe, tiptoe to the tomb
On Easter Day in the morn-ing.
On Easter Day in the morn-ing.

We're ready to add the tune.
Let's sing 'my turn' *Point to self, 'your turn' Leader's hands out to group.*

Tiptoe, tiptoe to the tomb
on Easter Day, on Easter Day.
**Tiptoe, tiptoe to the tomb
on Easter Day, on Easter Day.**

Tiptoe, tiptoe to the tomb
on Easter Day in the morn-ing.
**Tiptoe, tiptoe to the tomb
on Easter Day in the morn-ing.**

Let's try that all together.
Lead the children in singing:
**Tiptoe, tiptoe to the tomb
on Easter Day, on Easter Day.
Tiptoe, tiptoe to the tomb
on Easter Day in the morn-ing.**

We're ready to tell our story.
The women don't know that
Jesus has burst from the Dark Cave!
They still think Jesus has gone!

Let's be Jesus' friends, the women.
We're feeling very, very sad.
Can you show me sad?
Lead the children in showing a sad face and body.
We're fast asleep in bed.
Can you show me fast asleep?
Lead the children in being asleep.

65

It's time to get up,
but we're still feeling sad.
Let's get up really slowly.
Let's yawn and stretch and stand up.
Lead the children in getting up sadly and slowly.
Jesus has died. He's gone!
How are we feeling?
Lead the children in looking very sad.

We're going to the Dark Cave.
We want to say goodbye to Jesus properly.
Let's tiptoe on the spot.
Ssssh! We don't want anyone to see us. Ssssh!
Lead the children in singing quietly and sadly.

**Tiptoe, tiptoe to the tomb
on Easter Day, on Easter Day.
Tiptoe, tiptoe to the tomb
on Easter Day in the morning.**

We're here.
But look! *Point and gasp*
What's happened?! *Look confused and shocked*
Look! The stone is rolled away!

Let's show the stone that was rolled away with our arms.
'New Start' sign.
Has someone taken Jesus away? *Sound worried*
How are we feeling?
Can you show me with your face?
Accept the children's responses, which may range from sad/shocked/worried to happy/excited or confused.

We're feeling all sorts of things!
How confusing!
Let's sing 'Look! The stone is rolled away!'
and show the stone rolling with our arms.
Lead the children in singing in a confused voice with the 'New Start' sign.

**Look! The stone is rolled away
on Easter Day, on Easter Day.
Look! The stone is rolled away
on Easter Day in the morning.**

What's happening? *Hands out in question*
Let's tiptoe on the spot a bit closer.
Lead the children in tiptoeing.
Tiptoe, tiptoe, tiptoe . . . .

Let's bend down and look inside the cave . . . .
Lead the children in bending down and peering low.
Look! *Gasp and point*
There are two angels there!
Angels!

How do you think the women are feeling now?
Can you show me with your face?
Let's keep our faces looking like that,
And sing 'Look! *Point* Two angels in the cave!'

Lead the children singing in amazement.
**Look! Two angels in the cave!
On Easter Day, on Easter Day!
Look! Two angels in the cave!
On Easter Day in the morning.**

We've got to tell someone!
After 3, let's run on the spot
and sing 'Run and run to tell our friends . . .'

1, 2, 3 . . . Run!
Lead the children in singing faster and running on the spot.

**Run and run to tell our friends
on Easter Day, on Easter Day!
Run and run to tell our friends
on Easter Day in the morning!**

Excitedly:
Look! *Point* There's Peter and John!
After 3, let's shout: 'Look! Two angels in the cave!'
1, 2, 3: **Look! Two angels in the cave!**
Peter and John listened to the women.
And do you know what Peter and John did? *Rhetorical question*
They ran!

After 3, let's be Peter and John and run on the spot.
Let's sing: 'Run and run and run and run!'
1, 2, 3: Run!
Lead the children in singing even faster and running on the spot.

**Run and run and run and run
on Easter Day, on Easter Day!
Run and run and run and run
on Easter Day in the morning!**

Freeze!
John got to the cave first!
He bent down and looked inside.
Let's kneel down and look into the cave together.
Lead the group in kneeling and peering into an imaginary cave.

Then Peter came running up.
And he RAN inside the cave.
Who's feeling brave?
Let's get up and imagine
we've just stepped into the Dark Cave together.
Lead the children in standing up.

Let's look around . . . .
Lead the children in looking as described with hands shielding eyes.
Let's look left . . . .
and right . . . .
Behind us . . . *twirl around*
Let's look up . . . and down . . . .

Nothing!

The Dark Cave is empty!
Jesus is gone! *Look confused*

Gasp Jesus is RISEN!
Jesus is ALIVE!
How do you think Peter is feeling?
Can you show me with your face?

Let's keep our faces looking like that
and sing 'Look! The cave is empty!'
Lead the children in singing in amazement as you look around the cave on the spot.

**Look! The cave is e-empty,
on Easter Day, on Easter Day!
Look! The cave is e-empty,
on Easter Day in the morning!**

Peter and John were amazed!
Can you show me your amazed faces?
Freeze!

Let's shout our special Easter shout of joy.
Either: Alleluia! Jesus is risen!
He is risen indeed! Alleluia!
Or: Praise the Lord!
Alleluia!

Our story for today ends here.
Come back next time to hear the story of two friends meeting the Risen Jesus on a walk.

The Walk to Emmaus

→ Luke 24.13–35
→ Poem: 'Do this to remember me' © Sharon Moughtin.

Appropriate for mixed groups of babies, toddlers and children up to the age of 9.

In Luke's story of the road to Emmaus, it's only when the 'stranger' breaks the bread that the disciples' eyes are opened to recognize him as Jesus. This story therefore begins with a recap of Jesus' Last Supper. For this story, you'll need to have ready two or more trays: one set holding a piece of bread for each child and adult; the other set holding a cup with a small amount of grape juice at the bottom for each child and adult.

For the storytelling while the children are finishing their bread, you may like to use three 'small world' people to represent the two friends and Jesus, the stranger. There is a tradition that the two friends are a man (Cleopas) and a woman (unnamed).

Tip

You could use everyday bread or pitta bread for this action. Try to have a gluten free option also available. It might be helpful to cut the bread into small squares beforehand with scissors. There are benefits in making connections both with the kind of bread that you use in your church's communion service and with the kind that your children will be familiar with from home, school or nursery. As this story is told in the 'Journey to the Cross' unit as well, you could move between the different kinds of bread to support the children in making these connections.

If you prefer, you could tell the story with cups and plates (or wooden egg cups and wooden coasters acting as chalices and patens) for the children and simply imagine the bread and wine on them. Or you could even mime the actions without any props.

If your group is familiar with the 'Jesus, open up my eyes' song from the 'Getting Ready for Bible Storytelling' Building Block (p. 156), you may like to begin with the following material:

Today's story is all about our 'Open up my eyes' song.
It's the story of when Jesus opened up his FRIENDS' eyes
Trace cross on eyes.
and helped them hear his voice in their Bible stories.
Hands behind ears.

Let's watch out for the moment
the stranger breaks the bread!
Breaking bread action.
That's when the friends' eyes are opened!
Trace cross on eyes.

All other groups:
Today we're going to tell one of the stories
about Jesus after he burst from the Dark Cave.

But first, let's remember the story
of what Jesus did just BEFORE he died.
At Jesus' last dinner with his friends,
Jesus said, 'Do this to remember me.'

If appropriate:
Can anyone tell me what Jesus asked his friends to
remember him with?
Accept the children's responses.

Optional: What's in the Box? (see p. 7)
Invite one of the children to open the box. Inside will be bread and a cup or chalice.

What's in the box? *Ask the child to respond*
Show cup and bread.

Jesus told his friends to remember them with bread and wine.
This morning we're going to tell that story together.

If appropriate:
We tell this story every week in church.
It's one of our most important stories!

Jesus and his friends were at
a very special party called 'the Passover'.
They sat down to eat together,
like we're sitting here.
Then Jesus did something new.

Invite two children to take around small pieces of bread in two baskets for everyone who wants to receive them.

Name and *Name* are going to
bring around some bread now.
If you'd like some bread,
can you hold your hands out like this?
Model to the children holding out cupped hands.

Name and *Name* will give you a piece.
Keep the bread in your hands till everyone has some.
Don't eat it yet!

If your group is familiar with the 'I am going to follow Jesus' song from the 'Journey to the Cross' unit on p. 151, you may like to sing this as you wait for your bread. Or you could sing another appropriate song that the group is familiar with. Once all the children and adults who wish to receive bread have done so:

After dinner, Jesus did something new.
Can you say these words after me and copy my actions,
'my turn' *Point to self,* 'your turn' *Leader's hands out to group?*

Jesus took the bread.	*Take bread*
Jesus took the bread.	*Take bread*
He said, 'Thank you, God!'	*Hold bread up if this is in your tradition*
He said, 'Thank you, God!'	*Hold bread up if this is in your tradition*
Jesus broke the bread.	*Break bread*
Jesus broke the bread.	*Break bread*
Then he shared it.	*Mime handing bread out in a circle*
Then he shared it.	*Mime handing bread out in a circle*
This is my body,	*Hold bread or point to it*
This is my body,	*Hold bread or point to it*
Broken for you.	*Hold bread together then separate again*
Broken for you.	*Hold bread together then separate again*
Do this to remember me!	*Hold bread up if this is in your tradition*
Do this to remember me!	*Hold bread up if this is in your tradition*

69

Invite the children to eat their bread slowly, really tasting and enjoying it. Once the children's hands are empty, distribute cups with just 1–2 cm of grape juice at the bottom. These cups are best distributed by adults or responsible older children.

While you finish eating, we're going to bring around cups. If you'd like a cup, can you hold your hands out like this? Model to the children *Keep the cup in your hands till everyone has one. Don't drink from it yet!*

If your group is familiar with the 'I am going to follow Jesus' song from the 'Journey to the Cross' unit (p. 151), you may like to sing this as you wait for your cup. Or you could sing another appropriate song that the group is familiar with. Once all the children and adults who wish to receive a cup have done so:

When they'd finished eating, Jesus took the cup. Can you say these words after me and copy my actions, 'my turn' Point to self, 'your turn' Leader's hands out to group?

Jesus took the cup.	Take cup in both hands
Jesus took the cup.	Take cup in both hands
He said, 'Thank you, God!'	Hold cup up if this is in your tradition
He said, 'Thank you, God!'	Hold cup up if this is in your tradition
Jesus poured the wine.	Mime pouring wine
Jesus poured the wine.	Mime pouring wine
Then he shared it.	Mime handing cup out in a circle
Then he shared it.	Mime handing cup out in a circle
This is my blood,	Lift cup or point to it
This is my blood,	Lift cup or point to it
Poured out for you.	Mime pouring wine
Poured out for you.	Mime pouring wine
Do this to remember me!	Hold cup up if this is in your tradition
Do this to remember me!	Hold cup up if this is in your tradition

Invite the children to drink the grape juice slowly and to really taste and enjoy it.

Now as you finish your grape juice and bread, let's tell our Easter story of Jesus after he had risen.

If you're using 'small world' people, place the two friends in front of you.

Two of Jesus' friends were walking on the road to Emmaus.

Place the Jesus figure next to the two friends.

A stranger came and walked with them.
The friends looked sad.
To the group: Can you show me sad?
Lead the children in looking sad.

'What's wrong?' the stranger asked.
To the group: Can anyone tell us why the friends are looking sad? *Accept responses.*

Jesus had died on the cross. *Hold out arms in a cross shape*
The friends told the stranger about Jesus dying. *Cross shape*
The stranger said, 'Don't you understand?' *Shake head*
He started to tell them the stories of Moses [or: of the Bible] but it was getting late and dark.

'Come and eat with us,' said the friends.
The stranger said, 'Yes'.

If you're using 'small world' people, place them to the side as the group will now become these people.

70

and then . . .
Let's tell the story with OUR bodies now.
Can you repeat after me and help me with the actions?
This time mime the actions, without bread.

The STRANGER took the bread.	*Mime taking bread*
The STRANGER took the bread.	*Mime taking bread*
He said, 'Thank you, God!'	*Hold bread up if in your tradition*
He said, 'Thank you, God!'	*Hold bread up if in your tradition*
The STRANGER broke the bread.	*Mime breaking bread*
The STRANGER broke the bread.	*Mime breaking bread*
Then he shared it.	*Mime handing bread out in a circle*
Then he shared it.	*Mime handing bread out in a circle*

Then the eyes of the friends were opened.

If your group is familiar with the 'Jesus, open up my eyes' song:
Just like we ask Jesus to open up OUR eyes in our song.
Singing: Jesus open up my eyes, Alleluia! *Trace cross on forehead*

I wonder who it was breaking bread?
Accept responses.

It was Jesus!
Jesus is RISEN!
Jesus is ALIVE!

I wonder how the friends felt when they realized it was Jesus?!
Can you show me with your face?
Follow the children's suggested expressions.

Let's shout our special Easter shout of joy!
Either: Alleluia! Jesus is risen!
He is risen indeed! Alleluia!
Or: Praise the Lord!
Alleluia!

But Jesus had already gone!
I wonder how the friends felt when they saw that Jesus had gone?
Then the friends got up and ran to tell the other disciples.

The Good Shepherd

For groups that follow the church seasons, the Good Shepherd is traditionally told on the fourth week of Easter in the Lectionary. This material provides the opportunity to join in with this tradition. There are three options to recognize the different emphases that the story can have for different age groups and for different traditions. Choose which version works best in your setting.

Option 1: 'There was once a flock of sheep'

→ John 10.11–15
→ Song: 'The Good Shepherd song'. Words: © Sharon Moughtin.
→ Tune: 'Mary had a little lamb' (traditional).

[Musical notation: "There was once a flock of sheep, There was once a flock of sheep. There was once a flock of sheep. Baaaaaa!"]

Appropriate for mixed groups of babies, toddlers and children up to the age of 7. Groups that include children up to the age of 9 may prefer to use Option 2 or Option 3 as they may find acting out being sheep a little young for them. Choose which version works best in your setting.

Optional: What's in the Box? (see p. 7)

71

Invite one of the children to open the box. Inside will be a picture of a sheep, or a toy sheep.

What's in the box? *Ask the child to respond*

Today churches all over the world tell a story that Jesus told about sheep and a shepherd.
We're going to tell the story together.

To tell Jesus' story we need to be sheep!
What do sheep say?
Accept responses.
Freeze!

Can you show an action for sheep?
Accept one of the actions. This could be about the sheep's tail, ears, munching or more. This will become the 'sheep action'.

Now can you show me how a sheep looks and sounds when it feels scared?
Lead the group in looking and sounding like a scared sheep: **Baaaa!**
And happy?
Lead the group in looking and sounding like a happy sheep: **Baaaa!**
And cross?
Lead the group in looking and sounding like a cross sheep: **Baaaa!**

We're ready to tell our story.

Sheep live in groups called 'flocks'.
We're going to be a little flock of sheep.
This flock didn't have their own shepherd. *Shake head*
A different person came every day to look after them.

Let's sing 'There was once a flock of sheep'.
Let's show our sheep action as we sing.

Lead the group in the 'sheep action':
**There was once a flock of sheep,
flock of sheep, flock of sheep.
There was once a flock of sheep . . .**
Interrupt the singing: And wait!
What do sheep sound like when they're happy?
Baaaa!

But look! What's that over there?! *Point and look scared*
It's a wolf!
A big, bad wolf!
Hold your hands out like claws, ready to pounce.

How are the sheep feeling?!
Can you show me?

Let's sing and be the big bad wolf together. *Make as if ready to pounce*
Then we'll turn into the sheep for our scared baas at the end.
Let's sing 'Look! Here comes a big bad wolf!'
Hold your hands out like claws, ready to pounce on the word 'wolf'.

Lead the children in pouncing on the word 'wolf' as you sing.
Look! Here comes a big, bad wolf, *Pounce*
a big, bad wolf, *Pounce* **a big, bad wolf!** *Pounce*
Look! Here comes a big, bad wolf! *Pounce*
Baaaaa! *Lead the group in looking and sounding scared*

It's all right. Our shepherd will help us . . . .
But look! *Point*
Our shepherd's running away! *Shocked*

flock of sheep, flock of sheep.
There was once a flock of sheep . . .
Baaaa!

But look! What do you think I can see?!
Give the children opportunity to respond, then go straight into . . .

Hold your hands out like claws, ready to pounce on the word 'wolf'.
Look! Here comes a big, bad wolf, *Pounce*
A big, bad wolf, *Pounce* **a big, bad wolf!** *Pounce*
Look! Here comes a big, bad wolf! *Pounce*
Baaa! *Sounding scared*

Oh no! What's the shepherd going to do?
Give the children opportunity to respond.

How are we feeling now with no shepherd? *Shake head*
The wolf can catch us!
We need to get away!!
After 3, let's sing: 'The sheep they ran and ran and ran!'
And run on the spot like the sheep!
And show our really scared and tired Baa at the end!
1, 2, 3 . . . Run!
Lead the children in running on the spot and singing:
**The sheep, they ran and ran and ran,
ran and ran, ran and ran!
The sheep, they ran and ran and ran!
Baaaa!** *Lead the group in sounding terrified and exhausted*

Let's sit down for a moment.
Oh dear! Poor sheep! That shepherd wasn't very good!

Jesus said, 'Then there was another flock of sheep.' *Hold up hand*
Let's be the other flock of sheep,
happily chewing our grass.

Now this flock has a GOOD shepherd.
Our shepherd loves us!
Let's pretend that our hand is our shepherd's hand. *Hold up hand*
Let's stroke our arm like the shepherd stroking us.
Lead the children in stroking your arm with your hand.

How are you feeling?

Let's practise our baas now . . . .
Baaa!

Let's sing 'There was once a flock of sheep'.
Let's show our sheep action as we sing:
There was once a flock of sheep,

This shepherd is the Good Shepherd.
He won't run! *Shake head*
He won't leave us!
He'll keep us safe!

Let's stand up and be the Good Shepherd together.
Let's put our feet firmly on the ground: 1, 2 . . .
Lead the children in placing feet.
And fold our arms.
Lead the children in folding arms.

We're NEVER going to leave the sheep.
Let's sing 'I will never, never leave . . .' *Shake head gently*
I wonder how the sheep are going to feel at the end?
I will never, never leave, *Shake head gently*
never leave, never leave.
I will never, never leave. *Shake head gently*
Baaa!

This time it was the wolf who ran off!
The sheep were safe!
After 3, let's sing 'The wolf, it ran and ran and ran'.
Let's be the wolf, running on the spot as fast as we can.
1, 2, 3 . . . Run!

Lead the children in running on the spot as you sing:
The wolf, it ran and ran and ran,
ran and ran, ran and ran!
The wolf, it ran and ran and ran!
Freeze! *Interrupt the singing*

Wait!
How do you think the sheep will sound now?
The wolf has gone!
The sheep are safe!
Baaaa!
Lead the children in repeating the joyful, calm, etc., singing of the sheep two or three times.

We're safe! The Good Shepherd will never leave us!
Let's sit down for a moment.

Jesus said, 'I am the Good Shepherd!'
You're my little sheep, my little lambs. *Point to the children*
I love you and I will never leave you. *Shake head*

Let's close our eyes for a moment.
Let's imagine Jesus coming to us.
Let's sing the Good Shepherd's song quietly:
'I will never, never leave!'
Let's imagine Jesus singing it to us.
Instead of singing our 'baas' at the end,
Let's sing 'thank you, thank you, Je-sus'.

I will never, never leave,
never leave, never leave.
I will never, never leave.
Thank you, thank you, Je-sus!
Repeat if appropriate.

Option 2: David the shepherd king

→ 1 Samuel 17.34–36
→ Song: 'Shepherd king'. Words: © Sharon Moughtin.
→ Tune: 'Sur le Pont d'Avignon' (traditional).

Shep-herd child, shep-herd child, pro-tect-ing, lead-ing, lead-ing.
Shep-herd child, shep-herd child, Da-vid is a shep-herd child.

Appropriate for mixed groups of babies, toddlers and children up to the age of 9.
Groups that only include children up to the age of 7 may prefer to use Option 1.

If appropriate:
Today, churches around the world
are celebrating Good Shepherd Sunday.

Jesus said, 'I am the Good Shepherd!'
But what does that mean?
To understand what Jesus means, we need to tell David's story.
It's a very old story,
one that Jesus would have known well!

David was a shepherd child.
His family job was to look after the family sheep on the hills.
He had to make sure the family sheep

had good food, clean water, and stayed safe!

We have a song for David.
Let's learn it 'my turn', 'your turn'.
And while we sing, let's walk on the spot.
Let's imagine leading our family sheep
to find the best grass and good clean water.

We're a shepherd so let's pick up our crook.
Mime picking up an imaginary crook.
A crook is like a stick to hook the sheep and bring them back.
Demonstrate hooking a sheep with your crook.

Walk on spot as you sing.
Shepherd child, shepherd child, *Walk with crook*
protecting, leading, *Cross arms then walk with crook*
protecting, leading. *Cross arms then walk with crook*
Shepherd child, shepherd child, *Walk with crook*
protecting, leading, *Cross arms then walk with crook*
protecting, leading. *Cross arms then walk with crook*

Then:
Shepherd child, shepherd child, *Walk with crook*
David is a shepherd child. *Cross arms then walk with crook*
Shepherd child, shepherd child, *Walk with crook*
David is a shepherd child. *Cross arms then walk with crook*

Let's sing that all together:
Shepherd child, shepherd child, *Walk with crook*
protecting, leading, *Cross arms then walk with crook*
protecting, leading. *Cross arms then walk with crook*
Shepherd child, shepherd child, *Walk with crook*
David is a shepherd child. *Cross arms then walk with crook*

But, wait a minute, what do we mean by protecting?!
Shepherd children looked after their sheep
away from the family home.
It wasn't always completely safe!
Sometimes a lion or a bear would come
and try to steal a lamb to eat it up!

Can you imagine being a shepherd child,
looking out for lions or bears?
How would that feel?
Can you show me?
Accept responses.

David was a good shepherd!
He didn't just make sure his sheep
had good food and clean water.
He PROTECTED them from wild animals.

Let's be David.
We're out on the hills in the dark, protecting our sheep.
Look there's a bear! *Point*
It's taken a sheep to eat it!
After 3, let's run as fast as we can on the spot,
then show David rescuing the sheep!
1, 2, 3 . . . Run !
Lead the group in running on the spot.
And rescue! *Mime grabbing the sheep*
Phew! That was close!
Let's take our sheep back to the flock: the other sheep.
Mime putting the lamb down safely.

But look! *Point*
Now there's a LION!

The lion has taken a lamb to eat it!
After 3, let's run as fast as we can on the spot,
then show David snatching the lamb from the lion's mouth!
1, 2, 3 . . . Run !
Lead the group in running on the spot.
And rescue! *Mime grabbing the sheep*
I hope it's all right. Let's have a look . . . .
Yes – the lamb's fine. Phew.
Let's take our sheep back to the flock.
Mime putting the lamb down safely.

David was a good shepherd!
Let's sing our song again.
This time, instead of just walking with our crook,
when we sing 'protecting',
let's show bending down
and snatching the lamb from the lion's mouth!

Shepherd child, shepherd child, *Walk with crook*
protecting, leading. *Rescue lamb then walk with crook*
protecting, leading. *Rescue lamb then walk with crook*
Shepherd child, shepherd child, *Walk with crook*
David is a shepherd child. *Cross arms then walk with crook*

Now God was looking for a king to protect and lead God's People.
Who do you think God chose? *Rhetorical question*
One of the adult leaders who were used to leading people?
No! God chose David, the shepherd child,
even when he was still a child!
God saw that David had great skills
not just to look after sheep,
but to look after people, too!

So David the shepherd child
became David, the shepherd King.
Let's sing our song again.
But this time let's sing 'shepherd KING!'
Let's bang our imaginary crook on the floor for 'shepherd'.
Crook action.
And show a crown on our head with our hands when we sing 'king'.
Crown action.
This time, we're not leading sheep, we're leading people.
Let's cross our arms on our chest again to show 'protect'.

Shepherd king, shepherd king, *Crook action then crown action*
protecting, leading. *Cross arms then walk with crook*
protecting, leading. *Cross arms then walk with crook*
Shepherd king, shepherd king, *Crook action then crown action*
David is a shepherd king. *Crook action then crown action*

David was a great king. The greatest king of God's People!
God loved David.
The name David even means loved!
And David loved God!

For David, God was like HIS shepherd!
David sang a song about God being a shepherd.
People sing it all the time – it's Psalm 23.
You could read it later.

David saw that God protects and leads us like a shepherd does.
Let's sing 'Shepherd God! Shepherd God!
God is the shepherd God!'
As we sing 'protecting' let's cross our arms on our chest in love.
And for the rest of the song let's imagine God goes before us.
Let's follow God, marching on the spot, as we sing.

Lead the group in marching as you sing.

Shepherd God, shepherd God, *Crook action then crown action*
protecting, leading. *Cross arms then walk with crook*
Shepherd God, shepherd God, *Crook action then crown action*
protecting, leading. *Cross arms then walk with crook*
Shepherd God, shepherd God, *Crook action then crown action*
God is a shepherd God. *Crook action then crown action*

Jesus said 'I am the Good Shepherd'.
I want to lead you.
I want to protect you.

When Jesus said those words he was remembering David,
the shepherd child who became a shepherd king
and sang a song about a shepherd God.
Let's sit down for a moment.
When the group is ready:
Jesus is the shepherd GOD.
Jesus wants to protect and lead us.

Optional:
But Jesus said even more than this.
Let's close our eyes.
Let's hear some of Jesus' words to us.

These are simplified phrases taken from John 10.
Jesus says: I am the GOOD Shepherd.
The Good Shepherd calls you by name.
Listen to my voice.
I have called you by name,
you are mine.
I will never leave you.
I will stay close to you.

Those words from Jesus are for us.
Let's keep our eyes closed.

Let's imagine Jesus sitting with us here in our room.
Let's sing our shepherd God song to Jesus as a thank you prayer.

Reflectively with eyes closed.
Shepherd God, shepherd God,
protecting, leading, protecting, leading.
Shepherd God, shepherd God,
Jesus is the shepherd God.
Spoken: Amen

Option 3: God's my shepherd

→ 1 Samuel 17.34–36; Psalm 23
→ Song: 'God's my shepherd'. Words: © Sharon Moughtin.
→ Tune: 'Twinkle twinkle' (traditional). Note: this is basically the same tune as 'Baa baa black sheep' but in 'Twinkle twinkle' (and here in 'God's my shepherd') the last two lines are repeated.

God's my shep-herd, I have all I need. My God leads me in green fields.
E - ven when it's dark as night. God is with me, I am nev - er out of sight!
God's my shep-herd, I have all I need. My God leads me in green fields.

Appropriate for mixed groups of babies, toddlers and children up to the age of 9.
This option provides children with the opportunity to learn the psalm, 'The Lord's my Shepherd'. Groups that only include children up to the age of 7 may prefer to use Option 1.

Optional: Today, churches around the world
are celebrating Good Shepherd Sunday.

Jesus says 'I am the Good Shepherd!'
But what does that mean?
To understand what Jesus means,
we need to tell David's story.

It's a very old story,
one that Jesus would have known well!
David was a shepherd child.
His family job was to look after the family sheep on the hills.
He had to make sure the family sheep
had good food, clean water, and stayed safe!

Shepherd children looked after their sheep
away from the family home.
It wasn't always completely safe!
Sometimes a lion or a bear would come
and try to steal a lamb to eat it up!

Can you imagine being a shepherd child,
looking out for lions or bears?
How would that feel?
Can you show me?
Accept responses.

David was a GOOD shepherd!
He didn't just make sure his sheep
had good food and clean water.
He kept them safe from wild animals.

Let's be David.
We're out on the hills in the dark,
protecting our sheep.

Look there's a bear! *Point*
It's taken a sheep to eat it!
After 3, let's run as fast as we can on the spot,
then show David rescuing the sheep!
1, 2, 3 . . . Run!
Lead the group in running on the spot.
And rescue! ***Mime grabbing the sheep***
Phew! That was close!
Let's take our sheep back to the flock.
Mime putting the lamb down safely.

But look! *Point*
Now there's a LION!
The lion has taken a lamb to eat it!
After 3, let's run as fast as we can on the spot,
then show David snatching the lamb from the lion's mouth!
1, 2, 3 . . . Run !
Lead the group in running on the spot.
And rescue! ***Mime grabbing the sheep***
I hope it's all right. Let's have a look . . . .
Yes – the lamb's fine. Phew.
Let's take our sheep back to the flock.
Mime putting the lamb down safely.

David the shepherd child was very good at looking after sheep.
He was a good shepherd!
David was also a good singer.
The Bible celebrates lots of David's songs.
One of them is about God being like a Good Shepherd.
People sing it all the time,
especially when they're feeling sad or scared.
Let's learn David's song:
'my turn' *Point to self,* 'your turn' *Leader's hands out to group.*

78

Let's imagine we're the Good Shepherd
finding green fields for our sheep.
We're a shepherd so let's pick up our crook. *Mime picking up an imaginary crook.*
A crook is like a stick to hook the sheep and bring them back. *Demonstrate hooking a sheep with your crook.*

Let's walk with our crook as we sing *Lead the group in singing while walking on spot with imaginary crook in hand.*

God's my shepherd, I have all I need.
My God leads me in green fields.
God's my shepherd, I have all I need.
My God leads me in green fields.

David knew that being a shepherd
didn't just mean giving good things
like green fields and rivers of water to drink.
It means taking care of you when life is scary:
when everything feels dark!
Let's crouch down to show we're scared. *Lead the group in crouching down.*

Let's close our eyes
and cover them with our hands. *Lead the group in covering eyes.*
Can you sing:
'my turn' *Point to self,* 'your turn' *Leader's hands out to group.*

Even when it's dark as night *Crouch down with eyes covered*
God is with me, I am never out of sight. *Stay crouched down*
Even when it's dark as night, *Crouch down with eyes covered*
God is with me, I am never out of sight. *Stay crouched down*

Then we sing the first two lines again to end
as we walk along like God the Good Shepherd again.
Shall we see if we can sing that all together?

God's my shepherd, I have all I need. *Walk on spot with crook*
My God leads me in green fields. *Crouch down with eyes covered*
Even when it's dark as night, *Stay crouched down*
God is with me, I am never out of sight. *Walk on spot with crook*
God's my shepherd, I have all I need.
My God leads me in green fields.

Now God was looking for a king to protect and save God's People.
Who do you think God chose? *Rhetorical question*
David!
David had great skills not just to look after sheep,
but to look after people, too!
David was a great king. The greatest king of God's People!
God loved David.
The name David even means loved!
And David loved God!

Sometimes David made some really bad choices!
But even when David got it wrong
and got a bit lost, like a lost sheep,
David always called out to God for help.
Even when he became a shepherd KING,
People imagine him still singing the song
he sang as a shepherd child,
Shall we sing David's song together?

God's my shepherd, I have all I need. *Walk on spot with crook*
My God leads me in green fields. *Crouch down with eyes covered*
Even when it's dark as night, *Crouch down with eyes covered*

79

God is with me, I am never out of sight.
God's my shepherd, I have all I need. *Walk on spot with crook*
My God leads me in green fields.

Today we remember Jesus saying
'I am the Good Shepherd.'
When Jesus said that he was remembering David,
the shepherd child who became a shepherd king
and sang a song about the shepherd God.

Let's sit down for a moment.
When the group is ready:

Jesus is the shepherd GOD.
Jesus wants to protect and lead us.
Let's close our eyes.
Let's hear some of Jesus' words to us.

These are simplified phrases taken from John 10.
Jesus says: I am the GOOD Shepherd.
The Good Shepherd calls you by name.
Listen to my voice.
I have called you by name,
you are mine.
I will never leave you.
I will stay close to you.

Those words from Jesus are for us.
Especially when life feels dark or scary or sad.
Let's keep our eyes closed.
Let's imagine Jesus sitting with us here in our room.
Let's sing David's song to Jesus,
The shepherd king and shepherd God.

God's my shepherd, I have all I need. *Walk on spot with crook*
My God leads me in green fields.
Even when it's dark as night, *Crouch down with eyes covered*
God is with me, I am never out of sight.
God's my shepherd, I have all I need. *Walk on spot with crook*
My God leads me in green fields.

Thomas's Story

→ John 20.19-29
→ Song: 'Alleluia! Jesus is risen!' Words: © Sharon Moughtin.
→ Tune: 'Down in the jungle where nobody goes' (traditional).

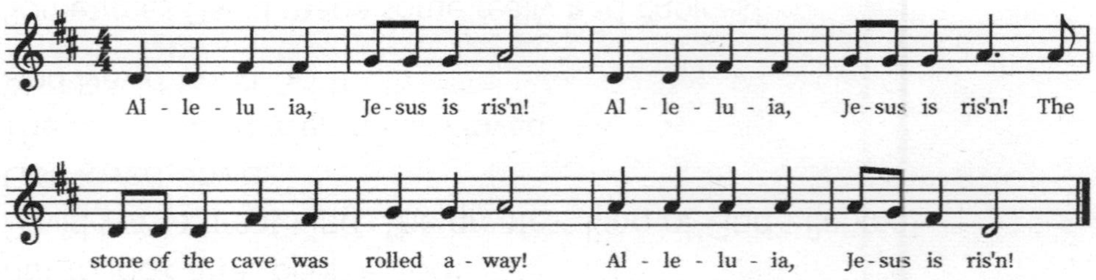

[Musical notation: Alleluia, Jesus is ris'n! Alleluia, Jesus is ris'n! The stone of the cave was rolled away! Alleluia, Jesus is ris'n!]

Appropriate for mixed groups of babies, toddlers and children up to the age of 9.
Groups that only include children up to the age of 7 may prefer to focus on other stories in the 'Jesus Is Alive! Alleluia! (Easter)' unit.

> This story uses the 'New Start' sign (the winding action from 'Wind the bobbin up') to show the rolling away of the stone on Easter Day that brings about that great 'new start' for the whole world. This is among the very few Sowing Seeds signs and actions that are fixed. See p. 8 or the website for a description and explanation.

80

Today we're going to tell the story
of when Thomas met the Risen Jesus!
To tell our story we need to learn a song.
Let's sing it:
'my turn' *Point to self,* 'your turn' *Leader's hands out to group.*
Singing: We're hiding, hiding, hiding away. [Ssssh!]
We're hiding, hiding, hiding away. [Ssssh!]
And again!
We're hiding, hiding, hiding away. [Ssssh!]

Then these next words stay the same every time.
Let's show the stone of the cave rolling away
with our 'roly poly' action as we sing.
Singing: The stone of the cave was rolled away! . . .
'New Start' sign. Hold final note.
The stone of the cave was rolled away!
'New Start' sign. Hold final note.

Then. . . .
Singing: We're hiding, hiding, hiding away. [Ssssh!]
We're hiding, hiding, hiding away. [Ssssh!]

Let's try that all together.
Lead the group in singing:
We're hiding, hiding, hiding away. [Ssssh!]
We're hiding, hiding, hiding away. [Ssssh!]
The stone of the cave was rolled away! *'New Start' sign*
We're hiding, hiding, hiding away. [Ssssh!]

We're ready to tell our story.
We're Jesus' friends the disciples.
On Easter Day, the stone of the cave was rolled away. *'New Start' sign*
Now what do you think we're doing? *Hide behind hands as if afraid*
Accept responses.

We're hiding!
Let's all hide behind our hands! Sssssssh!

Jesus is gone!
We don't know where he is!
And we're scared!
After 3 let's lock the door with our key.
Hold out an imaginary key as if about to lock the door.
1, 2, 3 . . . **Lock** *Lead the group in turning the key*
Now let's hide again! *Lead the group in hiding behind hands*
Let's sing together like we're really scared!

We're hiding, hiding, hiding away. [Ssssh!]
We're hiding, hiding, hiding away. [Ssssh!]
The stone of the cave was rolled away! *'New Start' sign*
We're hiding, hiding, hiding away. [Ssssh!]

What shall we do now?
I don't know!! . . . *Hands out, looking confused*
Let's keep on hiding.

We're hiding, hiding, hiding . . .
Look! Who's that?! *Point into the centre of the room*
How did . . .?
Look! It's Jesus!
How are we feeling now?
Can you show me with your whole body?
Accept responses.

Then Jesus said . . .
Let's stand up tall and be Jesus together.
Let's hold our hands out and say Jesus' words 'my turn', 'your turn'.
Peace be with you! *Hold hands outwards*
Peace be with you! *Hold hands outwards*

81

The most joyful you've ever felt! With your whole body!
Alleluia! *Hands up!*
Let's sing, 'Al-le-lu-ia! Jesus is risen!' *Hands up then waved*
Let's sing like we're full right up to the top of our heads with joy!

Alleluia! Jesus is risen! *Hands up then waved*
Alleluia! Jesus is risen! *Hands up then waved*
The stone of the cave was rolled away! *'New Start' sign*
Alleluia! Jesus is risen! *Hands up then waved*

The disciples were so excited.
But someone wasn't there.
Thomas wasn't there. *Shake head*
Thomas missed it! *Look sad and hold hands out*
How do you think Thomas felt when he found out what happened?
Can you show me with your body?

The disciples told Thomas the story of what had happened.
Let's be the disciples and sing about Jesus' hands and feet!
If appropriate: Let's sing double fast, because we're so excited!

See his hands and see his side! *Touch hands then side*
See his hands and see his side! *Touch hands then side*
The stone of the cave was rolled away! *'New Start' sign*
See his hands and see his side! *Touch hands then side*

Thomas had missed it. He'd missed Jesus! *Shake head*
Can you show me how he's feeling again?
The friends wanted Thomas to join in
celebrating 'Alleluia! Jesus is risen!'
But Thomas didn't want to. *Shake head*
He wanted to see Jesus' hands and side.
Actually, he wanted to TOUCH Jesus' hands and side.
Touch hands then side.
To put his own fingers there!

Look! Look at Jesus' hands!
They have marks on them!
It's the marks of the cross, where the nails were!
Let's touch the palms of our hands one by one
to show where the marks are.
Lead the group in touching the centre of your own hands one by one.

And look at his side!
Let's touch our own side.
It's the mark where the spear went into his side!
How are we feeling?
Can you show me with your body?
Let's sing 'See his hands and see his side!'

And let's touch the palms of our hands and our side as we sing.
See his hands and see his side! *Touch your hands, then your side*
See his hands and see his side! *Touch your hands, then your side*
The stone of the cave was rolled away! *'New Start' sign*
See his hands and see his side! *Touch your hands, then your side*

It really is Jesus!
I can see the marks on his hands and his side!
But he's alive!
Jesus is alive!
How are we feeling?!
Can you show me? *Accept responses*

Then Jesus breathed on them. *Breathe out*
After 3, let's breathe out like Jesus,
1, 2, 3 . . . *Lead the group in breathing out*
Receive the Holy Spirit!

And the disciples were filled with joy.
Can you show me full of joy?

82

Let's be Thomas.
Let's sing 'I want to TOUCH his hands and TOUCH his side!'
And let's point at ourselves and touch our hands and side as we sing.

Point **I want to touch his hands and touch his side!**
Touch hands then side.
Point **I want to touch his hands and touch his side!**
Touch hands then side.
The stone of the cave was rolled away! *'New Start' sign*
Point **I want to touch his hands and touch his side!**
Touch hands then side.

And the friends said . . .
Lead the group in singing joyfully:
Alleluia! Jesus is risen! *Hands up then waved*
Alleluia! Jesus is risen! *Hands up then waved*
The stone of the cave was rolled away! *'New Start' sign*
Alleluia! Jesus is risen! *Hands up then waved*

But Thomas said even louder:
Point **I want to touch his hands and touch his side!**
Touch hands then side.
Point **I want to touch his hands and touch his side!**
Touch hands then side.
The stone of the cave was rolled away! *'New Start' sign*
Point **I want to touch his hands and touch his side!**
Touch hands then side.

This carried on for a long time!
Thomas was very brave standing up against all his friends!
He really wanted to see Jesus for himself!

Either (if you're feeling confident!):
Split the room into two.

Let's have two groups.
One group can be the friends singing our 'Alleluia' song.
We want Thomas to join in!
Let's sing really loud!

Then the other group can be Thomas.
We're not ready to join in!
We want to see Jesus for ourselves!
We're going to try and sing as loud as the group.

Ready . . . go!
I want to touch his hands and touch his side!
I want to touch his hands and touch his side!
The stone of the cave was rolled away!
I want to touch his hands and touch his side!

Alleluia! Jesus is risen!
Alleluia! Jesus is risen!
The stone of the cave was rolled away!
Alleluia! Jesus is risen!
When appropriate, interrupt the singing.

Or: simply continue being Thomas as a whole group.

No one's listening!
Let's be Thomas and sing EVEN LOUDER!
Point **I want to touch his hands and touch his side!**
Touch hands then side.
Point **I want to touch his hands and touch his side!**
Touch hands then side.
The stone of the cave was rolled away! *'New Start' sign*
Point **I want to** *Interrupt the singing*

All groups:
But look! Who's that?! *Point into the centre of the room*

83

How did . . .?!
Look! It's Jesus!
How are we feeling now?
Can you show me with your whole body?

Then Jesus said . . . .
Let's stand up tall and be Jesus together.
Let's hold our hands out and say Jesus' words
'my turn' *Point to self,* 'your turn' *Leader's hands out to group.*
Peace be with you! *Hold hands outwards*
Peace be with you! *Hold hands outwards*

Then Jesus turned to Thomas and said . . . .
Touch my hands and touch my side! *Touch hands then side*
Touch my hands and touch my side! *Touch hands then side*

What did Thomas do?
What did Thomas THINK he wanted to do?
Accept responses.
Thomas THOUGHT he wanted
to touch Jesus' hands and touch his side.

But when Thomas looked at the Risen Jesus.
He didn't see Jesus' hands. *Shake head*
He didn't see Jesus' side. *Shake head*
When Thomas looked at Jesus, Thomas saw GOD! *Look amazed*
Thomas saw that Jesus is God!
And he bowed down low and worshipped!

Let's be Thomas.
Let's kneel down low before Jesus.

And Thomas said:
'You are my Lord! You are my God!'
That was the first time Jesus was called God!

Thomas saw something no-one else had seen!
Let's say Thomas's words together,
'my turn' *Point to self,* 'your turn' *Leader's hands out to group.*
You are my Lord! You are my God!
You are my Lord! You are my God!

Let's sing that together in amazement and awe.
Awe is when you are so amazed you can't even stand up.
Let's bow before Jesus.

Lead the group in bowing as you sing:
You are my Lord! You are my God!
You are my Lord! You are my God!
The stone of the cave was rolled away! *'New Start' sign*
Jesus, you are my Lord! You are my God!

THEN Thomas was ready to join in the friends' song!
He was really ready!
Let's be Thomas and sing really joyfully!
Let's sing even louder than the friends!
Loud enough for the stars to hear!

Alleluia! Jesus is risen! *Wave hands in air joyfully*
Alleluia! Jesus is risen! *Wave hands in air joyfully*
The stone of the cave was rolled away! *'New Start' sign*
Alleluia! Jesus is risen! *Wave hands in air joyfully*

Let's sit down for a moment.
When the group is ready:
In our story, Thomas felt left out.
Everyone else had seen something about Jesus:
his hands and his side.
And Thomas hadn't. *Shake head*
But when THOMAS saw Jesus, he saw God!
We don't have to see the same as everyone else.

Sometimes Jesus wants to show us something different.

Let's close our eyes for a moment.
When the group is ready:
Let's imagine Jesus coming to us.
Now does Jesus do anything? Or does Jesus say anything?
I wonder what you see when you see Jesus?

Let's open our eyes. The disciples' song became Thomas's song.
Jesus wants it to become our song too.
Let's sing our 'Alleluia!' song one more time.
Let's sing it as a prayer and ask God to make it into our song too.

Lead the group in singing reflectively:
Alleluia! Jesus is risen!
Alleluia! Jesus is risen!
The stone of the cave was rolled away! *'New Start' sign*
Alleluia! Jesus is risen!

The Catch of Fishes

→ John 21.1–14
→ Song: 'Back in Galilee'. Words: © Sharon Moughtin.
→ Tune: 'Row, row, row your boat' (traditional).

Row, row, row the boat, back in Gal-i-lee. 'Throw the net then pull it in... What can we see?

Appropriate for mixed groups of babies, toddlers and children up to the age of 9.

To tell our story, we need to learn a song.
Let's sit on the floor and pretend to row a boat.
Lead the children in sitting down and rowing in time:
Row and row and row and row....
And freeze!

Let's learn the words to our song:
'my turn' *Point to self*, 'your turn' *Leader's hands out to group*.

Sing the words with the tune.
Row, row, row the boat, *Rowing action*
Row, row, row the boat, *Rowing action*

back in Galilee. *Rowing action*
back in Galilee. *Rowing action*

Throw the net then pull it in . . . .
Mime throwing a net out of the boat then pulling it in.
Throw the net then pull it in . . . *Net out, then in*

What can we see? *Mime looking in the nets*
What can we see? *Mime looking in the nets*

Let's try singing that all together.
Lead the children in singing:
Row, row, row the boat, *Rowing action*
back in Galilee. *Rowing action*
Throw the net then pull it in . . . *Net out, then in*
What can we see? *Mime looking in the nets*

We're ready to tell our story.
Jesus has burst from the Dark Cave!
Jesus is alive!

Some of Jesus' friends, the disciples, have seen Jesus.
But they don't understand. *Shake head*
What does it mean that Jesus is alive?
Jesus isn't with his friends every day any more. *Shake head*
They have nothing to do.
Can you show me how you look when you have nothing to do?
The disciples had nothing to do! *Look fed up and bored*

If appropriate:
Can anyone tell me what Peter did before he met Jesus?
Accept all responses.

Before Peter met Jesus he was a fisherman.
So what do you think Peter decided to do?
Accept responses.

Optional: What's in the Box? (see p. 7)
Invite one of the children to open the box. Inside will be fish: either plastic or paper fish or a picture of a shoal of fish.
What's in the box? *Ask the child to respond*

Peter said, 'Come on, let's go fishing!' *Beckon action*
So Jesus' friends went back home to Galilee.
They got in their boat . . .
Lead the children in miming getting in the boat.
and fished all night.
Let's row our boat out and sing our song.

Row, row, row the boat, *Rowing action*
back in Galilee. *Rowing action*
Throw the net then pull it in . . . *Net out, then in*
What can we see? *Mime looking in the nets*

Let's have a look!
Lead the children in looking in the imaginary nets.
What have we caught?
Nothing! *Shake head*
I wonder how Peter and the disciples are feeling now?
Can you show me?

Let's sing our song feeling like Peter.
Lead the children in singing the song in the mood one of the children has chosen. For instance, fed up, cross, sad, bored, unsure, etc.

Row, row, row the boat, *Rowing action*
back in Galilee. *Rowing action*
Throw the net then pull it in . . . *Net out, then in*
What can we see? *Mime looking in the nets*

Let's have a look!
Lead the children in looking in the imaginary nets.
What have we caught?
Nothing! *Shake head*
I wonder how Peter and the disciples are feeling now?
Can you show me?

Upset: Nothing! Oh no!
Have we forgotten how to fish?
I wonder how Peter and the disciples are feeling now?
Can you show me?

Lead the children in singing the song in the mood one of the children has chosen.

Row, row, row the boat, *Rowing action*
back in Galilee. *Rowing action*
Throw the net then pull it in . . . *Net out, then in*
What can we see? *Mime looking in the nets*

Let's have a look!
Lead the children in looking in the imaginary nets.
What have we caught?
Nothing! *Shake head*

Sadly: We really HAVE forgotten how to fish!
We can't do ANYTHING right without Jesus!
I wonder how Peter and the disciples are feeling now?
Can you show me?

This time, let's sing our song and row really quietly and slowly and sadly like we're really missing Jesus.

Row, row, row the boat, *Rowing action*
back in Galilee. *Rowing action*
Interrupt the singing and point.

Wait! Look! Who's that?
A stranger was standing far away on the beach.

The stranger said: *Hands cupped around mouth*
'Have you caught anything?'

The disciples said . . .
Well, what do you think they said?
Accept responses.
The disciples said, 'No!' *Hands cupped around mouth*
The stranger said: *Hands cupped around mouth*
'Throw your net on the OTHER SIDE of the boat!' *Point*
There are fish there!

Now the stranger didn't really look like a fisherman. *Shake head*
Look suspicious: He didn't look like he'd know anything about fishing!
But the disciples were so sad and fed up
that they shrugged their shoulders.
Let's shrug our shoulders.
Lead the children in shrugging shoulders.
'We may as well try,' they said.
So they tried again.

Let's sing our song together, but still a bit fed up.
Row, row, row the boat, *Rowing action*
back in Galilee. *Rowing action*
Throw the net then pull it in . . . *Net out, then in*
What can we see? *Mime looking in the nets*

Let's have a look!
Lead the children in looking in the imaginary nets.
What have we caught?
Still nothing? . . .

No! Not nothing!
Oh my goodness!
This net is too heavy to pull in!
Lead the children in imagining pulling a net that's too heavy.
It's full to bursting with fish!
How is this net not breaking!

Then one of the disciples said:
'I know who the stranger is!'
Who do you think it is?
Accept responses.
It's Jesus!
And do you know what Peter did?

He jumped straight into the water
and swam as fast as he could to Jesus!
Let's swim on the spot as fast as we can!
Lead the children in swimming.
Faster! Faster!

And the other friends rowed their boat
as fast as they could to the shore.
Let's sit down and row as fast as we can to the shore,
pulling our heavy nets . . . .
Lead the children in rowing fast.

And do you know what Jesus said to them? *Rhetorical question*
Say in a calm, matter-of-fact voice:
Jesus said, 'Come and have breakfast!'

87

Peter's Story

→ John 18.15-27, 21.15-19
→ Song: 'I am going to follow Jesus'. Words: © Sharon Moughtin.
→ Tune: 'Bobby Shaftoe' (traditional).

I am going to fol-low Je-sus, I am going to fol-low Je-sus,

I am going to fol-low Je-sus, fol-low, fol-low Je-sus!

Appropriate for mixed groups of babies, toddlers and children up to the age of 9.

Optional: What's in the Box? (see p. 7)

Invite one of the children to open the box. Inside will be screwed up paper, looking like rubbish.
What's in the box? *Ask the child to respond*
Today we're going to tell the story of someone
who'd made a bad choice.
Such a bad choice he felt he should be thrown away
like rubbish.

Today we're going to tell Peter's story.
Before Jesus died on the cross,
Jesus' friends, the disciples, followed Jesus everywhere.
Let's march on the spot:
1, 2, 3, 4! 1, 2, 3, 4!

Continue marching on the spot as you sing:
I am going to follow Jesus,
I am going to follow Jesus,

So they did!

Let's kneel down. *Lead the children in kneeling*
Let's make a fire.
Lead the children in miming building a fire from wood.
Let's light our fire.
Lead the children in miming striking a match and lighting the wood.
1, 2, 3 . . . Tssss!

They cooked the fish together.
Lead the children in cooking the fish on the fire.
And they ate it! *Lead the children in taking a bite of fish*
Mmmm! Delicious!

Then let's say this:
'my turn' Point to self, 'your turn' Leader's hands out to group.

Jesus took the bread.   *Take bread*
Jesus took the bread.   *Take bread*
He said, 'Thank you, God!'   *Hold bread up if this is in your tradition*
He said, 'Thank you, God!'   *Hold bread up if this is in your tradition*
Jesus broke the bread.   *Break bread*
Jesus broke the bread.   *Break bread*
Then he shared it.   *Mime handing bread out in a circle*
Then he shared it.   *Mime handing bread out in a circle*

And then the disciples knew absolutely
that this was the Risen Jesus!

**I am going to follow Jesus,
follow, follow Jesus!**

The disciples followed Jesus everywhere!
But one dark night, Jesus said,
'I'm going somewhere and you can't follow me.' *Shake head*
Jesus meant the cross. *Hold arms out in cross shape*

Peter said, *Point to self*
'I will follow you EVERYWHERE!'
Let's be Peter.
Can you show me really brave and proud and confident?
Lead the children in looking brave, proud and confident.
Let's go!

Lead the children in singing the song looking brave and marching confidently on the spot.

**I am going to follow Jesus,
I am going to follow Jesus,
I am going to follow Jesus!
follow, follow Jesus!**

But Jesus shook his head. *Shake head*
Let's shake our heads together.
Lead the children in shaking heads.
'No, Peter!
A cockerel will crow three times.'

Who can show me what a cockerel crowing sounds like?
Give the children a few moments to crow like a cockerel.
Freeze!

Let's crow three times like a cockerel together.
Ready . . . .

Count crows on fingers as you lead the children in crowing.
Jesus said, 'Before the cockerel crows three times,
You will choose NOT to follow me.'

That night Jesus was taken away!
Everyone was very scared.
Can you show me scared?
Lead the children in looking scared.

Peter tried to follow Jesus.
Let's tiptoe like Peter in the dark.
Let's sing like we're really quite scared!
Tiptoe and sing quietly and hesitatingly:
**I am going to follow Jesus,
I am going to follow Jesus,
I am going to follow Jesus . . .
follow, follow Jesus . . .**

Then a woman saw Peter.
She said, 'Do you follow Jesus?'
And do you know what Peter said?

Peter said, 'No! *Shake head*
I do not follow Jesus!'
Let's sing that in a very quiet, scared voice.
Lead the children in singing timidly:
**No, I do not follow Jesus,
No, I do not follow Jesus,
No, I do not follow Jesus,
follow, follow Jesus!**

Peter crept away and sat by a fire.
Let's sit down and warm our hands by the fire.

Lead the children in sitting and miming warming hands.
But some men asked him: 'Do you follow Jesus?'

What do you think Peter said?
Accept responses.
Peter said, 'No, *Shake head*
I do not follow Jesus.'
Let's sing in an even quieter and more scared voice.

Lead the children in singing as if very scared:
No, I do not follow Jesus,
No, I do not follow Jesus,
No, I do not follow Jesus,
follow, follow Jesus!

But another man said, 'Yes you do! I saw you! *Point*
This time Peter jumped up.
Let's jump up together.
Lead children in jumping up.
Let's sing: *Loudly and angrily*
'No! *Stamp* I do not follow Jesus!'

Lead the children in singing loudly and angrily:
No! Stamp I do not follow Jesus!
No! Stamp I do not follow Jesus!
No! Stamp I do not follow Jesus,
follow, follow Jesus!

And at that very moment Peter heard a terrible sound.
What do you think it was?
Crow like a cockerel: Cock-a-doodle doo!

Let's crow like a cockerel three times.
Count crows on fingers as you lead the children in crowing three times.

I wonder how Peter felt.
Can you show me with your face?
Accept the children's responses.

Let's sit down for a moment.
That was before Jesus died.
Now Jesus has risen! *Sound excited*
Jesus is alive!

Sound more concerned:
And Jesus is standing in front of Peter.
I wonder how Peter is feeling?
He said that he didn't follow Jesus! *Shake head*
Can you show me with your face?

Then Jesus asked Peter three questions.
They were questions that would give Peter a whole new start.

Question number 1. Let's hold one finger up.
Lead the children in holding up one finger.
Jesus asked, 'Peter, do you love me?'
In a very quiet, sad voice, Peter said . . . 'Yes.' *Thumbs up*

Question number 2. Let's hold two fingers up.
Lead the children in holding up two fingers.
Jesus asked, 'Peter, do you love me?'
What do you think Peter said?
Accept responses.
In a little bit louder voice, Peter said . . .
Encourage the children to join in: **'Yes.'** *Thumbs up*

Question number 3. Let's hold three fingers up.
Lead the children in holding up three fingers.
Jesus asked, 'Peter, do you love me?'

90

When we make mistakes and feel good for nothing,
let's remember Peter's story.
God can always, always, always give us a new start.
God can do amazing things when we show we're sorry.

If your group is familiar with it, you may wish to use the Sorry Song (see p. 158) at this point, even if you haven't chosen it as a Building Block for the rest of the unit.

The Ascension

Option 1: Jesus goes up!

→ The Ascension
→ Luke 24.42–53
→ Song: 'Go! And wait for the Holy Spirit!' Words: © Sharon Moughtin.
→ Tune: 'London Bridge is falling down' (traditional).

We are eat - ing fish at the beach! Fish at the beach! Fish at the beach!

We are eat - ing fish at the beach! A - le - lu - ia!

Appropriate for mixed groups of babies, toddlers and children up to the age of 7. Groups that include children up to the age of 9 may prefer to use Option 2. The storytelling is very similar, but the song in Option 2 is slightly more challenging. Choose which version works best in your setting.

Optional: What's in the Box? (see p. 7)

Invite one of the children to open the box. Inside will be an 'Alleluia!' (written or printed).

This time Peter got a bit fed up.
Jesus wasn't listening properly!
Let's stand up.
After 3, let's shout, 'Yes!' and stamp our feet!

1, 2, 3: Yes! Stamp

Then Jesus said to Peter:
In a matter-of-fact, gentle voice, smiling:
'Follow me!'
And that was how Jesus gave Peter a new start.
Peter was Jesus' follower again!

Let's sing our song.
And this time, let's sing it really joyfully!
Like we really mean it!
Let's stand up and follow!

1, 2, 3, 4! 1, 2, 3, 4!

Continue marching happily as you sing:
**I am going to follow Jesus,
I am going to follow Jesus,
I am going to follow Jesus,
follow, follow Jesus!**

Let's sit down for a moment.
In our story today, Peter got it really wrong.
But Jesus gave him a brand new start.
Peter became the leader of all the disciples!
Then the leader of the whole Church!

If you're going to make keys later:
Jesus put Peter in charge and gave him some special keys:
the keys to heaven!

What's in the box? *Ask the child to respond. Don't worry if the child can't read it: she or he might say 'a word' or 'writing' or 'a piece of paper' or 'a drawing', etc.*
The writing/word on this piece of paper says 'Alleluia!'

Today's the last week of Easter.
So our song today ends every time with the joyful shout of Easter.

If appropriate:
Can anyone tell me what our joyful Easter word is?
Accept children's responses.
Alleluia! *Hands raised*

Let's practise:
'my turn' *Point to self,* 'your turn' *Leader's hands out to group.*
Sing to the tune of the last line of 'London Bridge is falling down':
'Alleluia!' *Hands raised*
'Alleluia!' *Hands raised*
And again: 'Alleluia!' *Hands raised*
'Alleluia!' *Hands raised*

We're ready to tell our story.
Jesus was sitting with his disciples, eating fish.

Let's kneel down. *Lead the children in kneeling*
Let's make a fire.
Lead the children in miming building a fire from wood.
Let's light our fire.
Lead the children in miming striking a match and lighting the wood.
1, 2, 3 . . . Tsssss!
Let's cook our fish.
Lead the children in cooking the fish on the fire.
Now let's eat it!

Lead the children in taking a bite of fish.
Mmmm! Delicious!

Let's sing: 'We are eating fish at the beach!' *Eating action*
And remember our special 'Alleluia!' *Hands raised* at the end!

Don't worry about teaching this song. Its tune and shape are so recognizable that the children will naturally join in when you start singing.
We are eating fish at the beach! *Eating action*
Fish at the beach! Fish at the beach! *Eating action*
We are eating fish at the beach! *Eating action*
Alleluia! *Raise arms to form a 'V' shape in the air*

So the disciples were eating fish at the beach.
Then Jesus said, 'Time to go! Get up!'
Let's get up! *Lead the children in standing*

Jesus led the disciples up a hill.
Put your hand up if you've ever climbed a very high hill.
It's hard work!
Can you show me walking up a hill on the spot?
Climb and climb and climb and climb!
Let's keep on climbing and sing:
'Climb the hi-ill, 1, 2, 3!'

Climb the hi-ill, 1, 2, 3!
1, 2, 3! 1, 2, 3! *Climb the hill together*
Climb the hi-ill, 1, 2, 3!
Alleluia! *'V' shape in the air*

Phew! We're at the top.
Wow! Look at the amazing view! *Hand sheltering eyes*
Lead the children in looking around!
Let's look left! And right!

Look! *Point upwards*
Look! *Point again* Jesus is going up!
Up and up and up! *Point higher and higher*
The disciples were amazed!
Can you show me your amazed face?

Look! Jesus is going up!
Lead the children in singing with amazement:
Look! Jesus is going up, *Point upwards*
going up, going up! *Point upwards*
Look! Jesus is going up! *Point upwards*
Alleluia! *'V' shape in the air*

Lead the children in looking upwards with your hand sheltering your eyes.
The disciples watched Jesus go up and up and up . . . .
Till they could only see his feet disappearing into a cloud!

Gasp Jesus is going!
Let's wave goodbye to Jesus.
Who likes waving goodbye?
Let's wave and sing goodbye as loudly as we can!

Wave goodbye to Je-e-sus! *Waving with both arms*
Je-e-sus, Je-e-sus! *Waving with both arms*
Wave goodbye to Je-e-sus! *Waving with both arms*
Alleluia! *'V' shape in the air*

Jesus has gone!
How do you feel when someone special comes visit, then goes again?
It can be fun waving goodbye.
Then how does it feel when they've gone?
Can you show me your face?
Jesus has gone! What shall we do now?

And in front of us! And behind us!
We can see everything!

Then Jesus said, 'Listen!' *Hand behind ear*
Let's say Jesus' words together:
'my turn' *Point to self, 'your turn' Leader's hands out to group*:

Go! And wait for the Holy Spirit! *Point*
Go! And wait for the Holy Spirit! *Point*

Let's sing Jesus' words together.
Go and wait for the Holy Spirit, *Point*
the Holy Spirit, the Holy Spirit! *Point*
Go and wait for the Holy Spirit *Point*
Alleluia! *'V' shape in the air*

Hold hands out in a questioning shape.
But who or what is the Holy Spirit? *Look confused*
The disciples haven't met the Holy Spirit yet! *Shake head*
Jesus said, 'The Holy Spirit will make you strong!' *Strong action*
Can you show me an action for strong?
Accept the children's actions.

When the Holy Spirit comes, it will be in fire!
Can you make your bodies into flames of fire
by waving and swaying them?
Lead the children in swaying with hands stretched upwards like flames of fire.
Let's sing:
'The Holy Spirit *Fire action* will make you strong!' *Strong action*

The Holy Spirit *Fire action* **will make you strong,** *Strong action*
make you strong, make you strong! *Strong action*
The Holy Spirit *Fire action* **will make you strong!** *Strong action*
Alleluia! *Hands upwards*

Option 2: You will tell the world about me!

→ The Ascension
→ Acts 1.8–14
→ Song: 'Alleluia! Jesus is risen'. Words: © Sharon Moughtin.
→ Tune: 'Down in the jungle where nobody goes' (traditional).

(musical notation)

Al-le-lu-ia, Je-sus is ris'n! Al-le-lu-ia, Je-sus is ris'n! The stone of the cave was rolled a-way! Al-le-lu-ia, Je-sus is ris'n!

Appropriate for mixed groups of babies, toddlers and children up to the age of 9. Groups that only include children up to the age of 7 may prefer to use Option 1. The storytelling is very similar, but the song in Option 2 is slightly more challenging. Choose which version works best in your setting.

> This story uses the 'New Start' sign (the winding action from 'Wind the bobbin up') to show the rolling away of the stone on Easter Day that brings about that great 'new start' for the whole world. This is among the very few Sowing Seeds signs and actions that are fixed. See p. 8 or the website for a description and explanation.

Optional: What's in the Box? (see p. 7)

Invite one of the children to open the box. Inside will be an 'Alleluia!' (written or printed).

What's in the box? *Ask the child to respond. Don't worry if the child can't read it: she or he might say 'a word' or 'writing' or 'a piece of paper' or 'a drawing', etc.*

Look confused and leave a moment's pause.

Can anyone remember what Jesus told us to do?
  If necessary: 'Go and wait for . . .'
Accept responses.

So what shall we do?
Lead the children straight into singing:

Go and wait for the Holy Spirit, *Point*
the Holy Spirit, *Point* **the Holy Spirit!** *Point*
Go and wait for the Holy Spirit! *Point*
Alleluia! *'V' shape in the air*

Can anyone remember what the Holy Spirit will do?
  If necessary: The Holy Spirit will make us . . . ?
Accept the children's responses.

Lead the children in singing:

The Holy Spirit *Fire action* **will make us strong,** *Strong action*
make us strong, make us strong! *Strong action*
The Holy Spirit *Fire action* **will make us strong!** *Strong action*
Alleluia! *Hands upwards*

That's where our story ends for today:
with waiting . . .

If appropriate:
  Can anyone remember who the disciples are waiting for?
  Help the children out if necessary: The . . . Holy . . . Spirit!

Come next time to find out what happens when the Holy Spirit comes . . .

94

The writing/word on this piece of paper says 'Alleluia!'

Today's the last week of Easter.
So our song today starts with the joyful shout of Easter.

If appropriate:
Can anyone tell me what our joyful Easter word is?
Accept children's responses.
Alleluia! *Hands raised*

If your group doesn't know the 'Alleluia! Jesus is risen!' song from Thomas's Story (p. 80):
To tell our story, we need to learn a song.
It's Jesus friends, the disciples' song.
Let's sing it 'my turn', 'your turn'.

Alleluia! Jesus is risen! *Hands up then waved*
Alleluia! Jesus is risen! *Hands up then waved*

We sing that twice,
then these next words stay the same every time.
Let's show the stone of the cave
rolling away with our 'roly poly' action as we sing.
Singing: The stone of the cave was rolled away! . . . .
'New Start' sign. Hold final note.
The stone of the cave was rolled away!
'New Start' sign. Hold final note.

Then . . . .
Singing: Alleluia! Jesus is risen! *Hands up then waved*
Alleluia! Jesus is risen! *Hands up then waved*

Let's try that all together.
Lead the group in singing:
Alleluia! Jesus is risen! *Hands up then waved*

Alleluia! Jesus is risen! *Hands up then waved*
The stone of the cave was rolled away!
'New Start' sign.
Alleluia! Jesus is risen! *Hands up then waved*

We're ready to tell our story.

All groups:
We're Jesus' friends the disciples.
On Easter Day, the stone of the cave was rolled away. *'New Start' sign*
Then Jesus appeared to his friends, the disciples!
The disciples were filled with joy.
Can you show me full of joy!
The most joy you've ever felt! With your whole body!
Alleluia! *Hands up!*

Let's sing the disciples' 'Alleluia! Jesus is risen!' song.
Hands up then waved.
Let's sing like we're full right up to the top of our heads with joy!

Alleluia! Jesus is risen! *Hands up then waved*
Alleluia! Jesus is risen! *Hands up then waved*
The stone of the cave was rolled away! *'New Start' sign*
Alleluia! Jesus is risen! *Hands up then waved*

The disciples were so excited!
Now they wanted Jesus to be king.
Whenever they saw Jesus they kept on saying to him,
'Jesus, Jesus, you could be king!' *Crown action*

Let's be the excited disciples and sing to Jesus.
Let's jump up and down as we sing:
Lead the group in jumping up and down as you sing:
Jesus, Jesus, you could be king! *Crown action*

Accept responses
Then Jesus started going up!
If appropriate: He 'ascended': that means went up!
Up, up, up into the clouds. *Point higher and higher*
The disciples were amazed!
Can you show me amazed?!
Let's sing 'Look! Jesus is going up!'

Lead the children in singing with amazement:
Look! Jesus is going up. *Point upwards*
Look! Jesus is going up. *Point upwards*
The stone of the cave was rolled away! *'New Start' sign*
Now, look! Jesus is going up! *Point upwards*

Lead the children in looking upwards with your hand sheltering your eyes.
The disciples watched Jesus go up and up and up . . . .
Till they could only see his feet disappearing into a cloud!

Gasp Jesus is going!
But he was going to be king!
Why is he going?!
How do you think the disciples are feeling now?
Can you show me?
Accept responses.

The disciples kept on looking upwards.
Let's try and see Jesus far away up there! *Point upwards*
Then suddenly.
Look! There were two angels.
Standing with the disciples!
How do you think the disciples are feeling now?
Can you show me!
Accept responses.

Jesus, Jesus, you could be king! *Crown action*
The stone of the cave was rolled away! *'New Start' sign*
Jesus, Jesus, you could be king! *Crown action*

But Jesus said 'Only God knows when.'
Then Jesus said, 'The Holy Spirit will make you strong!'
Can you show me an action for strong?
Accept the children's actions.

But what is Jesus talking about?
Who or what is the Holy Spirit? *Look confused*
The disciples haven't met the Holy Spirit properly yet! *Shake head*
Still, Jesus said, 'The Holy Spirit will make you strong!'
Choose one of the actions, this will become the 'strong action'
Let's sing Jesus' words.

The Holy Spirit will make you strong! *Strong action*
The Holy Spirit will make you strong! *Strong action*
The stone of the cave was rolled away! *'New Start' sign*
The Holy Spirit will make you strong! *Strong action*

And Jesus kept on speaking!
Jesus said: 'You will tell the world about me!'
The whole world!
That's a big job!
Let's point to each other and sing:
'You will tell the world about me!'

You will tell the world about me! *Point at each other*
You will tell the world about me! *Point at each other*
The stone of the cave was rolled away! *'New Start' sign*
You will tell the world about me! *Point at each other*

How do you think the disciples are feeling now?
Can you show me?

So the disciples went back to Jerusalem and they waited.
That's where our story ends for today:
with waiting . . .
Who do you think they were waiting for?
Help the children out if necessary:
The . . . Holy . . . Spirit!

Come back next time to find out what happens when the Holy Spirit comes . . .

Come, Holy Spirit!

→ **The Day of Pentecost**
→ **Acts 2.1-4**
→ **Song:** 'Holy Spirit, come!' Words: © Sharon Moughtin.
→ **Tune:** 'Wind the bobbin up' (traditional).

Ho - ly Spi-rit, come! Ho - ly Spi-rit, come! Come, come! Spi-rit come! Ho - ly Spi-rit, come!

Ho - ly Spi-rit, come! Come, come! Spi-rit, come! Fire on the ceil-ing! Fire on the floor!

Fire at the win - dow! Fire at the door! The fire of the Spi - rit:

can you see? Ho - ly Spi - rit, dance in me!

Appropriate for mixed groups of babies, toddlers and children up to the age of 9.

97

Then the angels started speaking.
'Why are you staring into the sky?' they said.
'Jesus has gone.
But he'll be back . . .'

The disciples looked at each other.
Let's look at each other.
Lead the group in looking at each other.
What shall we do?
What did Jesus say?

Jesus said, 'You will tell the world about me!'
Remember?
Let's remind each other and point at each other as we sing.
You will tell the world about me! *Point at each other*
You will tell the world about me! *Point at each other* 'New Start' sign
The stone of the cave was rolled away! 'New Start' sign
You will tell the world about me! *Point at each other*

But how are we going to do that?
Without Jesus?
What are we going to do?
We're not strong enough to do that! *Look sad*

But wait! Jesus said something else!
Jesus said, 'The Holy Spirit . . .
Encourage the group to join in: . . . **will make you strong**!'
Let's sing Jesus' words again.

The Holy Spirit will make you strong! *Strong action*
The Holy Spirit will make you strong! *Strong action*
The stone of the cave was rolled away! 'New Start' sign
The Holy Spirit will make you strong! *Strong action*

The 'New Start' sign (the winding action from 'Wind the bobbin up') is among the very few Sowing Seeds signs and actions that are fixed. Here it recalls the rolling away of the stone on Easter Day that brings about that great 'new start' for the whole world as well as the prayer for the Holy Spirit to come to bring a 'new start' for the disciples who will become apostles. See p. 8 or the website for a description and explanation.

Optional: What's in the Box? (see p. 7)

Invite one of the children to open the box.
Inside will be a picture of fire.
What's in the box? *Ask the child to respond*
Today's story is about fire!

To tell our story today, we need to learn a song.

You may find this introduction helpful for learning the song together.
Let's learn the words:
The fire of the Spirit! Can you see?
'my turn' *Point to self*, 'your turn' *Leader's hands out to group.*
The fire of the Spirit! Can you see?
Holy Spirit, dance in me!
Holy Spirit, dance in me!

Say the words (without the tune) in the rhythm of the song:
The fire of the Spirit! Can you see?
The fire of the Spirit! Can you see?
Holy Spirit, dance in me!
Holy Spirit, dance in me!

Let's try singing that. *Add the tune*
The fire of the Spirit! Can you see? *Point out*
The fire of the Spirit! Can you see? *Point out*
Holy Spirit, dance in me! *Point to self*
Holy Spirit, dance in me! *Point to self*

That's the end of the song.
Let's learn the middle words.
Can you say after me
Say in the rhythm of the song:
Fire on the ceiling! *Point up*
Fire on the floor! *Point down*
Fire on the ceiling! *Point up*
Fire on the floor! *Point down*
Fire at the window! *Point to window*
Fire at the door! *Point to door*
Fire at the window! *Point to window*
Fire at the door! *Point to door*

Then it's the part we already know.
Start singing and encourage the children to join in.
The fire of the Spirit: *Waving bodies like flames* can you see? *Waving bodies like flames*
Holy Spirit, dance in me! *Waving bodies like flames*

Let's try that one more time this time, let's sing:
Start singing and encourage the children to join in. The children will probably recognize the tune by now so the tune here won't need to be taught 'my turn', 'your turn'.

Fire on the ceiling! *Point up*
Fire on the floor! *Point down*
Fire at the window! *Point to window*
Fire at the door! *Point to door*
The fire of the Spirit: can you see? *Point out*
Holy Spirit, dance in me! *Point to self*

We're ready to tell our story.
Jesus has gone!
He's gone up and up and up to heaven! *Point up higher and higher*

98

If you told 'Jesus goes up!' Option 1 p. 91):
Let's wave goodbye to Jesus.
Lead the children in waving goodbye.
'Goodbye, Jesus!'

Before Jesus went up,
Jesus told his friends about someone coming
who would make them strong.
So the disciples went to wait.

If appropriate:
Can anyone remember who they're waiting for?
Help the children out if necessary: The . . . Holy . . . Spirit!

So at the beginning of our story,
the disciples are waiting.
But they're not just waiting.
They're praying!
They're praying, 'Holy Spirit, come!'
'New Start' sign. This will be the 'come' action for the song.

Let's be Jesus' friends, the disciples, and pray:
Lead the children in singing quietly:
Holy Spirit, come! *'Come' action throughout*
Holy Spirit, come!
Come, come! Spirit, come!

Lead the children in looking around.
Can anyone see the Holy Spirit?
Not yet . . .

Let's keep praying . . . .
Holy Spirit, come! *'Come' action throughout*
Holy Spirit, come!
Come, come! Spirit, come!

Lead the children in looking around.
Any sign of the Holy Spirit?
Sigh Not yet . . . .
Let's keep praying . . . .

Holy Spirit, come! *'Come' action throughout*
Holy Spirit, come!
Come, come! Spirit, come!

The disciples prayed for nine whole days.
Let's count to 9.
Lead the children in counting on their fingers.
1, 2, 3, 4, 5, 6, 7, 8, 9 . . .
That's a long time to pray!

Holy Spirit, come! *'Come' action throughout*
Holy Spirit, come!
Come, come! Spirit, come!

Lead the children in looking around.
Is the Holy Spirit here yet?
No! Shall we give up?!
Nothing seems to be happening *Sigh*
But it's what Jesus TOLD us to do!
Let's keep praying.

Holy Spirit, come! *'Come' action throughout*
Holy Spirit, come!
Come, come! Spirit, come!
Ssssssssshhhh! What's that?
Look around and upwards and put hand to your ear.

Blow into the air.
Can you hear that?
There's a sound like wind blowing!
Blow, and encourage the children to join in blowing.
Louder . . . Blow louder and louder . . . Blow even louder . . .
Then lead the children in banging hands on the floor, louder and louder . . .

And look! *Point* What's that?
Fire! There's fire everywhere!
Let's show the fire with our bodies:
Lead the children in swaying your whole body to look like a fiery flame.

It's waving and swaying everywhere!
Look! The whole room is filled with fire!
Lead the group in singing:
Fire on the ceiling! *Point up in shock*
Fire on the floor! *Point down*
Fire at the window! *Point to window in shock*
Fire at the door! *Point to door*
The fire of the Spirit: can you see? *Point all around*
Holy Spirit, dance in me! *Sway like a flame*

And look! *Point to a child in surprise*
Now the fire is dancing on your head!

And your head! *Point to another child*
On all our heads!
Put hands together above head and wave them side to side to show a flame dancing on your head.
Let's show the fire dancing on our head.
Lead the children in the same action.

The fire danced on the disciples' heads!
I wonder how the disciples are feeling now?
Can you show me with your face?
Follow the children's suggested expressions.

Then all of a sudden the fire was gone!
Even the flames on the disciples' heads had gone!
Quick! Let's hide the flames behind our back.
Lead the children in placing hands behind back.

Let's sit down for a moment.
When the group is ready:
The flames had gone!
But the FIRE hadn't gone away!
The fire had gone INSIDE the disciples! *Trace circle on heart*

All the power and light and dancing
of the fire had gone INSIDE them!
Making them feel strong and not afraid:
full of fire and life!

The fire was the Holy Spirit!
The Holy Spirit had come!
And the disciples weren't afraid or lonely or sad any more,
because the Spirit was inside them!

Shall we tell the story again with our song.
Let's be the disciples, praying and waiting.
Lead the children in singing:
Holy Spirit, come! *'Come' action throughout*
Holy Spirit, come!
Come, come! Spirit, come!

Lead the children in looking around.
Can anyone see the Holy Spirit?
Not yet . . .

Let's keep praying . . . .

Holy Spirit, come! *'Come' action throughout*
Holy Spirit, come!
Come, come! Spirit, come!

Lead the children in looking around.
Any sign of the Holy Spirit?
Sigh Not yet . . . .
Let's keep praying . . . .

Holy Spirit, come! *'Come' action throughout*
Holy Spirit, come!
Come, come! Spirit, come!

Lead the children in looking around.
Is the Holy Spirit here yet?
No! Shall we give up?!
Accept children's responses.
Jesus told us to wait!
Let's keep praying.

Holy Spirit, come! *'Come' action throughout*
Holy Spirit, come!
Come, come! Spirit, come!

Ssssssssh! What's that?
Look around and upwards and put hand to your ear.

Blow into the air.
Can you hear that?
Blow, and encourage the children to join in blowing.
Louder . . . *Blow louder* and louder . . . *Blow even louder* . . .
Then lead the children in banging hands on the floor, louder and louder . . .

And look! *Point* What's that?
Lead the group in singing:
Fire on the ceiling! *Point up in shock*
Fire on the floor! *Point down*
Fire at the window! *Point to window in shock*
Fire at the door! *Point to door*
The fire of the Spirit! Can you see? *Point all around*
Holy Spirit, dance in me! *Sway like a flame*

Let's sit down for a moment.
In our story, the Holy Spirit came on the disciples like fire!
The Holy Spirit made them feel strong and not afraid.

I wonder if you ever feel like the Holy Spirit is in you?
Dancing and making you strong?
I wonder if you'd like to pray for the Holy Spirit?
I'm going to pray our song now as a prayer.
If you like, you can join in and ask the Holy Spirit to come inside you.

We can't always SEE the Holy Spirit.
But the Spirit is like God's fire,
dancing around us and inside us.
And if we learn to see with God's eyes, *Point to eyes*
we might learn to see it!

Shall we sing our song again.
This time, let's sing it for ourselves.
Let's make Jesus' friends' song into our song.

Sing quietly and reflectively:
Holy Spirit, come! *'Come' action throughout*
Holy Spirit, come!
Come, come! Spirit, come!

Holy Spirit, come!
Holy Spirit, come!
Come, come! Spirit, come . . .

We can't always SEE the Holy Spirit.
But the Spirit is like God's fire dancing INSIDE us.
I wonder if you can feel the Spirit dancing inside YOU?
End with a short moment of silence.

If appropriate: Today's the Day of Pentecost!
It's the day that all around the world
we remember the day the Holy Spirit came in fire
and we pray for the Holy Spirit to dance in us!

1, 2, 3, the Trinity! (Trinity Sunday)

→ Song: '1, 2, 3, the Trinity!' Words: © Sharon Moughtin.
→ Tune: © Sharon Moughtin.

Appropriate for mixed groups of babies, toddlers and children up to the age of 9. Different options are available within the storytelling according to the ages represented in your group.

> **Tip**
> The Easter season is now over. Churches following the liturgical year may prefer to use 'Holy Spirit, come!' (the song from the previous story) as a Gathering Song. If your group would like to do this, start from the recap of the story on p. 100. The following introduction may be helpful:
>
> In our story last time, the Holy Spirit came like fire!
> Let's remember the story with our song.
> Let's be the disciples praying and waiting . . .

Two versions of the Trinity song are available, depending on the ages of the children present. The second version has been provided for groups which include children aged 5+ or for all-age worship settings. It allows for more development, but may be too much for younger children to sing unsupported by an older group. Choose which version is most appropriate for your group.

Optional: What's in the Box? (see p. 7)
Invite a child to open the box.
Inside is golden fabric or tinfoil (or something similar) that is breaking out of the box as it's too big!

What's in the box?
Accept the child's response.

Look, it doesn't fit! It's too big for our box!

Today we're not going to tell a story!
Today we're going to learn something big!
Can you show me big with your body?
Lead the children in standing and stretching out with their whole bodies.

102

Even bigger! And bigger!
Impossibly big!
Freeze!

Imagine the biggest thing you can imagine!
God is big!
God is bigger than the biggest thing you can imagine.

Let's sit down for a moment.
When the group is ready:
God is so big that we can't know all about God.
We can't squeeze God *Show hands squeezing*
into our heads or our words.
Sometimes God doesn't make sense. *Shake head*
That means God is a 'mystery'. *Hands out in question*
Can you say 'mystery'?
Mystery!
A mystery is something that's too big *Stretch out wide with arms*
to understand all of it.

We're going to learn a song today
That's all about God being so big
That God is a mystery!
It's too BIG to make sense. *Shake head*

Our song starts with counting: 1, 2, 3 *Count on fingers*
Then we show a shape with three sides.
Can anyone tell me what shape has three sides?
Lead the children in showing a triangle with their fingers.

Let's sing the words:
'my turn' *Point to self*, 'your turn' *Leader's hands out to group.*
1, 2, 3, the Trin-it-y! *Count on fingers followed by a triangle shape*
1, 2, 3, the Trin-it-y! *Count on fingers followed by a triangle shape*

Either:
The Trinity is: *Count to 3 on fingers in time with the words*
Father, Son and Holy Spirit.
Let's try that:
'my turn' *Point to self*, 'your turn' *Leader's hands out to group.*

Father, Son and Holy Spirit.
Counting to three in time with the song.
Father, Son and Holy Spirit.
Counting to three in time with the song.

Or:
Then another way of showing the Trinity
is by drawing a cross on ourselves.
Father, Son and Holy Spirit.
Cross yourself in time with the song.
Father, Son and Holy Spirit.
Cross yourself in time with the song.

All groups:
Let's put that all together.
Lead the children in singing:
1, 2, 3, the Trinity! *Count on fingers followed by a triangle shape*
Father, Son and Holy Spirit. *Cross self or count to 3 again*

Groups using the first easier version:
Then we sing again:
1, 2, 3, the Trinity! *Count on fingers followed by a triangle shape*
1, 2, 3, the Trinity! *Count on fingers followed by a triangle shape*

Groups using the second developed version:
Then we sing:
Let us praise the Trinity! *Hands up in praise*
Let us praise the Trinity! *Hands up in praise*

Then this is the bit that's impossible to understand.
God is One: let's show one finger with one hand. *One finger*
AND God is Three! *Three fingers*
Let's show three fingers with our other hand at the same time. *Three fingers.*
Look from one hand to the other, looking confused.

Let's say that
'my turn' *Point to self,* 'your turn' *Leader's hands out to group.*
Look from one hand to the other, looking confused.
God is One and God is Three! *One hand shows one, the other three*
God is One and God is Three! *One hand shows one, the other three*
God is a mystery! *Hands turned upwards, confused face*
God is a mystery! *Hands turned upwards, confused face*

Let's try singing that all at once.
Sing very slowly and clearly, giving the children the chance to keep up with at least the actions.

1, 2, 3, the Trinity! *Count on fingers followed by a triangle shape*
Father, Son and Holy Spirit. *Cross self or count to 3 again*
Either repeat: **1, 2, 3, the Trinity!**
Count on fingers followed by a triangle shape.
Or: **Let us praise the Trinity!** *Hands up in praise*
God is One and God is Three! *One hand shows one, the other three*
God is a mystery! *Hands turned upwards, confused face*
Repeat until the children are confident with at least the actions.

Let's show one finger! *Lead the children in showing one finger*
Number 1 is God the Father!
God the Father made the world!
Who can show us an action for 'the world'?

Choose one of the actions for the group to use, or leave the children free to make their own actions.
Let's sing 'God the Father made the world!'

God the Father made the world! *World action*
God the Father made the world! *World action*
God the Father made the world! *World action*
Sing louder at this point to make the words clear to the children, who will otherwise carry on with 'God the Father made the world'.
God is One and God is Three! *One hand shows one, the other three*
God is a mystery! *Hands turned upwards, confused face*
Groups with younger children could repeat this verse.

Groups with older children from KS1 could repeat the Trinity refrain:
'1, 2, 3, the Trinity . . .'
1, 2, 3, the Trinity! *Count on fingers followed by a triangle shape*
Father, Son and Holy Spirit. *Cross self or count to 3 again*
Let us praise the Trinity! *Hands up in praise*
God is One and God is Three!
One hand shows one, the other three.
God is a mystery! *Hands turned upwards, confused face*

So we have . . .
If appropriate see if the children can help you remember.
Number 1: *Show one finger* God the . . . **Father.**

Now let's show two fingers. *Lead the children in showing two fingers*
Number 2 is God the Son.
God the Son is JESUS!
Jesus was born as a baby. *Rock baby in arms*
He died on the cross. *Stretch arms out*
And then he burst from the Dark Cave. *Crouch down and jump up*
What action shall we use for Jesus?

Choose one of the actions for the group to use (or another that the children have suggested), or leave the children free to make their own actions.
Let's sing 'God the Son is Jesus'.

God the Son is Jesus! *Jesus action*
God the Son is Jesus! *Jesus action*
God the Son is Jesus! *Jesus action*
God is One and God is Three! *One hand shows one, the other three*
God is a mystery! *Hands turned upwards, confused face*
Groups with younger children could repeat this verse.

Groups with older children from KS1 could repeat the Trinity refrain:
'1, 2, 3, the Trinity . . .'
1, 2, 3, the Trinity! *Count on fingers followed by a triangle shape*
Father, Son and Holy Spirit. *Cross self or count to 3 again*
Let us praise the Trinity! *Hands up in praise*
God is One and God is Three!
One hand shows one, the other three.
God is a mystery! *Hands turned upwards, confused face*

So we have . . . .
   If appropriate, see if the children can join in at the dots.
Number 1: *Show one finger* God the . . . **Father.**
Number 2: *Show two fingers* God the . . . **Son.**

Now let's show three fingers. *Lead the children in showing three fingers*
Number 3 is God the HOLY SPIRIT!

God the Holy Spirit came like a dove on Jesus.
Can you show me the Spirit coming down like a dove, a bird?
Lead the children in showing a bird flying down.
Then the Holy Spirit came like fire on Jesus' friends!
Can you show me the fire of the Holy Spirit?
Lead the children in swaying their body like flames.

Now the Holy Spirit lives in you and me! *Point at children then self*
The Holy Spirit makes us strong!
Who can show us STRONG?
What action shall we use for the Holy Spirit?
Choose one of the actions for the group to use (or another that the children have suggested), or leave the children free to make their own actions.
Let's sing 'God the Spirit lives in us!'

God the Spirit lives in us! *Spirit action*
God the Spirit lives in us! *Spirit action*
God the Spirit lives in us! *Spirit action*
God is One and God is Three!
One hand shows one, the other three.
God is a mystery! *Hands turned upwards, confused face*
Groups with younger children could repeat this verse.

Groups with older children from KS1 could repeat the Trinity refrain:
'1, 2, 3, the Trinity . . .'
1, 2, 3, the Trinity! *Count on fingers followed by a triangle shape*
Father, Son and Holy Spirit. *Cross self or count to 3 again*
Let us praise the Trinity! *Hands up in praise*
God is One and God is Three!
One hand shows one, the other three.
God is a mystery! *Hands turned upwards, confused face*

So we have . . . .
   If appropriate see if the children can join in at the dots.
Show one finger God the . . . **Father.**
Show two fingers God the . . . **Son.**
Show three fingers And God the . . . **Holy Spirit!**

So today we celebrate the Trinity!
Father, Son and Holy Spirit!
   If appropriate, see if the children can join in after the dots.

One finger God the . . . **Father** made the . . . **world**.
Two fingers God the . . . **Son** is . . . **Jesus**.
Three fingers And God the . . . **Spirit**, lives in . . . **us!**

Let's sing our Trinity song again.
1, 2, 3, the Trinity!
Count on fingers followed by a triangle shape.
Father, Son and Holy Spirit. *Cross self or count to 3 again*
Either repeat: **1, 2, 3, the Trinity!**
Count on fingers followed by a triangle shape.
Or: **Let us praise the Trinity!** *Hands up in praise*
God is One and God is Three! *One hand shows one, the other three*
God is a mystery! *Hands turned upwards, confused face*

So today we've learned a big mystery about God.
God is too big . . .
Let's show big again!
Lead the children in showing a big shape with their arms.

God is too big to squash into our thinking. *Squeeze with hands*
Or to squeeze into our words. *Squeeze with hands*
God is a MYSTERY! *Hands turned upwards, confused face*

We're going to sing our Trinity Song two more times to finish.
Let's sing the first one really quietly to God.
Then let's stand up and sing the second time really loudly
to let the whole world know about the Trinity!

Quietly, seated:
1, 2, 3, the Trinity! *Count on fingers followed by a triangle shape*
Father, Son and Holy Spirit. *Cross self or count to 3 again*
Either repeat: **1, 2, 3, the Trinity!**
Count on fingers followed by a triangle shape.
Or: **Let us praise the Trinity!** *Hands up in praise*
God is One and God is Three! *One hand shows one, the other three*
God is a mystery! *Hands turned upwards, confused face*

Let's stand up! Let's sing so the whole world can hear!
Singing strongly:
1, 2, 3, the Trinity!
Count on fingers followed by a triangle shape.
Father, Son and Holy Spirit. *Cross self or count to 3 again*
Either repeat: **1, 2, 3, the Trinity!**
Count on fingers followed by a triangle shape.
Or: **Let us praise the Trinity!** *Hands up in praise*
God is One and God is Three! *One hand shows one, the other three*
God is a mystery! *Hands turned upwards, confused face*

Part 2
Bible storytelling for baby and toddler groups

Introduction

This material is designed for groups of babies and toddlers (and their parents/carers) which don't currently include any children above the age of 2½. Groups which include children over the age of two and half may find the material in Part 1 more helpful.

For tips on how to involve babies actively alongside older children when telling stories from Part 1, see p. 7.

You may like to make simple song sheets for each unit to help the adults, but most of the songs provided here simply repeat the first line, making it easy to join in. And everyone can join in the actions even if they're not sure of the words!

Choose a simple structure for your group's time together, like the one outlined here, and keep this pattern the same for every session. Alternatively, you may simply like to choose one song to sing from the units below each time you gather. Please use and adapt the material as best suits your group.

Welcome Song: this stays the same across every unit
Introduction to the Unit: this changes every unit and helps to introduce the theme
Choice of Songs from the Unit: these change every unit: choose them from the material below or beyond
Optional: Prayer Song: this can stay the same across every unit, or you might like to use an alternative every so often
Closing Song: this stays the same across every unit

If your session will be followed by a time for refreshments, suggestions for relevant toys and sensory equipment for the children to play with that can support their understanding of the unit can be found in Part 3: Creative Response starter ideas. Make sure that all the choices you make are appropriate to the ages and development stages of your group.

> **Tip: Presentation folders**
>
> Presentation folders can really help when leading Sowing Seeds. They're much easier to manage than loose sheets, especially when doing actions! We've found that A5 folders are best, and the Bible storytelling has been formatted to slip easily into A5 folders.

Basic Structure

Welcome Song

→ Song: 'The Sowing Seeds welcome song'. Words © Sharon Moughtin.
→ Tune: 'Glory, glory, alleluia!' (traditional).

Wel-come Name— to St Mar-y's! Wel-come Name— to St Mar-y's! Wel-come Name— to St Mar-y's! You are wel-come in the name of the Lord.

Welcome your group, which is, if possible, seated in a circle.
Let's start by going round the circle
and saying our name out loud.
My name's _____.
Go round the circle so that every adult and child has the chance to say his or her name (and introduce any dolls, teddies or toys). If any of the children don't want to say their name or aren't able to, you (an adult) could say it for them and wave.

When you're ready, start the song. Go around the circle the same way as above. See if each of you can remember the others' names and insert them into the song.

Welcome Name 1 to St Mary's*
Welcome Name 1 to St Mary's*
Welcome Name 1 to St Mary's*
You are welcome in the name of the Lord!
* Insert the name of your church or children's group.

Introducing the Unit

A simple introduction to each unit and its theme can be found below.

Choice of Songs from the Unit

Choose the songs from the units below that you think might work in your setting. How many songs you sing each week will depend on your group. It may even be just one!

In practice we've found that it is best not to change too abruptly between units/ seasons with this age group. This would mean having to learn more than one new song in a single week! Instead, we've found it makes sense to add one new song, when the group feels ready, and say goodbye to one old song (which may be from the same unit or the previous unit) every now and again, moving around the year that way.

Every group is different and so is every leader! Over time, you will find the number of songs and the rhythm that works for your group.

Prayer Song

Option 1: Thank You, God

→ Song: 'My hands were made for love'. Words © Sharon Moughtin.
→ Tune: 'Hickory, dickory, dock' (traditional).

My hands were made — for love. My hands were made — for love. Thank you for the love they've shown! My hands were made — for love.

Alternative prayer songs include the Sorry Song (p. 158) and the 'Jesus, hear your prayer!' song (p. 170).

Invite the children to sit in a circle for a moment of quiet.
It's time to remember all the things we've done this week.
It's time to say 'thank you' to God
for when we've been part of showing God's love.

110

Option 2: Prayers for Other People

→ **Song:** 'The Sowing Seeds little prayers song'. Words © Sharon Moughtin.
→ **Tune:** 'Frère Jacques' (traditional).

For our food,— For our food,— thank you, God. thank you, God. For our teach-ers, For our teach-ers, thank you, God. thank you, God.

For Rach-el's Nan-ny, For Rach-el's Nan-ny, hear our prayer. hear our prayer. For peo-ple with no homes,— for peo-ple with no homes,— hear our prayer. hear our prayer.

Either choose what you'd like the group to pray for before the session, or ask the toddlers and adults at this point if there is anything or anyone that they'd like to pray for. You will need two different 'thank you' suggestions and two different 'hear our prayer' suggestions.

> **Tip**
> Try to encourage at least one prayer for other people outside the group.

Invite the adults and the children to sing after you, repeating your words and their actions. Sometimes it might be almost impossible to fit a toddler's own words in! It's really valuable to do this where possible, however, resisting the urge to try and 'neaten' their suggestions.

Let's wiggle our fingers!
I wonder when you've shown love
with your hands this week?

Wiggle fingers as you sing.
My hands were made for love!
My hands were made for love!
Thank you for the love they've shown.
My hands were made for love!

Let's wiggle our feet!
I wonder when you've shown love
with your feet this week?

Wiggle feet as you sing.
My feet were made for love!
My feet were made for love!
Thank you for the love they've shown.
My feet were made for love!

Let's put our hands gently on our neck.
Ahhhhh!
Let's sing 'Ahhh!'
Can you feel your throat vibrating and dancing?
I wonder when you've shown love
with your voice this week?

Hold neck and feel your voice 'dancing' as you sing.
My voice was made for love!
My voice was made for love!
Thank you for the love it's shown.
My voice was made for love!

For our foo-ood,
For our foo-ood,
Thank you, God!
F-or our frie-ends,
F-or our frie-ends,
Thank you, God!
For Rachel's Nanny,
For Rachel's Nanny,
Hear our prayer!
Hear our prayer!
For people with no homes,
For people with no homes,
Hear our prayer!
Hear our prayer!

Having sung your prayers, you could insert a Prayer Action (see the choices on p. 173), repeat the process or move straight on to close with the following (or other words that remain the same each week).

For today,	*Point hands down for 'now'*
For today,	*Point hands down for 'now'*
Thank you, God!	*Open hands upwards to God or hands together in prayer*
Thank you, God!	*Open hands upwards to God or hands together in prayer*
Fo-r your love,	*Cross hands on chest*
Fo-r your love,	*Cross hands on chest*
Thank you, God!	*Open hands upwards to God or hands together in prayer*
Thank you, God!	*Open hands upwards to God or hands together in prayer*

Closing Song

→ Song: 'I've got peace like a river' (traditional).
→ Tune: Traditional.

For this song you may like to use a long piece of blue fabric.

Either: invite the children each to hold a small section of the fabric, helped by adults, and to raise and lower it so it 'flows' like a river as you sing.
Or: Invite the children to lie beneath the fabric as two adults wave it over their heads.
Or: If you don't have any blue fabric, invite the group to join in raising and lowering their hands like the waters of a flowing river as you sing.

I've got peace like a river,
I've got peace like a river,
I've got peace like a river in my soul.
I've got peace like a river,
I've got peace like a river,
I've got peace like a river in my soul.

112

The Journey to the Cross unit (Lent)

Introducing the Unit

Week 1: This week we're starting on a journey with Jesus.
All other weeks: We're on a journey with Jesus.

It's a journey to the big city!

If appropriate: a big city like Manchester! Adapt as appropriate

The Journey to the Cross songbox

Choose from this songbox or elsewhere in this book the songs that you think might work in your setting to add to the simple structure of your session (see p. 110). Don't try to learn them all in one day! In practice, we've found it works to add a new song and to say goodbye to an old song every now and again, when your group feels ready, moving around the year that way. With this unit, there is a connection between the songs. At the point where your group has only introduced one or two of the new songs, you could end the group by encouraging them to come back next time to find out what happens next.

Lent is a time when the Church turns its attention to baptism so if some of these songs from the 'John the Baptist' unit (Book 1, p. 130) end up being used in the Lent season as well, this is entirely appropriate.

Lent is also a good time to explore the Prayer Songs (see pp. 170–3). You may like to try more than one over the weeks.

'I am going to follow Jesus'

→ Words: © Sharon Moughtin.
→ Tune: 'Bobby Shaftoe' (traditional).

Our song is all about following Jesus.
Let's get ready to follow Jesus.

Either: Let's get up and march on the spot.
Or: lead the parents/carers in lying their babies in front of them and gently moving their babies' legs to the beat.

1, 2, 3, 4! 1, 2, 3, 4!

Continue 'marching' as you sing:
**I am going to follow Jesus,
I am going to follow Jesus,
I am going to follow Jesus,
follow, follow Jesus!**

If you have imaginative aids, you may like to distribute them at this point.
Let's practise following Jesus!
Choose one of the toddlers/babies to be 'Jesus'.
Name is going to be Jesus!
To the toddler or parent/carer: 'Jesus!' Can you show us an action?'
Let's all copy what 'Jesus' does.
Let's 'follow Jesus'.

Continue 'following' the toddler/baby's actions as you sing:
**I am going to follow Jesus,
I am going to follow Jesus,
I am going to follow Jesus,
follow, follow Jesus!**

Invite another toddler/baby to be 'Jesus' and repeat as appropriate.
When the group is ready to finish:

In Lent, we follow Jesus!
If you're using a cross, show it to the group again at this point.
We follow Jesus to the cross.

'Jesus came riding on a donkey'

→ Matthew 21.1–11; Mark 11.1–10; Luke 19.28
→ Words: © Sharon Moughtin.
→ Tune: 'Sing hosanna' (traditional).

For this song, you may like to distribute branches, leaves, green imaginative aids (or a mixture). Check that whatever you distribute is child-safe (and not toxic). You might like to try singing the song while moving around the room.
Let's sing our song about the day Jesus went to the big city, Jerusalem!
Let's follow Jesus with our song!

Jesus came riding on a donkey *Hold reins and jig up and down*
and the people all danced and sang! *Wave hands above head*
They threw down their cloaks before him *'Glory of the Lord' sign (see p. 147)*
and waved gre-en palm leaves in their hands! *Wave hands above head*
Sing hosanna! Sing hosanna! *Wave hands above head*
Sing hosanna *Wave hands* **to the King of Kings!** *Crown action twice*
Sing hosanna! Sing hosanna!
Sing hosanna *Wave hands above head* **to the king!** *Crown action*
Repeat.

'Love is stronger'

→ Words: © Sharon Moughtin.
→ Tune: 'She'll be coming round the mountain'.

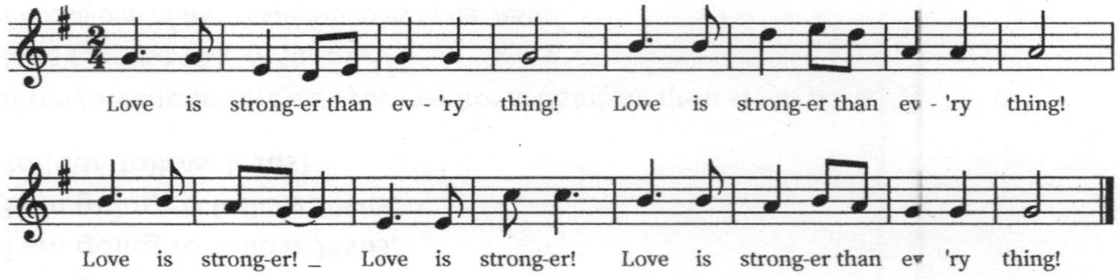

This song provides an opportunity to introduce the 'Love is stronger' song from the 'Story of the Cross' (see p. 53). This might be particularly helpful for settings where you would like to include babies and toddlers in the 'Story of the Cross' on Good Friday.

We have a song about love!
Love *Crossed arms* is stronger *Clench fists gently* than everything! *Arms out*
Love *Crossed arms* **is stronger** *Clench fists gently* **than everything!** *Arms out*
Love *Crossed arms* **is stronger** *Clench fists gently* **than everything!** *Arms out*
Love *Cross arms* **is stronger** *Clench fists*
Love *Cross arms* **is stronger** *Clench fists*
Love *Crossed arms* **is stronger** *Clench fists gently* **than everything!** *Arms out*
Repeat until the group is sounding confident.

Love is stronger than everything!
Even when things get hard!
Who's had a hard time this week?
Invite the group to share stories of either the babies/toddlers or their adults having a difficult time.

Adapt the words to reflect this.

'When the king says . . .'

→ **Words:** © Sharon Moughtin.
→ **Tune:** 'If you're happy and you know it!'.

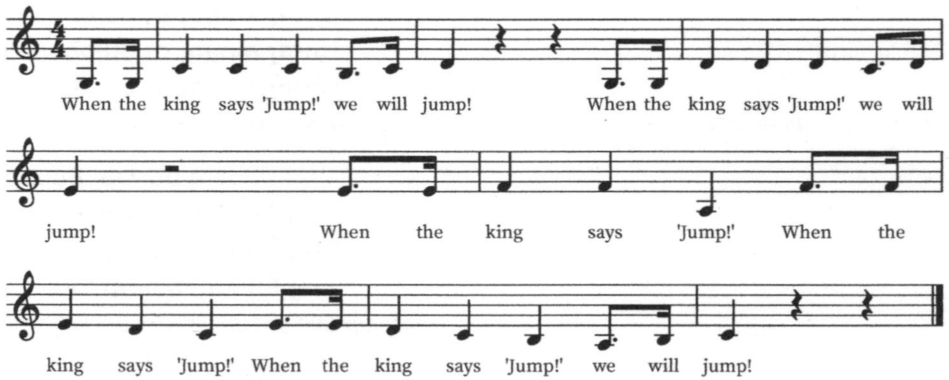

[Musical notation: When the king says 'Jump!' we will jump! When the king says 'Jump!' we will jump! When the king says 'Jump!' When the king says 'Jump!' When the king says 'Jump!' we will jump!]

This song is designed as a companion to 'The Sowing Seeds footwashing song' which follows.

Jesus is the king! *Crown action*
The King of Kings! *Crown action twice*
When Jesus was alive, it was different being a king!
You got to tell everyone what to do . . . And they obeyed!
Imagine that!
Let's practise being servants and kings!
Invite a child to be 'king' and place a real or imaginary crown on her or his head. Ask the child what she or he would like the group to do (sweep the floor, jump, draw, etc.). If appropriate make a suggestion. Then lead the rest of the group in being the servants.

We're King *Name*'s servants, we have to do as the king says!

Lead the children in miming and singing.

When the king says '___!'
We will ___!
When the king says '___!'
We will ___!
When the king says '___!'
When the king says '___!'

Example: Childminder:
Jeffrey had a hard time this week when he fell over and hurt his knee.
Leader: Ouch! It can really hurt when we fall over.
But Love *Crossed arms* is stronger *Clench fists gently* than hurting! *Hold knee*

Lead the group in singing:
Love *Crossed arms* **is stronger** *Clench fists gently* **than hurting.** *Hold knee*
Love *Crossed arms* **is stronger** *Clench fists gently* **than hurting.** *Hold knee*
Love *Cross arms* **is stronger** *Clench fists*
Love *Cross arms* **is stronger** *Clench fists*
Love *Crossed arms* **is stronger** *Clench fists gently* **than hurting.** *Hold knee*

Example 2: Grandma: Amelie had a hard time this week when she lost her teddy.
Leader: Oh no! It can be so hard when we lose a special friend.
It can make us want to cry! *Tears on face*
But Love *Crossed arms* is stronger *Clench fists gently* than tears! *Tears on face*

Lead the group in singing:
Love *Crossed arms* **is stronger** *Clench fists gently* **than tears.** *Tears on face*
Love *Crossed arms* **is stronger** *Clench fists gently* **than tears.** *Tears on face*
Love *Cross arms* **is stronger** *Clench fists*
Love *Cross arms* **is stronger** *Clench fists*
Love *Crossed arms* **is stronger** *Clench fists gently* **than tears.** *Tears on face*

Love is stronger than everything!
When people are sad or hurt it can help so much if we show them love.
By giving them a hug, or drawing them a picture, or showing our love in a different way.

Let's sing our song one more time.
Let's sing, 'Love is stronger than everything!' *Throw arms out*

Love *Crossed arms* **is stronger** *Clench fists gently* **than everything!** *Arms out*
Love *Crossed arms* **is stronger** *Clench fists gently* **than everything!** *Arms out*
Love *Cross arms* **is stronger** *Clench fists*
Love *Cross arms* **is stronger** *Clench fists*
Love *Crossed arms* **is stronger** *Clench fists gently* **than everything!** *Arms out*

When the king says '___!'
We will ___!
Choose another child to be 'king' and repeat with different actions as appropriate.

Jesus is the king! *Crown action*
The King of Kings! *Crown action twice*
What will King Jesus ask us to do?

> Either: Come back next time to find out!
> Or: move straight on to 'The Sowing Seeds footwashing song'.

The Sowing Seeds footwashing song

↳ John 13.1–17
↳ Words: © Sharon Moughtin.
↳ Tune: 'Bobby Shaftoe' (traditional).

If you haven't just sung 'When the king says . . .' above.
Jesus is the king! *Crown action*
The King of Kings! *Crown action twice*

King Jesus did something very surprising!
He knelt down and washed his friends' feet! *Mime washing*
Kings don't kneel on the floor! *Crown action and shake head*
Kings don't wash feet! *Crown action and shake head*
But King Jesus did!

Lead the group in miming washing feet as you sing.
Washing, washing, washing feet,
washing, washing, washing feet,
washing, washing, washing feet,
washing, washing feet.

Lead the group in miming drying feet as you sing together.
Drying, drying, drying feet,
drying, drying, drying feet,
drying, drying, drying feet,
drying, drying feet.

Then King Jesus said:
'You . . .' *Point around the group*
'must be SERVANTS like me!'
So let's kneel down and wash each other's feet.
You may even like to try using real water for one or more weeks. For tips on holding a real footwashing, see pp. 39–40.

Lead the group in 'washing feet' as they sing:
Washing, washing, washing feet,
washing, washing, washing feet,
washing, washing, washing feet,
washing, washing feet.

If you're using actual water, you may like to extend the song with the following:
I am going to follow Jesus,
I am going to follow Jesus,
I am going to follow Jesus,
follow, follow Jesus!

Lead the group in singing as they dry feet.
Drying, drying, drying feet,
drying, drying, drying feet,
drying, drying, drying feet,
drying, drying feet.

If you're using actual water, you may like to extend the song with the following:
I am going to follow Jesus,
I am going to follow Jesus,
I am going to follow Jesus,
follow, follow Jesus!

'Do this to remember me'

→ Luke 22.14–23
→ Words: © Sharon Moughtin

You may like to tell the story of the Last Supper. For this you may like to use bread and grape juice, or simply use hand actions. See p. 50 for more details and the 'Do this to remember me' poem, which is also given below.

Can you say these words after me and copy my actions,
'my turn' *Point to self,* 'your turn' *Leader's hands out to group.*

Jesus took the bread.	Take bread in one hand
Jesus took the bread.	Take bread in one hand
He said, 'Thank you, God!'	Hold bread up if this is in your tradition
He said, 'Thank you, God!'	Hold bread up if this is in your tradition
Jesus broke the bread.	Break bread
Jesus broke the bread.	Break bread
Then he shared it.	Mime handing bread out in a circle
Then he shared it.	Mime handing bread out in a circle
This is my body,	Hold bread or point to it
This is my body,	Hold bread or point to it
broken for you.	Hold bread back together then separate it again
broken for you.	Hold bread back together then separate it again
Do this to remember me!	Hold bread up if this is in your tradition
Do this to remember me!	Hold bread up if this is in your tradition
Jesus took the cup.	Take cup in both hands
Jesus took the cup.	Take cup in both hands
He said, 'Thank you, God!'	Hold cup up if this is in your tradition
He said, 'Thank you, God!'	Hold cup up if this is in your tradition
Jesus poured the wine.	Mime pouring wine
Jesus poured the wine.	Mime pouring wine
Then he shared it.	Mime handing cup out in a circle
Then he shared it.	Mime handing cup out in a circle
This is my blood,	Lift cup or point to it
This is my blood,	Lift cup or point to it
poured out for you.	Mime pouring wine
poured out for you.	Mime pouring wine
Do this to remember me!	Hold cup up if this is in your tradition
Do this to remember me!	Hold cup up if this is in your tradition

Jesus Is Alive!
Alleluia! unit (Easter)

The 'Jesus Is Alive! Alleluia!' unit gathers together some of the most famous Bible stories about the Risen Jesus.

Optional: Throughout this unit, you might like to have an Easter Garden visible to the group. This Easter Garden could be as simple as an empty plant pot laid on its side with a large stone next to it. It could be an Easter Garden created by one of the toddlers (see p. 136). Or you might like to plant a larger garden together. Choose what's right for your group.

Introducing the Unit

If you have an Easter Garden, show it to the group
    This is our Easter Garden with the Dark Cave in the middle.

Week 1:
    Today we're starting to tell some of the stories
    about when Jesus burst from the Dark Cave.

Following weeks:
    Today we're telling some of the stories
    about when Jesus burst from the Dark Cave.

Jesus Is Alive! Alleluia! songbox

Choose from this songbox or elsewhere in this book the songs that you think might work in your setting to add to the simple structure of your session (see p. 110). Don't try to learn them all in one day! In practice, we've found it works to add a new song and to say goodbye to an old song every now and again, when your group feels ready, moving around the year that way.

'He is risen, risen, risen!'

→ **Words:** © Sharon Moughtin.
→ **Tune:** 'Wide awake' © Mollie Russell-Smith and Geoffrey Russell-Smith, also known as 'The dingle, dangle scarecrow'. It is now published by EMI Harmonies Ltd.

The music for 'Wide awake' is under copyright so can't be reproduced here but can be found online by searching for 'Dingle dangle scarecrow'. A sung version of 'When all the world was sleeping' can be found on the Sowing Seeds website.

> This song uses the 'New Start' sign (the winding action from 'Wind the bobbin up'). This is deliberate. The 'New Start' sign is created to echo the rolling away of the stone from the tomb, which won a new start for all of us. This is among the very few Sowing Seeds signs and actions that are fixed. See p. 8 for a description and explanation. It's worth introducing this even at this very young age so the children do not have to 'unlearn' actions for the songs later.

Let's tell the story of Easter Day with our song.
If there are toddlers in the group, encourage them to follow you in the actions.

On Good Friday, Jesus died on the cross. *Stretch arms out*
His friends took Jesus' body down from the cross. *Mime holding Jesus' body gently*
They put it gently into the Dark Cave *Mime placing Jesus' body in the cave*
and rolled the stone across. *Mime rolling a large stone across*
They went home feeling very, very, very sad. *Touch face to show tears*

Nothing happened for one whole night and day after that.
But then the night after, something amazing happened!

Let's sing our song about the Dark Cave!
Let's curl up on the floor like we're in the Dark Cave with Jesus.

Lead the group in helping the babies and toddlers to curl up on the floor or crouch low to sing.

**When all the world was sleeping
and the sun had gone to bed . . .**
up jumped Lord Jesus Jump up with hands in the air or raise baby high above head and this is what he said: Hands out, palms up or bring baby back down
'I am risen, risen, risen, *Wave hands high in the air or in front of baby*
I have won us a new start! *'New Start' sign over head or in front of baby*
'I am risen, risen, risen, *Wave hands high in the air or in front of baby*
I have won us a new start! *'New Start' sign over head or in front of baby*

Let's tell our story again!
Let's curl up on the floor like we're in the Dark Cave with Jesus.
Repeat song.

'On Easter Day in the morning'

→ John 20.1–10
→ Words: © Sharon Moughtin.
→ Tune: 'I saw three ships come sailing in' (traditional).

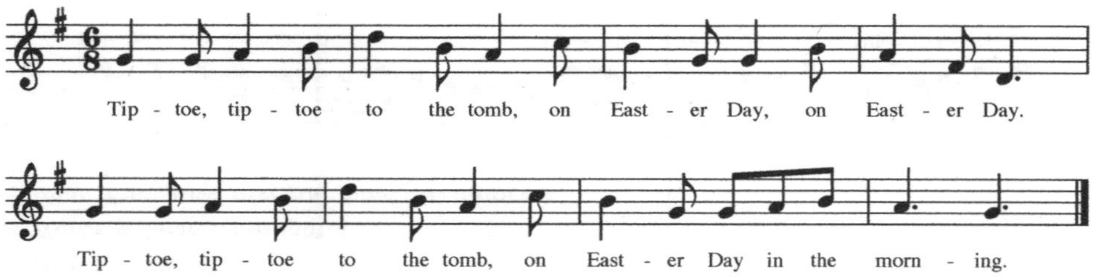

Jesus is alive! But no one knows yet!
Let's sing our song about when Jesus' friends found out!
Lead the toddlers in tiptoeing on the spot and singing quietly and sadly. Invite any parents/carers with babies to 'cycle' their babies legs as if walking.

**Tiptoe, tiptoe to the tomb,
on Easter Day, on Easter Day.
Tiptoe, tiptoe to the tomb,
on Easter Day in the morning.**

Lead the toddlers in the winding action from 'Wind the bobbin up' as you sing. Invite any parents/carers with babies to wind their babies' arms around for them.

**Look! The stone is rolled away
on Easter Day, on Easter Day.
Look! The stone is rolled away
On Easter Day in the morning.**

Lead the group in singing in amazement and pointing, or flapping wings like angels.

**Look! Two angels in the cave!
On Easter Day, on Easter Day!
Look! Two angels in the cave!
On Easter Day in the morning.**

We've got to tell someone!
After 3, let's show running with our arms. *Move arms quickly as if running* Invite any parents/carers with babies to 'cycle' their babies' legs a little faster.
1, 2, 3 . . . Run!

Lead the group in singing faster and making a running motion.

**Run and run to tell our friends
on Easter Day, on Easter Day!
Run and run to tell our friends
On Easter Day in the morning!**

Excitedly:
Look! *Point* There's Peter and John!
And do you know what Peter and John did? *Rhetorical question*
They listened to the women! And they ran!

Lead the group in singing even faster and making a running motion with their arms.

**Run and run and run and run
on Easter Day, on Easter Day!
Run and run and run and run
on Easter Day in the morning!**

Lead the group in looking around in amazement as you point and sing.

**Look! The cave is e-empty,
on Easter Day, on Easter Day!
Look! The cave is e-empty,
on Easter Day in the morning!**

Gasp Jesus is RISEN!
Jesus is ALIVE!

'Back in Galilee'

→ John 18.15–27
→ Words: © Sharon Moughtin.
→ Tune: 'Row, row, row your boat' (traditional).

For this song you may find it helpful to have a net or (white cloth with black netting drawn on it) plus ten or more cardboard fish.

Let's tell another story about Jesus after he burst from the Dark Cave!
For this story, we need to get into our boats!

Lead the toddlers in sitting on the floor. Encourage parents/carers to get ready to make a rowing action with their baby as they would for the traditional nursery rhyme 'Row, row, row your boat'.

Row, row, row the boat, *Rowing action*
back in Galilee. *Rowing action*
Throw the net then pull it in . . . *Mime throwing net out, then in*
What can we see? *Mime looking in the nets*

Let's have a look! *Lead the group in looking in the imaginary nets*
What have we caught? Nothing! *Shake head*

Optional: Show the group an empty net
The nets looked like this one!
Empty.

Repeat this singing and looking three times.
Oh no! Have we forgotten how to fish?
Wait! Look! Who's that?
A stranger was standing far away on the beach.
The stranger said: *Hands cupped around mouth*
'Throw your net on the OTHER SIDE of the boat!' *Point*

Shall we try it?
Row, row, row the boat, *Rowing action*
back in Galilee. *Rowing action*
Throw the net then pull it in . . . *Mime throwing net out, then in*
What can we see? *Mime looking in the nets*

Let's have a look! *Lead the group in looking in the imaginary nets*
The net's full of fish!
I can see so many fish!

Optional: Show the group the net full of cardboard fish
The nets looked like this one!
Full of fish!

Let's count ten of them together!
Lead the group in counting on fingers: 1, 2, 3, 4, 5, 6, 7, 8, 9, 10!
And more!
So many fish!

I know who the stranger is!
It's Jesus! Jesus is alive!

'The Good Shepherd'

→ John 10.11–15
→ Words: © Sharon Moughtin.
→ Tune: 'Mary had a little lamb' (traditional).

There was once a flock of sheep, flock of sheep, flock of sheep. There was once a flock of sheep. Baaaaaa!

For this song, you may like to show the children a sheep at this point.

At Easter, churches all over the world tell a story that Jesus told about sheep and a shepherd.
Shall we tell the story with our song?
To tell Jesus' story we need to be sheep!
What do sheep say?
Accept responses.

Now can you show me how a sheep looks and sounds when it feels scared?
Lead the group in looking and sounding like a scared sheep: **Baaaa!**
And happy?
Lead the group in looking and sounding like a happy sheep: **Baaaa!**
And cross?
Lead the group in looking and sounding like a cross sheep: **Baaaa!**
We're ready for our song.
Let's show our sheep ears/tails wiggling as we sing.

There was once a flock of sheep, *Wiggle ears/tails or other sheep action*
flock of sheep, flock of sheep.
There was once a flock of sheep.
Baaa!

But look! What's that over there?! *Point*
It's a wolf!
A big, bad wolf!
Hold your hands out like claws, ready to pounce.

Lead the group in pouncing on the word 'wolf' as you sing.
Look! Here comes a big, bad wolf, *Pounce*
a big, bad wolf, *Pounce* **a big, bad wolf!** *Pounce*
Look! Here comes a big, bad wolf! *Pounce*
Baaaa! *Lead the group in looking and sounding scared.*

It's all right. Our shepherd will help us . . .

But look! *Point*
Our shepherd's running away! *Shocked*
The wolf can catch us!
We need to run!!

Lead the toddlers in running on the spot or with a running action with their arms. Encourage adults to 'cycle' their babies' legs to show running as you sing.

The sheep, they ran and ran and ran,
ran and ran, ran and ran!
The sheep, they ran and ran and ran!
Baaa! *Lead the group in sounding terrified and exhausted*

Oh dear! Poor sheep! That shepherd wasn't very good!
Jesus said, 'Then there was another flock of sheep.'
Now this flock has a GOOD shepherd.
Let's sing 'We are all little sheep again'
And show our sheep ears/tails wiggling as we sing.

There was once a flock of sheep,
flock of sheep, flock of sheep.
There was once a flock of sheep.
Baaa!

But look! What do you think I can see?!
Give the group opportunity to respond, then go straight into . . .
Hold your hands out like claws, ready to pounce on the word 'wolf'.

Look! Here comes a big, bad wolf, *Pounce*
A big, bad wolf, *Pounce* **a big, bad wolf!** *Pounce*
Look! Here comes a big, bad wolf! *Pounce*
Baaa! *Sounding scared*

121

Oh no! What's the shepherd going to do?
Give the group opportunity to respond.

This shepherd is the Good Shepherd.
He won't run! *Shake head*
He'll keep us safe!
Let's find the person we came with and give them a big hug as we sing.
Let's sing 'I will never, never leave . . .'

And this time instead of a baa at the end, let's sing 'never, never leave'

**I will never, never leave,
never leave, never leave.
I will never, never leave,
never, never leave.**

Jesus said, "I am the Good Shepherd!"
You're my little lambs. *Point around the group*
I love you and I will never leave you. *Shake head.*

'Go! And wait for the Holy Spirit!'

→ Luke 24.42-53
→ Words: © Sharon Moughtin.
→ Tune: 'London Bridge is falling down' (traditional).

We are eat - ing fish! Yum! Yum! Fish! Yum! Yum! Fish! Yum! Yum!

We are eat - ing fish! Yum! Yum! All - e - lu - ia!

One day Jesus went UP *Point up* to heaven.
Our song starts with climbing! Let's go!

Lead any toddlers in climbing on the spot. Encourage any parents/carers with babies to cycle their legs to show climbing.

**Climb the hi-ill, 1, 2, 3!
1, 2, 3! 1, 2, 3!
Climb the hi-ill, 1, 2, 3!
Alleluia!** *'V' shape in the air*

Then Jesus said:

'Go and wait for the Holy Spirit, *Point*
the Holy Spirit, the Holy Spirit! *Point*
Go and wait for the Holy Spirit.' *Point*
Alleluia! *'V' shape in the air*

When the Holy Spirit comes, it will be in fire! *Sway arms and body to show flames*
The Holy Spirit *Fire action* **will make you strong,** *Strong action*
make you strong, make you strong! *Strong action*
The Holy Spirit *Fire action* **will make you strong!** *Strong action*
Alleluia! *'V' shape in the air*

Look! *Point upwards*
Lead any toddlers in pointing up as you sing. Encourage any parents/carers with babies to lift their babies up for each line of the song.
Look! Jesus is going up. *Point upwards*
going up, going up! *Point upwards*
Look! Jesus is going up! *Point upwards*
Alleluia! *'V' shape in the air*

Jesus is going! Let's wave goodbye to Jesus.
Wave goodbye to Je-e-sus! *Wave*
Je-e-sus, Je-e-sus! *Wave*
Wave goodbye to Je-e-sus! *Wave*
Alleluia! *'V' shape in the air*

Jesus has gone! What shall we do now?
Lead the group straight into singing with the same actions as before.

'Go and wait for the Holy Spirit, *Point*
the Holy Spirit, the Holy Spirit! *Point*
Go and wait for the Holy Spirit.' *Point*
Alleluia! *'V' shape in the air*

When the Holy Spirit comes, it will be in fire! *Sway arms and body to show flames*
The Holy Spirit *Fire action* **will make you strong,** *Strong action*

make you strong, make you strong! *Strong action*
The Holy Spirit *Fire action* will make you strong! *Strong action*
Alleluia! *'V' shape in the air*

'Holy Spirit, come!'

→ Acts 2.1–4
→ Words: © Sharon Moughtin.
→ Tune: 'Wind the bobbin up' (traditional).

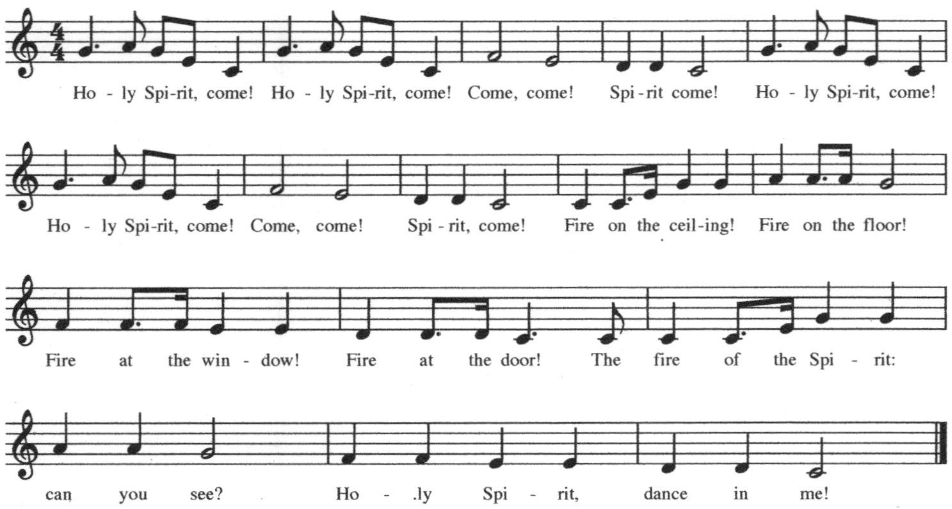

They're singing 'Holy Spirit, come!'
'New Start' sign. This will be the 'come' action for the song.

**Holy Spirit, come! *'Come' action throughout*
Holy Spirit, come!
Come, come! Spirit, come!**

Lead the group in looking around.
Can anyone see the Holy Spirit?
Not yet . . .
Let's keep praying . . . .

**Holy Spirit, come! *'Come' action throughout*
Holy Spirit, come!
Come, come! Spirit, come!**

Blow into the air.
Can you hear that?
Blow and encourage the group to join in blowing.
Louder . . . Blow louder and louder . . . Blow even louder
Then, if appropriate, lead the toddlers in banging hands on the floor, louder and louder.
And look! *Point* What's that?

Lead the group in singing:
Fire on the ceiling! *Point up in shock*
Fire on the floor! *Point down*
Fire at the window! *Point to window in shock*
Fire at the door! *Point to door*
The fire of the Spirit: can you see? *Point all around*
Holy Spirit, dance in me! *Sway like a flame*

Shall we tell our story again?
Repeat from the beginning of the song.

The 'New Start' sign (the winding action from 'Wind the bobbin up') is among the very few Sowing Seeds signs and actions that are fixed. Here it recalls the rolling away of the stone on Easter Day that brings about that great 'new start' for the whole world as well as the prayer for the Holy Spirit to come to bring a 'new start' for the disciples who will become apostles. See p. 8 for a description and explanation.

Let's sing our song about the day the Holy Spirit came!
At the beginning of our song, Jesus' friends are waiting . . . and praying.

Part 3
Creative Response starter ideas

Introduction

Sowing Seeds aims to create a space for children to encounter God for themselves. An important part of this is giving young children the opportunity to respond creatively to what they've heard and experienced. This chapter provides starter ideas for each unit to encourage this.

These starter ideas deliberately offer very simple templates (all designed by children), or other open-ended activities, as starting points for the children to explore for themselves. Our hope is that in their hands these resources and initial ideas will be transformed into wholly unique and individual responses, according to the children's gifts, interests and abilities.

When leading a time of Creative Response, we recommend providing children with choices rather than a single option. Choice-making encourages children to begin to take responsibility for their own responses and their own relationship with God. Some young children can be overwhelmed by too much choice so it may help to begin by offering just two or three starter ideas to choose from. This will help to build their confidence and give them experience in exercising their imagination.

As the children grow in confidence, try providing only open-ended resources (paints, clay, play dough, collage materials (p. 188) and glue, recycling materials, Lego, Kapla blocks, or other interesting media (p. 189) for at least one week per unit to encourage their creativity and sense of personal responsibility.

Tip: Imagination and creativity can be vital to our relationship with God. After all, we're made in the image of God the Maker.

The Journey to the Cross unit (Lent)

These starter ideas are designed to spark imaginations and open up opportunities for the children to respond creatively in their different ways to the worship and storytelling you've taken part in together.

Story Starter Ideas relate directly to the Bible Storytelling of each session, including a print-and-go option.
Sensory Starter Ideas are designed for sensory explorers, including babies and toddlers. These can remain the same through the whole unit.
Unit Starter Ideas are designed to remain relevant throughout the whole unit. Keeping these resources available each time gives children the opportunity to deepen and develop their responses, while making preparation more manageable for leaders.

> ### Tip: Free response area
>
> In addition to any other resources you provide, keeping a free response area available every time will give the children the opportunity to create anything they wish in response to the story they've told, building their sense of confidence and personal responsibility. In this area you could simply provide blank paper and crayons, pencils, paints or pastels. If you have them, other interesting media (p. 189) will provide even more scope for the children to nurture and strengthen their imaginative skills.

Story Starter Ideas

Jesus Gives Up Everything for Us

☩ Invite the children to decorate a 'pancake' with their favourite toppings. What would it be like to give those things up for Lent? Jesus gave up everything for us! *Provide circle template (p. 218 or website), pencils/crayons/pastels/paints.*

☩ Invite the children to draw around their open hand and to write/draw on the shape what they plan to give up for Lent. Encourage them to put it up somewhere at home to remind themselves. *Provide paper, pencils/crayons.*

☩ Give the children the opportunity to make their own wilderness tray (see p. 11). *Provide sand, pebbles and a box or tub from recycling. Tubs with lids (e.g. margarine tubs, takeaway containers) are ideal.*

☩ Invite the children to make their own wilderness scene. All we can see in the wilderness is sand and rocks and sky! The children may like to draw Jesus in the wilderness, or to leave it empty. *Provide paper, glue, sand (or brown sugar) and small pebbles.*

☩ If your church gives up alleluias for Lent, you could give the group the opportunity to create a joint 'Alleluia! Alleluia!' poster, with as many alleluias (or part alleluias) as the children create. Invite the children to design one of the letters from 'alleluia' in bubble writing, or to decorate one of the 'alleluia' letters from the website. When the children are ready, attach the letters with string or glue them onto a large roll of paper. Your group may prefer to draw and decorate individual alleluias to take home. *Provide paper, pencils/crayons/paints/pastels, glue, scissors, string and tape, or a large roll of paper and glue. Optional: 'Alleluia!' template (website only).*

Tip

Think about whether your group would like to take part in the traditional custom of 'burying the alleluia' in preparation for Lent. Having made a group 'Alleluia!' banner (see above), you could sing or say 'Alleluia!' a number of times, then invite the children to wrap the group's 'Alleluia!' banner and place it in a box. 'Bury' the box either outside (make sure it's fully dry and in a waterproof container), under the communion table/altar, or somewhere dark for Lent. The 'Alleluia!' banner can then be brought out/dug up for Easter Day.

Jesus Is Tested in the Wilderness

☩ Invite the children to decorate a cross made from wood or card to remind them to walk the way of love like Jesus. You may like to show the children a photograph of one or more of the crosses that are used in your own church or local area or around the world as inspiration. However, encourage them to explore their own unique ideas and designs. *Provide wooden crosses or the cross template (p. 199 or website), pencils/crayons/paints and scissors. If you have collage materials (p. 188) and glue, make these available too. If you have string or wool, you could see if any children would like to make necklaces or bookmarks with their cross. If they are making necklaces, make sure the string/wool can easily snap when pulled and is attached as two separate ends to prevent accidents.*

☩ Invite the children to decorate a heart to remind them to walk the way of love like Jesus. *Provide large heart template (p. 209 or website), pencils/crayons/paints and scissors. If you have collage materials (p. 188) and glue, make these available too. If you have string or wool, you could see if any children would like to make necklaces or bookmarks with their hearts. If they are making necklaces, make sure the string/wool can easily snap when pulled and is preferably attached to the heart as two separate ends to prevent accidents.*

☩ Give older children the opportunity to make their own cross from simple materials. *Provide twigs/lollipop sticks and string/wool.*

☩ Invite the children to paint or draw a cross or a heart on a stone or safe piece of wood to carry in their pocket. *Provide smooth pebbles (check they aren't a choking hazard) or a piece of wood (check for splinters) and felt tips/pastels/paints.*

☩ Give the children the opportunity to make their own wilderness tray (see p. 11). *Provide sand, pebbles and a box or tub from recycling. Tubs with lids (e.g. margarine tubs, takeaway containers) are ideal for transporting home.*

Jesus Enters Jerusalem

☩ Invite the children to colour or collage palm leaves. *Provide the palm leaf template (p. 210 or website), scissors pencils/crayons, etc. If you have green collage materials (p. 188) and glue, make these available too. If you have lollipop sticks/twigs and masking tape, you could see if any children would like to add a branch to their palm leaf.*

☩ Give the children the opportunity to make palm leaf hats. *Provide palm leaf templates (p. 210 or website) printed on green paper, plus scissors, glue and paper hatbands (see p. 192).*

☩ Give the children the opportunity to contribute to a group giant palm branch with their handshapes. Show the children how to draw around their hand on green paper then cut it out. Invite them to write their name on their handshape(s) then stick them to a branch with sticky tack. Make it clear that the tack means they can take their hand home afterwards if they like! *Provide green paper, scissors, sticky tack and a stick or branch (suitably sized for your group).*

☩ Invite the children to make palm leaves by rolling and taping green paper into a roll they can hold in their hand, then cutting lengthways halfway down the roll all the way around, to create strip leaves. *Provide green paper, scissors, masking tape.*

☩ Give the children the opportunity to enter into the part of the story when the crowd are crying out for King Jesus! Invite them to make and decorate a crown for Jesus. *Provide hatbands for crowns (see p. 192 or website) or crown templates (p. 200), scissors, masking tape, collage materials (p. 188)*

☩ Invite the children to imagine what they would wave for Jesus if Jesus came to their place. You could take them outside into the churchyard to find branches/leaves/grasses to wave. Or you could provide materials to make placards/flags/banners, etc. *Provide an appropriate range of materials with lots of choice.*

Jesus Cleans the Temple

☩ You could give the children the opportunity to draw or paint a picture in a frame of a place where they feel close to God. *Provide picture frame template (p. 211 or website), paints/pastels/pencils/crayons.*

☩ This story also opens up an important opportunity for children to explore anger as a positive force for justice. Invite the children to explore the expressions on Jesus' face when he was cleaning out the Temple. *Provide the face template (p. 203 or website), scissors, pencils/crayons/pastels, etc.*

☩ Invite the children to create a picture of Jesus cleaning out the Temple. *Provide blank paper, or the large or small body templates (p. 215 or p. 196), scissors, pencils/crayons, etc.*

☩ Invite the children to help you clean out and tidy your group's resources or meeting space. *Provide (for example): damp cloths or wipes, brushes and dustpans, grimy resources (you could always add grime!), resources that need tidying and organizing, crayons/pens/pencils that need sorting, appropriate silver and a soft cloth, used fabric/paper/card that could be cut into squares and sorted into collage materials for the group to create with (p. 188), or ask those who clean your meeting space or church for more ideas. If appropriate in your space, you could even provide a water tray with soapy water.*

Jesus Is Like a Mother Hen

☩ Give the children the opportunity to make a thank you card for someone who's been like a mummy to them. They might like to make their card for Jesus, Mum, Dad, a carer, Grandma, Granddad, the church, a leader or someone else who has looked after them like a mummy. *Provide A4 card folded in half, pencils/crayons/pastels. You may also like to provide the mother hen and chick templates (p. 207 or website) for children who'd like to use these pictures in their own design. Encourage the children to explore their own ideas. Some children may prefer to use a postcard template (p. 212 or website).*

☩ Some places share Simnel cakes on Mothering Sunday (others at Easter). You could give the children the opportunity to decorate either a mini Simnel-like cake for someone who's looked after them like a mummy, or a large cake for your church to share with your congregation after the service. To decorate the cakes: spread apricot jam on the top, roll out the marzipan, cut out a circle shape from it and place it onto the jam layer. Next, roll the marzipan into small balls (traditionally 11) and 'glue' them to the top of the cake using the jam. Give the children space to develop the Simnel cake tradition in their own ways. *Provide a large sponge cake or one cupcake per child, marzipan, rolling pins, circle cutters (plate/cup/cutter with a similar circumference to the cake), apricot jam.*

Mary Anoints Jesus

✝ Mary anoints Jesus' feet! Give the children an opportunity to draw round one or more of their feet and to decorate them. *Provide paper, pencils/crayons/chalk/pastels and scissors.*

✝ The smell of Mary's special oil filled the whole room! Give the children the opportunity to explore scents with rose petals, lavender, rosemary, thyme or similar. They could even make scent bags from them or create scented water. *Provide scented herbs, scissors. Optional: scent bags or containers to hold a small amount of water, mini rolling pins to crush the herbs, or spoons and water (optional). If you're going to use water, think about how to prevent slipping hazards.*

✝ Give the children the opportunity to make a miniature clay jar. *Provide playdough, salt dough (see p. 190) or clay (airdrying clay would mean that children could take their bowls home), facilities for the children to wash and dry their hands afterwards. Optional: clay modelling tools.*

Jesus Washes the Disciples' Feet

If you've held an actual footwashing in your group, there may be little time for a Creative Response. Bear in mind that you may not have space to put your usual tables out and that the floor may be wet!

✝ Invite the children to draw around their foot and then to cut it out. If you have blue/green collage materials available, you could also invite the children to create a water collage around their footprint(s). *Provide coloured paper, pencils/crayons, scissors. Optional: blue/green collage materials (p. 188) and glue.*

✝ Give the children the opportunity to make a miniature clay bowl or jug for footwashing. *Provide playdough, salt dough (see p. 190) or clay (airdrying clay would mean that children could take their bowls home), facilities for the children to wash and dry their hands afterwards. Optional: clay modelling tools.*

✝ See John the Baptist unit Story Starter Ideas (River Jordan) for more water-themed creative starter ideas (Book 1, p. 152).

Jesus' Last Meal

✝ Give the children the opportunity to decorate their own cup or chalice from Jesus' Last Supper. If you have examples in your own church that are available, you could show these to the children but encourage the children to create their own unique designs. *Provide chalice template (p. 198), pencils/crayons, scissors. Optional: different-coloured collage materials (p. 188) and glue.*

✝ Invite the children to make an image of Jesus, Peter, themselves or someone they know at Jesus' Last Supper. *Provide large body template (p. 215), pencils/crayons/pastels, scissors. Optional: collage materials (p. 188) and glue.*

✝ Give the children the opportunity to spend time kneading and shaping bread dough into a roll to take home, bake and share. *Provide a simple bread dough for the children (use a readymade mix, see p. 190 for a recipe, or use your own recipe), a floured container or cling film to take the roll home in, and appropriate instructions for baking the bread. Optional: if you have the facilities, you may even like to bake the bread on site.*

✝ Give the children the opportunity to decorate a paper cup with the story of Jesus' Last Supper. If you have examples of decorated communion cups or chalices in your own church that are available, you could show these to the children. *Provide paper cups that can be drawn on, pencils/crayons, scissors. Optional: different-coloured collage materials (p. 188) and glue.*

✝ Invite the children to decorate mini wooden chalices and patens. *Provide felt-tip pens or good-quality pencils, wooden egg cups and coasters.*

✝ Give the children the opportunity to create their own artwork of Jesus' Last Supper. Show them examples of famous or local paintings then encourage them to use these as a starting point to paint or draw their own picture. *Provide paper, paints/pastels, famous paintings for inspiration (e.g. The Last Supper by Leonardo da Vinci, Joos van Cleve, Hans Holbein the Younger, Fra Angelico). Optional: picture-frame template (p. 211 or website) or an 'icon background' (a piece of card wrapped in tinfoil that's slightly larger than the paper provided).*

The Story of Love: The Story of the Cross: Good Friday

You might like to provide mini storytelling boxes for the children to take home with them. For each child, you will need:

- a box with a lid that the figure of Jesus can fit inside when wrapped in the cloth. See the website for examples;
- a thin red ribbon (for instance a 5 mm red ribbon around 40 cm long for the children's boxes);
- a mini figure of Jesus (with these and other templates, it may be easiest to cut these into simple squares that will fit into the box and let the children cut them out properly during the session);
- a mini cup/chalice and a tiny piece of pitta bread;
- a small twig of a plant (e.g. rosemary) to represent the Garden of Gethsemane;
- a short piece of string;
- wire or a bendy twig (for the children to twist into a crown);
- two small twigs and a piece of string for the children to make into a cross (younger children may need help with this). Make sure these are small enough to fit into the box before giving them to the children;
- a white piece of cloth (felt, cotton or kitchen paper) (big enough to wrap the figure in).

See the Sowing Seeds website for pdfs of a simplified version of the storytelling for children to take home.

† Invite the children to decorate a cross made from wood or card. You may like to show the children a photograph of one or more of the crosses that are used in your own church or local area or around the world as inspiration. However, encourage them to explore their own unique ideas and designs. *Provide wooden crosses or the cross template (p. 199), pencils/crayons/ paints and scissors. If you have collage materials and glue, make these available too. If you have string or wool, you could see if any children would like to make necklaces or bookmarks with their cross. If they are making necklaces, make sure the string/wool can easily snap when pulled and is attached as two separate ends to prevent accidents.*

† Invite the children to paint or draw a cross or a heart on a stone or safe piece of wood to carry in their pocket. *Provide smooth pebbles (check they aren't a choking hazard) or a piece of wood (check for splinters) and felt tips/pastels/paints.*

† Give the children the opportunity to make a stained-glass cross. Invite them to glue brightly coloured tissue/cellophane/ crepe paper to cross-shaped wax/baking paper. *Provide scissors, glue and brightly coloured tissue/crepe/cellophane paper (e.g. transparent sweet wrappers) plus baking/wax paper (the whiter the better, but brown paper still works) in the shape of a cross. You (or older children) can make a cross shape by folding square or rectangular wax/baking paper into quarters then cutting an L-shape into it (making sure you don't cut into any side that's a fold).*

† Give the children the opportunity to design a stained-glass window as a cross. *Provide stained-glass window template (p. 219) and crayons/pastels/pencils/felt tips.*

† Invite the children to make a cross with playdough, salt dough or airdrying clay. They may also like to etch patterns into it. *Provide playdough, salt dough (p. 190) or airdrying clay, clay modelling tools or plastic (safe) knives and forks.*

Sensory Starter Ideas (including for babies and toddlers)

You could provide:

✝ a plastic or soft donkey;

✝ a Jesus figure (Joseph from Nativity sets can work well);

✝ child-safe crosses (holding crosses are particularly appropriate);

✝ wooden/metal or other child-safe cup and plate or chalice and paten for children to explore and tell the story of Jesus' Last Meal. Alternatively you could provide wooden egg cups and coasters;

✝ purple imaginative aids;

✝ if your church ashes people on Ash Wednesday, you could provide a bowl of ash in a little oil for the children to explore, plus dolls or 'small world' people that can receive an ash cross on their forehead;

✝ building blocks to build Jerusalem, the Temple or the tallest tower from the 'Jesus Is Tested in the Wilderness' unit or other creations;

✝ resources for exploring real footwashing (a bowl of water and towel) or roleplaying footwashing (a bowl filled with blue fabric, a doll/teddy and towel);

✝ if you've used a wilderness tray and Jesus figure in the last unit, you could make it available for the children to explore for themselves towards the beginning of Lent (make sure the rocks/pebbles don't present a choking hazard);

✝ if your group is using a 'sorry tree' (p. 162) or 'prayer tree' (p. 173) during the session, you could leave this and tissue paper available for the children to continue adding their prayers or 'sorries' during the Creative Response time;

✝ board books that tell the story of Jesus' Last Week;

✝ dressing up: robes (to look like important people and to throw down before Jesus), palm leaves, cow and sheep masks, a till with money (for Jesus cleaning the Temple);

✝ playdough plus shape cutters of the animals that feature in the unit's stories (donkeys, cows, sheep, hens, chicks), people shape cutters and modelling tools if you have them;

✝ animal jigsaws or plastic models of the animals that feature in the unit's stories (donkeys, cows, sheep, hens, chicks);

✝ palm leaves and/or palm crosses for the children to explore;

✝ books with pictures of ancient Jerusalem;

✝ small tree branches that are growing spring leaves and/or blossom. You could take these out of water for the session itself for the children to explore, but replace them in water between sessions. Branches from different trees for the children to compare and contrast would be wonderful.

Unit Starter Ideas

✝ An important theme of Lent in Sowing Seeds is that God can create beautiful things from what looks like rubbish. Invite the children to use recyclable materials to create amazing sculptures. *Provide recycling materials such as boxes, tubes, cartons, egg boxes, paper, etc., along with masking tape, string, glue sticks.*

✝ Another important Lenten theme is saying sorry to God and letting God make us clean again. Invite the children to help you clean out and tidy your group's resources or meeting space. *Provide (for example): damp cloths or wipes, brushes and dustpans, grimy resources (you could always add grime!), resources that need tidying and organizing, crayons/pens/pencils that need sorting, appropriate silver and a soft cloth, or ask those who clean your meeting space or church for more ideas. If appropriate in your space, you could even provide a water tray with soapy water.*

✝ Invite some of the children to help sharpen pencils/crayons then to use the sharpenings to create pictures. *Provide pencils (good-quality pencils/crayons make this easier as the wood or wax doesn't disintegrate on sharpening), sharpeners, paper, PVA glue and glue sticks.*

✝ If your church ashes people on Ash Wednesday, you could invite the children to decorate then ash a body template. Who will their person look like? *Provide large or small body templates (p. 215 or p. 196), crayons/pencils/paints/pastels, scissors plus a bowl of ash and a drop of water/oil.*

✝ Give the children the opportunity to contribute to the group's resources by transforming used patterned paper, sweet wrappers, etc., into collage materials for the group to create. Invite the children to cut the paper into squares and other shapes, then to sort them into different containers. *Provide a range of recyclable materials that can become collage materials (p. 188). You could even encourage them to bring recyclable material to contribute themselves the next time they come.*

✝ Invite the children to make a picture of themselves in one of the stories you've told together. *Provide body templates (p. 215 or p. 196 or website) and pencils/crayons/paints. If it's Palm Sunday, you may also like to provide real or paper leaves and glue so the children can add leaves to their creations.*

✝ Lent means 'springtime'. Give the children the opportunity to plant seeds and watch them grow. *Provide plant pots, recyclable containers, appropriate compost/soil, seeds/bulbs.*

✝ Give the children the opportunity to witness new life growing from 'rubbish'. Invite the children to decorate a recyclable container that can act as a plant pot with collage materials. When they're ready, invite them to place a few pieces of folded paper towel and a discarded carrot top (top upwards) in the container. When they get home, they can put a little water on the paper towel and keep it damp (not soaked). Green leaves will grow up from the carrot top! *Provide recyclable containers, collage materials (p. 188), glue, paper towel (or cotton wool), discarded carrot tops.*

✝ Invite the children to explore different tree branches that are growing spring leaves or blossom. *Provide a range of tree branches (take these out of water for the session), notepads and pencils to take notes or make observational drawings, rulers, scales, magnifying glasses, torches, even a child microscope if you have one.*

✝ Invite the children to make a spring scene picture or their own mini spring garden in a box using real materials. *Provide either paper and glue or small boxes (e.g. recyclable tubs) plus natural materials such as grass, leaves, twigs, fallen blossom, etc. If you have a churchyard, you could even go and find some spring materials together there.*

✝ Give the children the opportunity to make a Lent or Holy Week wheel to tell six stories from Holy Week, with an arrow to move around the stories: for instance: Jesus Enters Jerusalem (Palm Sunday), Jesus Cleans the Temple, Jesus Washes the Disciples' Feet, the Last Supper, the Crucifixion and Easter Day. Your group of children may like to choose differently. *Provide wheel with arrow template (p. 214 or website), paper fasteners, pencils/crayons]/pens.*

Prayer

✝ Invite the children to make their own 2D version of your group's sorry/prayer tree. *Provide bare tree template (p. 194 or website) plus glue and squares of white/pink tissue paper (prayer tree, p. 173) or crumpled and torn white/pink tissue paper (sorry tree).*

✝ Give the children the opportunity to make their own 3D version of your group's sorry/prayer tree. *Provide appropriate twigs plus glue and squares of white/pink tissue paper (prayer tree) or crumpled and torn white/pink tissue paper (sorry tree).*

✝ Invite one or more children to create a prayer space for Lent (or beyond) in the room in which you hold your session. Encourage them to find or make symbols or pictures to place in the prayer space that help them feel close to God. This 'prayer space' could be packed into a box at the end of each session and re-created (the same or different) during the Creative Response each time. *Provide a wide range of materials and objects for the children to choose from: Bible, books, crosses, candles, pictures, icons, flowers, paper, crayons/pencils/pastels, recyclable materials, etc.*

✝ Give the children the opportunity to draw or paint a picture of a place where they feel close to God in a picture frame. *Provide picture-frame template (p. 211 or website), paints/pastels/pencils/crayons.*

The Way of the Cross

See the suggestions from the 'Jesus Is Tested in the Wilderness' story above (p. 128), or try one of the following:

✝ Give the children the opportunity to make a stained glass cross. Invite them to glue brightly coloured tissue/cellophane/crepe paper to cross-shaped wax/baking paper. *Provide scissors, glue and brightly coloured tissue/crepe/cellophane paper (e.g. transparent sweet wrappers) plus baking/wax paper (the whiter the better, but brown paper still works) in the shape of a cross. You (or older children) can make a cross shape by folding square or rectangular wax/baking paper into quarters then cutting an L-shape into it (making sure you don't cut into any side that's a fold).*

✝ Invite the children to make a cross with playdough, salt dough or airdrying clay. They may also like to etch patterns into it. *Provide playdough, salt dough (p. 190) or airdrying clay, clay modelling tools or plastic (safe) knives and forks.*

Holy Week

✝ Give the children the opportunity to make a Lent or Holy Week wheel to tell six stories from Holy Week, with an arrow to move around the stories. Examples of six stories include: Jesus Enters Jerusalem (Palm Sunday), Jesus Cleans the Temple, Jesus Washes the Disciples' Feet, the Last Supper, the Crucifixion and Easter Day. Your group may like to choose differently. *Provide wheel with arrow template (p. 214), paper fasteners, pencils/crayons]/pens.*

✝ Invite the children to decorate a heart to remind them of the strength of love. They may even want to write 'Love is stronger' on their heart. *Provide large heart template (p. 209), pencils/crayons/paints and scissors. If you have collage materials, and glue, make these available too. If you have string or wool, you could see if any children would like to make necklaces or bookmarks with their hearts. If they are making necklaces, make sure the string/wool can easily snap when pulled and is attached as two separate ends to prevent accidents.*

✝ Give the children the opportunity to make their own Easter Garden. *Provide a box or tub from recycling or a paper plate to hold the garden (tubs with lids such as margarine tub or takeaway containers are ideal for easy transportation home), plus a range of materials that could be used to create the garden such as: soil and grass/flower seeds, or green fabric/paper and real or paper flowers (for the garden), a paper cup, yoghurt pot, plant pot, section of an egg tray (for the cave), a suitably sized stone to seal the cave.*

Jesus Is Alive! Alleluia! unit (Easter)

These starter ideas are designed to spark imaginations and open up opportunities for the children to respond creatively in their different ways to the worship and storytelling you've taken part in together.

Story Starter Ideas

Jesus Is Risen! Alleluia!

- Invite the children to decorate an Easter egg in their own way. Will their egg be closed or open (they could cut a jagged or straight line across the egg to show its opening)? Will there be a chick inside? Or will it be hollow like the empty tomb? *Provide paper, Easter egg templates (p. 201 or website), scissors, crayons/pencils/pastels/paints. Optional: collage materials (see p. 188 or website), glue, chick templates (p. 216 or website), paper fasteners so the children can create an egg that opens and closes if they wish, with the fastener holding the two sections together at the corner.*

- Invite the children to decorate an Easter card or postcard to send. *Provide folded card, pencils/crayons/pastels. Optional: postcard template (p. 212 or website), Easter egg template (p. 201 or website), collage materials (p. 188), glue.*

- Give the children the opportunity to paint real Easter eggs to take home and eat. *Provide real eggs (boiled [!] that morning and refrigerated), paints, pastels or felt tips.*

- Invite the children to create Easter paper chains to celebrate Easter Day! *Provide strips of yellow/white or Easter-themed paper and glue.*

- See other Easter egg starter ideas from the unit starter ideas on p. 141.

The Women's Story

- Invite the children to make a picture or collage of the empty tomb. They may even like to add angels, Jesus' friends or the Risen Jesus there. *Provide the empty tomb template (p. 202 or website), scissors, glue, pencils/crayons/pastels. Optional: paper fasteners (so the stone can open and shut) and collage materials (p. 188; newspapers make great collage materials for the tomb).*

- Invite children to make one of the angels from the story. Remember to give them the space to imagine for themselves what angels look like. *Provide angel templates (p. 193 or website), body templates (p. 000 or p. 196), blank paper for those who would like to draw freestyle, pencils/crayons/pastels/paints. Optional: collage materials (p. 188), glue.*

- Give the children the opportunity to make their own Easter Garden (see p. 134). *Provide a box or tub from recycling or a paper plate to hold the garden (tubs with lids such as margarine tub or takeaway containers are ideal for easy transportation home), plus a range of materials that could be used to create the garden such as: soil and grass/flower seeds, or green fabric/paper and real or paper flowers (for the garden), a paper cup, yoghurt pot, plant pot, section of an egg tray or eggshells* (for the cave), a suitably sized stone to seal the cave.*

Tip

* Using eggshells creates a wonderful opportunity to make connections between the tomb and Easter eggs but they need to be handled carefully. Before the session, make sure you wash the eggshells thoroughly, then boil or bake them in the oven at 120 °C (250 °F, gas mark ½) for 15–20 minutes to sterilize them.

- Invite the children to make an Easter flower collage to celebrate the joy of Easter from magazines. They may even like to decorate a cross with their joyful flowers. *Provide paper/card, flower magazines, glue, scissors. Optional: cross template (p. 199 or website).*

- Give the children the opportunity to decorate Easter Garden cakes to celebrate Easter. *Provide cupcakes (pre-made or bought), green icing and flower sprinkles. Optional: desiccated coconut dyed green to be the grass, marzipan or royal icing that can be shaped into an empty tomb and stone.*

The Walk to Emmaus

- Invite the children to create finger puppets of Jesus' friends and the 'stranger' to tell the story themselves. Each child will need at least three finger puppets. *Provide finger puppet templates (p. 204), scissors, pencils/crayons, glue.*

- Give the children the opportunity to spend time kneading and shaping bread dough into a roll to take home, bake and share. *Provide a simple bread dough for the children (use a readymade mix, see p. 190 for a recipe, or use your own recipe), a floured container or cling film to take the roll home in, and appropriate instructions for baking the bread. Optional: if you have the facilities, you may even like to bake the bread on site.*

- Invite the children to make an icon of the Risen Jesus *Provide a card rectangle, tinfoil to wrap around the card to create a silver icon background and paper, pencils/crayons/pastels/paints, scissors. Optional: glue, collage materials (p. 188), body template (p. 215, p. 196 or website).*

The Good Shepherd

- Invite the children to show themselves, or friends/family, as a sheep: as part of a picture or collage, as a necklace, Easter card, puppet or anything they like. *Provide sheep template (p. 213 or website), pencils/crayons/pastels, etc. If you have cotton wool, lollipop sticks/twigs and masking tape, glue and any other collage materials (p. 188), make these available too. If they are making necklaces, make sure the string/wool can easily snap when pulled and is attached as two separate ends to prevent accidents.*

- Invite the children to make their own shepherd's crook and decorate it. *Provide sticks, plus coloured wool/string.*

- Give the children the opportunity to design a stained-glass window with an image of the Good Shepherd. *Provide stained-glass window template (p. 219) and crayons/pastels/pencils/felt tips.*

- If you're exploring Psalm 23, 'The Lord's my shepherd', you could invite the children to create a picture of God with them when things feel 'dark as night'. *Provide body template (p. 215, p. 196 or website) or blank paper, dark collage materials, scissors, yellow and gold collage materials, glue and crayons/pastels/pencils/felt tips.*

Thomas's Story

- Thomas saw the Risen Jesus! The Risen Jesus still had the marks of the cross on his hands and side and feet. Invite the children to create a picture of the Risen Jesus with those marks showing. *Provide body templates (p. 215, p. 196 or website), crayons/pencils/paints/pastels.*

- Thomas saw that Jesus is God! Give the children an opportunity to create pictures of what Thomas saw. *Provide body templates (p. 215, p. 196 or website), crayons/pencils/paints/pastels and a range of collage materials (including bright colours) with glue.*

The Catch of Fishes

- Invite the children to make their own fish. *Provide fish template (p. 206 or website), pencils/crayons/pastels, etc. If you have collage materials (p. 188), make these available too. Optional: add a card handle to a paper plate to make a frying pan, or decorate the fish with finger paints (see p. 191 for a recipe for edible finger paints).*

- Give the children the opportunity to build a fire from sticks. Once the fires are ready, you could mime lighting them (1, 2, 3 . . . Tssss *Strike imaginary match*) then sit around the fires, imagining Jesus there cooking fish with you. *Provide a range of sticks.*

- Give a small group of children the opportunity to work together to make a boat to sit in from whatever you have to hand. They may like to create a sea around themselves and a fishing net. They may like to act out fishing from the boat, or they may simply like to get caught up in the act of creating. *Provide a range of open-ended materials: chairs, tables, rugs, blue/white sheets and pillow cases, brush handles, etc.*

- Invite the children to make their own fish from paper plates. Cut a triangle from the edge to the centre of the plate (the hole becomes the mouth and the triangle can be glued to the other end of the fish to become its tail). The fish can then be painted, coloured or collaged. *Provide paper plates, scissors, glue, pencils/crayons/paints/pastels. Optional: collage materials (p. 188).*

- Give the children the opportunity to imagine swimming through the water to find Jesus through one of the water-themed (River Jordan) starter ideas in the 'John the Baptist' unit (Book 1, p. 152).

Peter's Story

- Peter is given the keys to God's kingdom! Peter's given a new start and an important job! Invite the children to make Peter's key (or set of keys) and to decorate them with joyful colours. *Provide key templates (p. 208 or website) and paints/pastels/pencils/crayons. Optional: string/wool to create a set of keys.*

- Give the children the opportunity to explore the different emotions from the story with face templates. Which part of the story will they choose? When Peter has said, 'No! I do NOT follow Jesus!'; when Jesus gives Peter a new start and says, 'Follow me!'; or another part of the story? Maybe the children would prefer to respond to a moment from their own life with their face picture. *Provide face templates (p. 203 or website), pencils/crayons/pastels/paints.*

- Invite the children to create Jesus' footsteps to follow by drawing around their own or each other's feet. What would they like to do with their footprint(s)? Decorate them? Make them into a necklace or card? *Provide paper, scissors, pencils/crayons/pastels/paints, plus string and collage materials (p. 188) if you have them. If they are making necklaces, make sure the string/wool can easily snap when pulled and is attached as two separate ends to prevent accidents.*

The Ascension

- Invite the children to make an image of the Risen Jesus the last time his friends saw him. You could invite them to attach string to the back so that Jesus can go 'up' from the ground. Some children may even like to create clouds from card, paper plates or an upturned open box, into which they can pull Jesus up. *Provide body template (p. 215, p. 196 or website), pencils/crayons/pastels, scissors. Optional: paper plate/card/box, string/wool.*

- Invite the children to create a waving hand by drawing around their own hand and cutting it out. They may like to attach their hand to a stick with masking tape, so they can wave goodbye to Jesus with it. *Provide card, pencils, scissors. Optional: lollipop stick/straw/real stick and masking tape.*

- Get ready for the fire of the Spirit at Pentecost by creating fire pictures! Invite the children to make their paintbrushes/fingers 'dance' with fire on paper with swirls and swooshes in reds/yellows/oranges to create images of fire. Ask the children if they're willing to make more than one painting and to leave one behind to be used during the Creative Response next time. *Provide blank paper, different shades of red/yellow/orange paint and paintbrushes (or use fingerpaints, see p. 191 for recipe).*

Come, Holy Spirit!

- Invite the children to dance with their pencils/crayons/pastels to colour their tongues of fire with fiery colours. The children may even like to attach their flames to a hatband to show the Spirit's fire resting on them. *Provide fire template (p. 205 or website), fire-coloured pencils/crayons/pastels/paints. Optional: hatband (see p. 192) and masking tape, fiery-coloured collage materials (p. 188) and glue.*

- Invite the children to collage fire. *Provide paper, fiery-coloured collage materials, glue.*

- Invite the children to collage a dove shape with fire. They may enjoy attaching red/yellow/orange streamers to it. *Provide bird template (p. 195 or website), fiery-coloured collage materials (p. 188) glue, scissors. Optional: streamer materials such as red/yellow/orange ribbon/wool/curling ribbon/crepe/tissue paper.*

- Give the children the opportunity to create Holy Spirit streamers by attaching yellow/orange/red streamers to a real stick. *Provide real sticks (check for sharp points), masking tape, streamer materials such as red/yellow/orange ribbon/wool/curling ribbon/crepe/tissue paper.*

- Invite younger children to dance like fire with paint on a paper plate (which allows for spillages). *Provide paper plates, red/yellow/orange paints, paintbrushes (or use fingerpaints, p. 191).*

- Give the children the opportunity to make a fire and wind shaker so they can make the sound of the Spirit rushing into the room. Invite the children to pour dried orange lentils/rice into a transparent bottle with a teaspoon. You could even ask them to feed little twigs in first, for the lentils to run through. Allow plenty of time for this and expect lots of lentils to escape! When the children are ready, they may need help with attaching the lid tightly. The children may like to attach fiery streamers to their bottles. *Provide plastic bottles with secure lids (transparent if possible), dried red lentils/rice. Optional: twigs, streamer materials such as red/yellow/orange ribbon/wool/curling ribbon/crepe/tissue paper.*

- If you made fire pictures last time, invite the children to take one of the pictures (it doesn't need to be their own and you could even contribute more yourself). Ask the children to dance like the fire of the Spirit again, this time using scissors to sway and turn through the fire paintings to create flame shapes. Use the freestyle red/yellow/orange cuttings that are created by this to create a large-scale fire collage. *Provide: fire paintings (dried), scissors, large roll of paper, glue.*

1, 2, 3, the Trinity!

- Invite the children to make a Trinity banner to celebrate the Trinity. You might like to create individual banners or a large group banner with lots of different pictures representing God the Father, God the Son and God the Holy Spirit. Starter ideas include: draw around your own hand, create something with a piece of plasticine/ball of mud/clay (God the Father, the Maker), a cross or empty cave (God the Son, Jesus), a dove or fire (God the Holy Spirit). However, encourage the children to create their own drawings. How would they like to show God the Father, God the Son and God the Holy Spirit? If you're making individual banners, they might like to glue their pictures to paper or attach them to string. *Provide lots of blank paper, bird template (p. 195 or website), cross template (p. 199 or website), empty tomb template (p. 202 or website), fire template (p. 205 or website), scissors, glue. Optional: string/wool/ribbon, masking tape, large pieces of paper.*

- Invite the children to create Trinity triangles from twigs or lollipop sticks to celebrate the Trinity. See if they'd like to attach string to them to create Trinity necklaces or hanging decorations. Before older children construct their triangle, they may like to draw pictures of God the Father, God the Son and God the Holy Spirit on the sticks. Give the children space to explore other shapes (beyond triangles) as images of the Trinity. *Provide twigs or lollipop sticks, glue sticks, pencils/felt tips, string.*

- Give the children the opportunity to focus on one Person of the Trinity. Who do they feel most close to? Father, Son or Holy Spirit? Invite them to create a picture of that Person of the Trinity. You may like to share your different responses as a group, ending with the Trinity song while holding your different pictures up in praise of God, Father, Son and Holy Spirit. *Provide lots of blank paper, pencils/pastels/paints/crayons. With very young children, you may like to offer the templates outlined in the first option above as starter ideas to collage or decorate. If they are making necklaces, make sure the string/wool can easily snap when pulled and is attached as two separate ends to prevent accidents.*

Sensory Starter Ideas (including for babies and toddlers)

Resources that you could provide for the children to explore for themselves include the following.

- a Jesus figure (the Joseph figure from a Nativity set can work well);

- child-safe crosses (holding crosses are particularly appropriate);

- an Easter Garden to explore. Note: If your group is using an Easter Garden during your time of saying sorry or prayers, you could leave this and flowers for the children to continue adding their prayers or 'sorries' during the Creative Response time;

- wooden/metal or other child-safe cup and plate or chalice and paten for children to explore and tell the story of Jesus' Last Meal and the Walk to Emmaus (wooden egg cups and coasters can also work well);

- yellow imaginative aids; lots of stones for building a Dark Cave. Check none of these present a choking hazard;

- flowers or pictures/magazines/books of flowers to explore;

- boats, fish and a net if you have one. Check that play with any net is closely supervised by a parent or trained helper;

- board books that tell the story of Jesus' Last Week and Easter;

- playdough and modelling tools to make all sorts of things: the empty cave, eggs, chicks, boats, fish, characters from the stories, or anything that sparks the children's imagination;

- mini fluffy chicks (the kind you get as cake decorations at Easter) in a bottle, so the babies can see them safely, with the lid taped shut;

- preloved Easter cards with Easter pictures on them;

- chick, sheep or fish jigsaws;

- musical instruments: Easter is a time of joy and celebration;

- sticks to make a fire like the disciples, a child-safe frying pan, fish (plastic/wood/printed). When you've made a fire together, you might like to sit around it, cooking fish and imagining Jesus there with you. I wonder how it feels to be with Jesus?

Unit Starter Ideas

- Invite the children to make edible Easter egg nests with mini eggs in. Melt chocolate just before the Creative Response and stir well to make sure it's cool to the touch with no hot spots. While the children are waiting, invite them to crush cornflakes in bowls with a spoon. Pour a little melted chocolate into each bowl and ask the children to combine the ingredients. When they're ready, invite them to place spoons of the mixture into cupcake cases, create a little hollow in the middle, then place two or three mini eggs in the hollow. Give the children the space to create their own versions of nests or simply to be caught up in the act of creation (and inevitable joyful eating). *Provide facilities to wash hands before and after this activity (!!), cornflakes (or another suitable cereal), cupcake cases, spoons, bowls, melted chocolate.*

- Simnel cakes are traditionally eaten at Easter (sometimes on Mothering Sunday). Give the children the opportunity to decorate either their own mini Simnel-like cake or a large Simnel cake for your church to share with your congregation after the service. To decorate the cakes: spread apricot jam on the top, roll out marzipan, cut out a circle shape from it with circle cutters and place it on the jam layer. Next, roll the marzipan into small balls (traditionally 11) and 'glue' them to the top of the cake using the jam. Give the children space to develop the Simnel cake tradition in their own ways. *Provide a large sponge or fruit cake (or one cupcake per child), marzipan, rolling pins, circle cutters (plate/cup/cutter with a similar circumference to the cake), apricot jam, safe knives or spoons to spread the jam.*

- The Easter stories open up lots of opportunities to explore a range of emotions. Invite the children to cut different expressions out of magazines and create a collage from them. *Provide newspapers/magazines. Check the headlines are suitable.*

- Use one of the other Easter egg starter ideas from 'Jesus Is Risen! Alleluia!' (p. 135).

- Invite the children to make an 'Alleluia! banner' to take home (if they didn't make one on the Sunday before Lent). Give the children the opportunity to write their own 'Alleluia!' in bubble letters or on bunting, or to use the 'Alleluia!' template (website only). Invite them to cut the letters out and then to tape them to a length of string to create a banner. Leave the children the imaginative space to create what they would like with their 'Alleluia!' letters. For example, this isn't the time to worry about spelling! *Provide card, 'Alleluia!' template (website only), pencils/crayons/pastels, scissors, masking tape, string/wool.*

- Easter is a time of joyful celebration! On Easter Day, the bells ring out! Give the children the opportunity to create musical instruments to celebrate. For instance, you could adapt the 'fire and wind shaker' starter idea from 'Come, Holy Spirit!' (p. 139) to become an Easter joy shaker, using yellows, golds and whites, instead of fiery colours. Or experiment with other musical instruments: elastic bands stretched over a strong box or tub to create a stringed instrument; paper or cellophane stretched over a strong cardboard cup or tub and secured with an elastic band to create a drum; straws with the end flattened and cut into a 'V'-shaped point to create a buzzing oboe! Give the children space and time to experiment! *Provide elastic bands, strong boxes and tubs, straws, scissors, masking tape, paper (or cellophane if you have it).*

- Invite the children to decorate the Easter stone that rolled away. *Provide smooth stones, felt tips/pastels/paints.*

- Invite the children to make the cross of the Risen Jesus beautiful by decorating it with flowers, or bright colours. *Provide wooden crosses or the cross template (p. 199 or website), pencils/crayons/paints and scissors. If you have collage materials (p. 188) or real flowers (such as daisies, buttercups, clover) and glue, make these available too. If you have string or wool, you could see if any children would like to make necklaces or bookmarks with their cross. If they are making necklaces, make sure the string/wool can easily snap when pulled and is attached as two separate ends to prevent accidents.*

- Give the children the opportunity to design a stained-glass window with an Easter theme such as the Empty Cave, the sunrise, or a cross made beautiful with flowers. *Provide stained-glass window template (p. 219) and crayons/pastels/pencils/felt tips.*

- Give the children the opportunity to draw their own cross of the Risen Jesus with bright colours on black paper (to echo the darkness of Good Friday and the joyful colours of Easter Day). *Provide black paper, bright pastels or chalks.*

- Invite the children to have a go at making a daisy chain or another creation from daisies. *Provide freshly picked daisies or go and pick them together outside. Optional: you could provide wool and plastic needles to support younger children in making a daisy chain. The needle can go through the head of the daisy if the stalk is too tricky.*

- If the Paschal/Easter candle is prominent in your church during Easter, you could give the children the opportunity to paint their own design on a candle to make their own Paschal candle. You might like to show them your church's Paschal candle as an example. *Provide candles that are large enough to paint on, paints, paintbrushes. It may help to keep last year's Paschal candle to show as an example in Sowing Seeds sessions.*
- Alternatively, invite the children to decorate a 2D candle template. *Provide candle template (p. 197 or website), pencils/crayons/pastels/paints.*

Part 4
The Building Blocks

Introduction

Sowing Seeds isn't just Bible storytelling. The Building Blocks provide a wide range of prayer, worship and creative materials to resource and nurture your group's time with God. Different groups work in different ways and so the idea is that you choose Building Blocks and options that are appropriate for your group to build your own session or service.

There's no single way of holding a Sowing Seeds gathering. Groups will continually be faced with developing and flexing as they change in number, experience and age range, as well as with adapting to new children who have different gifts and ways of being. Every group really is unique, and it will be for your own group to work out over time how Sowing Seeds can resource you.

The idea is for your group to explore the material and decide which Building Blocks you'd like to use to build your own session. It can be helpful to think of the Building Blocks as falling into four categories:

- beginning
- middle
- middle plus
- end.

Aim to build a session or service that has a beginning, a middle and an end, which best reflects the shape and feel of worship in your church or school. In other words, if your church tends to have informal worship, create a session with an informal feel. If your gathering is held during a communion service, then build a communion service for your children (up to the Peace, at which you can rejoin the wider congregation to share communion together). If your church uses liturgical colours, then use liturgical colours; if your church has an informal prayer time, then have an informal prayer time, etc.

Because Sowing Seeds has been written to be used across a whole range of traditions, it's likely that there will be material in this chapter that you would never use in your setting! Simply skip over that material and find the options that best fit your group.

Whatever choices you make, we advise that you stick to those choices for one whole week so your group can find a rhythm. This will encourage participation and allow for deeper engagement among the children and adults.

> **Tip**
>
> The material includes Building Blocks for every part of a communion service or a Service of the Word. However, it was never envisaged that any group would attempt to use all these Building Blocks each Sunday. That would be far too much for children and leaders alike! For this reason, we would suggest using only one Prayer Building Block each time.

The Sowing Seeds Website

When building your own session and service, the Sowing Seeds website can be an invaluable resource. All the Building Blocks are laid out there in a format that is easy to cut and paste into your own document. Using the website for the Building Blocks is generally far easier than trying to photocopy the material from this book. In contrast, the Bible Storytelling material has been designed for easy photocopying.

The website also provides a guide to each of the Building Blocks as well as examples of services you could build.

> **Tip**
>
> The members' code for this book on the website is: mustard252.

> **Tip: Presentation folders**
>
> Presentation folders can really help when leading Sowing Seeds. They're much easier to manage than loose sheets, especially when doing actions! And most of the session or service will stay the same for the whole unit, once your group has made your choices so will only need to be printed once: it's only the Bible storytelling material that will change. We've found A5 folders are best.

Teaching Your Group New Songs and Responses

Many of the songs and responses from the Sowing Seeds Building Blocks remain the same every week even when the units change. Still, there will always be a first time these songs and responses need to be learned. Tips on teaching new songs and said responses can be found on the website.

The Building Blocks

Welcome

Welcome your group.

Let's start by going around the circle
and saying our name out loud.
My name's _____.

Go around the circle so that every adult and child has the chance to say her or his name (and introduce any dolls, teddies or toys). If any of the children don't want to say their name, or aren't able to, you (or a parent or carer) could say it for them and wave.
It's time to sing our Welcome Song!

Welcome Song: Option 1

→ Song: 'The Sowing Seeds welcome song'. Words: © Sharon Moughtin.
→ Tune: 'Glory, glory, alleluia!' (traditional).

[Musical notation with lyrics:]
Wel-come Name _ to St Mar - y's! Wel-come Name _ to St Mar - y's!
Wel-come Name _ to St Mar - y's! You are wel-come in the name of the Lord.

Go around the circle the same way as above. See if you can remember one another's names and insert them into the song.

Welcome *Name 1* to *St Mary's**
Welcome *Name 1* to *St Mary's**
Welcome *Name 1* to *St Mary's**
You are welcome in the name of the Lord!

* Insert the name of your church or children's group, or sing 'our worship'.

Welcome Song: Option 2

→ Song: 'You are welcome in the name of the Lord' (traditional).
→ Tune: traditional.

[Musical notation for the song with lyrics:]
You are wel-come in the name of the Lord! You are wel-come in the name of the Lord! I can see all ov-er you the glor-y of the Lord! You are wel-come in the name of the Lord!

Welcome to St Mary's!
Let's wave with one hand. *Lead waving*
Then with our other hand. *Lead waving*
Then let's choose someone and show God's 'glory'!
Move arms up and down in front of you with fingers wiggling, palms facing out, towards one person.
And someone else! *Repeat*
Then let's wave with both hands all around the circle.
Lead waving.

We're ready to sing!
You are welcome in the name of the Lord!
Wave with right hand to one person.
You are welcome in the name of the Lord!
Wave with left hand to another person.
I can see all over you the glory of the Lord!
Move arms up and down in front of you with fingers wiggling,
palms facing out, towards one person and then another.
You are welcome in the name of the Lord!
Wave with both hands all around the circle.

Getting Ready to Worship

This option is designed with churches or schools who regularly use the sign of the cross or 'The Lord be with you' in mind, to support the children in joining in. If your church regularly uses other words of greeting you could use these here instead. If your church or school is more informal, then you could mirror that here.

Getting Ready to Worship: Option 1

→ Action: the sign of the cross.
→ Words: © Sharon Moughtin.

Invite the children to make the sign of the cross slowly with you. You could lead this 'my turn/your turn' or, as the children become more confident, invite a child to lead the action as the whole group says the words and makes the sign of the cross.

In my head,	*Touch head*
in my heart,	*Touch chest*
and all around me,	*Touch shoulders one by one*
Jesus is here.	*Open hands in front, facing upwards*

Getting Ready to Worship: Option 2

→ Action: 'The Lord be with you' (open hands).

Let's start by clenching our hands together tightly.
Lead children in clenching fists against your body to show a defensive posture.
When we close ourselves up like this,
it's hard to let anyone into our heart.
It's hard even to let God into our heart!

When we get ready to worship,
we show that we're open to God and to each other.

Open your hands out, facing up.
Can you show me your open hands?
We're ready to let God and each other in!

The Lord be with you.
Hold hands open to the children.

And also with you.
Invite the children to open their hands towards you.

Introducing the Unit

Choose an introduction according to which unit you're in and the age range of your group. This introduction can stay the same for the whole unit.

Introducing the Unit: The Journey to the Cross unit: Option 1

→ Optional focus: a cross.

> *Week 1:* This week we're starting on a journey with Jesus
> *All other weeks:* We're on a journey with Jesus
>
> *If you're using a cross, show the children the cross.*
> the journey to the cross.

The way of the cross is the way of love.
Let's cross our arms on our chest to show love.
Lead the children in crossing arms on chest.

Look down at your own arms.
Look! Our sign for love is a cross.
The way of love is the way of the cross.
For the first couple of weeks, you may like to trace your finger on the crossed arms of a child sitting next to you to show the cross shape she or he is making.

In our stories,
we're following Jesus on the way of love to the cross.

Introducing the Unit: The Journey to the Cross unit: Option 2

→ Focus: the liturgical colour purple.
→ Optional focus: a cross.

> *If your church uses visible liturgical colours:*
> Can anyone tell me what colour season we're in now?
> *If appropriate:* You may have seen it in church.

Week 1:
Today is the *first Sunday* of an important time for the Church.
It's the start of the season of Lent!

The special colour of Lent is purple.
It's the colour that reminds us to get ready!
We're getting ready to follow Jesus on a journey:
> *If you're using a cross, show the children the cross.*

the journey to the cross.

The way of the cross is the way of love.
Let's cross our arms on our chest to show love.
Lead the children in crossing arms on chest.

Look down at your own arms.
Look! Our sign for love is a cross.
The way of love is the way of the cross.
> *For the first couple of weeks, you may like to trace your finger on the crossed arms of a child sitting next to you to show the cross shape he or she is making.*

In Lent we follow Jesus to the cross.
> *If you're using a cross, or there's one in the building, show the group the cross.*

Introducing the Unit: The Journey to the Cross unit: Option 3

→ **Focus: the use of sackcloth during Lent.**
→ **Optional focus: a cross.**

If your church uses visible sackcloth as a sign of repentance for Lent, you may also like to choose Saying Sorry to God for your Prayer Building Block (p. 158) to support children as they make the connections between what they see in the church building and their own acts of worship.

Week 1:
Today is the *first Sunday* of an important time for the Church.
It's the start of the season of Lent!

In Lent our church wears sackcloth.
It's the colour that reminds us to say sorry.
In Lent we do lots of saying sorry to get ready.

We're getting ready to follow Jesus on a journey:
> *If you're using a cross, show the children the cross.*

the journey to the cross.

The way of the cross is the way of love.
Let's cross our arms on our chest to show love.
Lead the children in crossing arms on chest.

Look down at your own arms.
Look! Our sign for love is a cross.
The way of love is the way of the cross.
> *For the first couple of weeks, you may like to trace your finger on the crossed arms of a child sitting next to you to show the cross shape she or he is making.*

In Lent we follow Jesus to the cross.
> *If you're using a cross, or there's one in the building, show the group the cross.*

Introducing the Unit: Jesus Is Alive! Alleluia! unit: Option 1

> *If your group is using an Easter Garden (see p. 60), place it in the middle of the circle.*
> Can anyone tell me what this is?
> *Accept children's responses and ways of naming the garden.*

This is our Easter Garden
with the Dark Cave in the middle.

We're telling the stories of what happened
when Jesus burst from the 'tomb', the Dark Cave,
and won a new start for us.

If your church shouts a special 'Alleluia!' at Easter, you could introduce it here. Examples follow, but adapt these to introduce the children to the words that they will hear around them in your church services. Encourage them to join in in church, too!
We celebrate Easter with the Church's special shout of joy:
Alleluia!

Either: When I say, 'The Lord is risen!',
you can shout: **'He is risen indeed, Alleluia!'**

The Lord is risen!
He is risen indeed, Alleluia!
Repeat until the children are confident.

Or: When I say, 'Praise the Lord!',
you can shout: **'Alleluia!'**

Praise the Lord!
Alleluia!
Repeat until the children are confident.

Introducing the Unit: Jesus Is Alive! Alleluia! unit: Option 2

↳ **Focus: the liturgical colours, white and gold, and 'Alleluia!'.**

Can anyone tell me what colour season we're in now?

If appropriate: You may have seen it in church.

Accept responses.
At the moment, the Church is in Easter!
The special colours of Easter are white and gold!
The colours of joy and celebration!

If your group is using an Easter Garden (see p. 60), place it in the middle of the circle.
Can anyone tell me what this is?
Accept children's responses and ways of naming the garden.
This is our Easter Garden
with the Dark Cave in the middle.

At Easter, we celebrate Jesus
bursting from the 'tomb', the Dark Cave,
and winning a new start for us.

We celebrate Easter with the Church's special shout of joy:
Alleluia!

Either: When I say, 'The Lord is risen!',
you can shout: **'He is risen indeed, Alleluia!'**

The Lord is risen!
He is risen indeed, Alleluia!
Repeat until the children are confident.

Or: When I say, 'Praise the Lord!'
you can shout: **'Alleluia!'**

Praise the Lord!
Alleluia!
Repeat until the children are confident.

At Easter, we celebrate Jesus bursting out of the Dark Cave and winning new life for all of us!

Gathering Song

Choose a Gathering Song according to which unit you're in and the age range of your group. This Gathering Song can stay the same for the whole unit.

Gathering Song: The Journey to the Cross unit: Option 1

→ Song: 'I am going to follow Jesus'. Words: © Sharon Moughtin.
→ Tune: 'Bobby Shaftoe' (traditional).

I am going to fol-low Je-sus, I am going to fol-low Je-sus,
I am going to fol-low Je-sus, fol-low, fol-low Je-sus!

Our song [for Lent] is all about following Jesus.
Let's get ready to follow Jesus.
Let's get up and march on the spot:
Lead the children in marching in time to the beat:
1, 2, 3, 4! 1, 2, 3, 4!

Continue marching as you sing:
I am going to follow Jesus,
I am going to follow Jesus,
I am going to follow Jesus,
follow, follow Jesus!

Distribute imaginative aids (p. 187) if you have them.

Let's practise following Jesus!
Invite one of the children to stand in the centre of the circle or at the front.
Name is going to be Jesus!
To the child: 'Jesus!' Can you show us an action?
Let's all copy what 'Jesus' does.
Let's 'follow Jesus'.

Continue 'following' the child's action as you sing:
I am going to follow Jesus,
I am going to follow Jesus,
I am going to follow Jesus,
follow, follow Jesus!

Invite another child to be 'Jesus' and repeat as appropriate.
When the group is ready to finish:
In Lent, we follow Jesus!

> **Tip**
>
> The words to this song are so repetitive that you won't need to teach them to the children, they will naturally begin to join in as you sing.

For the 'Jesus Is Tested in the Wilderness' story:
The place we start is the 'wilderness'

If you're using a wilderness tray (see p. 11) place this in the centre of the circle.
This is the 'wilderness': sand, rocks and sky and nothing else.
Jesus went to the wilderness!
Place Jesus figure in the wilderness.

It's time to follow Jesus into the wilderness!
Lead the children in marching on the spot.
1, 2, 3, 4 . . . 1, 2, 3, 4 . . .

I am going to follow Jesus,
I am going to follow Jesus,
I am going to follow Jesus,
follow, follow Jesus!

For all other stories in this unit:
We follow Jesus all the way to the cross.
　If you're using a cross, show the cross to the group.
Lead the children in crossing arms on your chest.
Let's show the way of love –
the cross – on our chest as we follow Jesus.

Cross and uncross your arms across your chest as you sing:
I am going to follow Jesus,
I am going to follow Jesus,
I am going to follow Jesus,
follow, follow Jesus!

Gathering Song: The Journey to the Cross unit: Option 2

→ **Song:** 'Take up your cross' © Sharon Moughtin.
→ **Tune:** 'On Ilkla moor baht 'at' (traditional).

'Take up your cross and fol-low me!' Can you hear Jesus calling? 'Take up your cross and fol-low me!' 'Take up your cross and fol-low me!' O yes! I'll fol-low you! O yes! I'll fol-low you! O yes! I'll fol-low you!'

Jesus' friends, 'the disciples', followed Jesus everywhere.
Then one day Jesus said,
'If you want to come with me . . .
take up your cross and follow me!'
'Take up your cross' means 'pick up your cross'.

> *First week:*
> We've got a new song to learn.
> First of all, can you show me a cross shape with your body?
> *Lead the group in making a cross shape by stretching out arms and standing up straight.*
> 'My turn', 'your turn':
>
> 'Take up your cross and follow me!' *Cross arms on chest*
> **'Take up your cross and follow me!'** *Cross arms on chest*
> Can you hear Jesus calling? *Hand to ear*
> **Can you hear Jesus calling?** *Hand to ear*
>
> Let's sing that all together:
> **'Take up your cross and follow me!'** *Cross shape*
> **Can you hear Jesus calling?** *Hand to ear*
>
> And then we sing Jesus' words 'Take up' twice. Listen:
> 'Take up your cross and follow me!' *Cross shape*
> 'Take up your cross and follow me!' *Cross shape*
> Can you sing that?
> **'Take up your cross and follow me!'** *Cross shape*
> **'Take up your cross and follow me!'** *Cross shape*
>
> Let's practise saying yes to Jesus
> and taking up our cross to follow Jesus.
> O yes! I'll follow you! *Marching with crossed arms*
> O yes! I'll follow you! *Marching with crossed arms*
> O yes! I'll follow you! *Marching with crossed arms*
> **O yes! I'll follow you!** *Marching with crossed arms*
> **O yes! I'll follow you!** *Marching with crossed arms*
> **O yes! I'll follow you!** *Marching with crossed arms*
>
> Let's sing that all together:

All groups:
'Take up your cross and follow me!' *Cross shape*
Can you hear Jesus calling? *Hand to ear*
"Take up your cross and follow me!' *Cross shape*
'Take up your cross and follow me!' *Cross shape*

Let's practise saying yes to Jesus
and taking up our cross to follow Jesus.
O yes! I'll follow you! *Marching with crossed arms*
O yes! I'll follow you! *Marching with crossed arms*
O yes! I'll follow you! *Marching with crossed arms*

Jesus says 'Take up your cross and follow me!'
Taking up our cross means
following God's way of love like Jesus.
Lead group in crossing arms on chest.
Look! Our action for taking up the cross
is the same as the sign for love!
When Jesus calls us to take up the way of the cross. *Cross shape*
Jesus calls us to follow the way of love! *Cross arms on chest*

But what is the way of love?
The way of love is lots of things!
We'll find out in our story today!

As we get ready to hear today's story,
let's sing our song one more time,
and practise following Jesus.

'Take up your cross and follow me!' *Cross shape*
Can you hear Jesus calling? *Hand to ear*
'Take up your cross and follow me!' *Cross shape*
'Take up your cross and follow me!' *Cross shape*
O yes! I'll follow you! *Marching with crossed arms*
O yes! I'll follow you! *Marching with crossed arms*
O yes! I'll follow you! *Marching with crossed arms*
Repeat as appropriate.

Gathering Song: Jesus Is Alive! Alleluia! unit: Option 1

→ Song: 'When all the world was sleeping'. Words © Sharon Moughtin.
→ Tune: 'Wide awake' © Mollie Russell-Smith and Geoffrey Russell-Smith, also known as 'The dingle, dangle scarecrow'. It is now published by EMI Harmonies Ltd.

The music for 'Wide awake' is under copyright so can't be reproduced here but can be found online by searching for 'Dingle dangle scarecrow'. A sung version of 'When all the world was sleeping' can be found on the Sowing Seeds website.

Skip this Gathering Song if you're telling the 'Jesus Is Alive! Alleluia!' story this week as this song features as part of the Interactive Bible Storytelling.

Let's tell the story of Easter Day with our song.
On Good Friday, Jesus died on the cross.
Let's hold our hands out in love like Jesus on the cross.
Lead the children in stretching arms out to the side.

His friends took Jesus' body down from the cross.
Let's be Jesus' friends.
Lead the children in miming holding Jesus' body gently.

They put it gently into the Dark Cave
Lead the children in miming placing Jesus' body in the tomb,
and rolled the stone across.
Lead the children in rolling a large stone across.

They went home feeling very, very, very sad.
Nothing happened for one whole night and day after that.
But then the night after, something very, very special . . .
something amazing happened!

Lead the children in curling up on the floor or crouching to sing:
When all the world was sleeping
and the sun had gone to bed . . .
up jumped Lord Jesus *Jump up with hands in the air*
and this is what he said: *Hands out, palms up*

'I am risen, risen, risen, *Wave hands high in the air*
I have won us a new start!' *'New Start' sign (see p. 8) over head*
I am risen, risen, risen, *Wave hands high in the air*
I have won us a new start!' *'New Start' sign over head*
Repeat.

Gathering Song: Jesus Is Alive! Alleluia! unit: Option 2

→ Song: 'Let's praise the Lord! Alleluia!' (unknown)
→ Tune: 'Let's praise the Lord! Alleluia!' (unknown)

We're going to sing a song
that is full of the Church's 'Alleluia!' shout of joy now.

> *If your group is singing this song for the first time, you may find the following introduction helpful.*
> Let's learn the words to a new song,
> 'my turn' *Point to self*, 'your turn' *Leader's hands out to group*.
>
> *Singing:* 'Allelu, allelu, allelu, alleluia!
> Let's praise the Lord!
> **Allelu, allelu, allelu, alleluia!**
> **Let's praise the Lord!**
> *And again:* 'Allelu, allelu, allelu, alleluia!
> Let's praise the Lord!
> **Allelu, allelu, allelu, alleluia!**
> **Let's praise the Lord!**
>
> Then our words go the other way around!
> *Singing:* Let's praise the Lord! Alleluia!
> Let's praise the Lord! Alleluia!
> **Let's praise the Lord! Alleluia!**
> **Let's praise the Lord! Alleluia!**
>
> *Singing:* Let's praise the Lord! Alleluia!
> Let's praise the Lord!
> **Let's praise the Lord! Alleluia!**
> **Let's praise the Lord!**
>
> Let's try that all together.
> **Allelu, allelu, allelu, alleluia!**
> **Let's praise the Lord!**
> **Allelu, allelu, allelu, alleluia!**
> **Let's praise the Lord!**
> **Let's praise the Lord! Alleluia!**
> **Let's praise the Lord! Alleluia!**
> **Let's praise the Lord! Alleluia!**
> **Let's praise the Lord!**
> *Repeat until the children are confident. If you feel the group is ready, you could split the group as indicated below, or you may like to leave this for another week.*

We're going to split into two groups.
Split the group in half, making sure there are confident singers in both groups.

Over here *Indicate clearly* is the 'Alleluia!' team.
Over here *Indicate clearly* is the 'Let's praise!' team.

You're going to sing the 'Alleluias!' *Point to the 'Alleluia!' team*
You're going to sing the 'Let's praise the Lords!' *Point*

When you're singing, you can stand up!
When you're not singing, sit down again!

And remember. We're going to show 'Alleluia!' with our whole body.
Let's raise our hands to sing 'Alleluia!' and 'Praise the Lord!' *Arms in 'V' shape*

Let's go:
Allelu, allelu, allelu, alleluia! *'Alleluia!' team stand to sing with arms raised*
Let's praise the Lord! *'Let's praise' team stand to sing with arms raised*
Allelu, allelu, allelu, alleluia! *'Alleluia!' team stand to sing with arms raised*
Let's praise the Lord! *'Let's praise' team stand to sing with arms raised*

Getting Ready for Bible Storytelling

Getting Ready for Bible Storytelling: Option 1

→ **Action:** opening your group's box and naming this week's object.

This Building Block is especially helpful for groups that include babies and toddlers who might need support with some of the vocabulary in the story. See the beginning of the weekly storytelling material for ideas of items to place in your box.

Invite one of the children to open the box.
What's in the box? *Ask the child to respond*

Getting Ready for Bible Storytelling: Option 2

→ **Song:** 'Jesus, open up my eyes'. Words: © Sharon Moughtin.
→ **Tune:** 'Michael, row the boat ashore' (traditional).

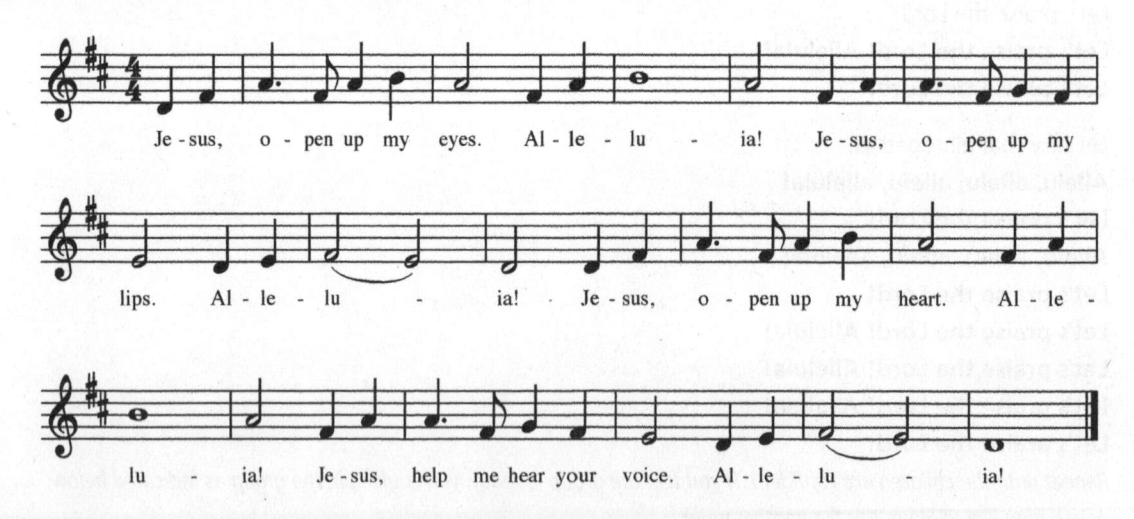

Je-sus, o-pen up my eyes. Al-le-lu-ia! Je-sus, o-pen up my lips. Al-le-lu-ia! Je-sus, o-pen up my heart. Al-le-lu-ia! Je-sus, help me hear your voice. Al-le-lu-ia!

This option has been created for churches who mark themselves with a cross three times before the reading of the Gospel in their church, to support children in understanding what is happening.

It's time to open the Bible.
Let's get ready!
Let's take our thumb *Lead children in showing thumb*
and draw our cross on our eyes, *Draw cross*
and our lips, *Draw cross*
and our heart. *Draw cross*
Let's ask Jesus to help us get ready to listen out for God!

Jesus, open up my eyes. Alleluia!
Trace a cross between your eyes.
Jesus, open up my lips. Alleluia!
Trace a cross on your lips.
Jesus, open up my heart. Alleluia!
Trace a cross on your heart.
Jesus, help me hear your voice. Alleluia!
Cup your hands behind your ears.

Interactive Bible Storytelling

See the Bible Storytelling material in Part 1 of this book.

Saying Sorry to God

Choose from one of the Saying Sorry options below according to which unit you're in.

Introduction to Saying Sorry: The Journey to the Cross unit

Cross arms on chest.
[In Lent/In life] we follow Jesus on the way of love,
the way of the cross. *Look down at your crossed arms*
Let's say sorry for the times
we haven't followed Jesus well.
When we haven't loved as Jesus loves.
Let's sing/say sorry to God with our Sorry Song.

Sometimes we get it wrong and make God or other people sad.
It's time to sing our Sorry Song.

Introduction to Saying Sorry: Jesus Is Alive! Alleluia! unit

Invite the children to sit in a circle for a moment of quiet.
Jesus burst from the Dark Cave.
Jesus showed us how strong love is!

But we don't always love like God loves. *Shake head*
Sometimes we get it wrong and make God or other people sad.
It's time to sing our Sorry Song.

Saying Sorry to God

→ Song: 'The Sowing Seeds Sorry Song'. Words: © Sharon Moughtin.
→ Tune: © Sharon Moughtin.

With my hands on my head, I re-mem-ber the things I've thought to-day, I re-mem-ber the things I wish I'd thought a diff'-rent way. I'm sor-ry, I'm sor-ry, I wish I could start a-gain. I'm sor-ry I'm sor-ry, I wish I could start a-gain.

> ### The 'I'm Sorry' and 'New Start' signs
> The 'I'm Sorry' and 'New Start' signs that appear repeatedly in this unit are among the very few Sowing Seeds signs and actions that are fixed. Usually, the children are trusted with the responsibility for creating the actions for the songs and storytelling as the hope is that this will become *their* story and *their* song (p. 2). However, the 'I'm Sorry' and 'New Start' signs have been chosen for the resonances they create through the material. Videos of both signs can be found on the website next to the Sorry Song Building Block in any of the units.
>
> ### The 'I'm Sorry' sign
> The 'I'm Sorry' sign not only conveys sadness. It calls to mind the waters of baptism being splashed over us. The echoes of an 'X' shape not only show that we know that we've got something wrong, but can also call to mind at the same time the cross of Jesus in the background. Start with your hands lightly crossed in front of your forehead, then move them in opposing arcs downwards towards your chest and round in opposing circles, and back just in front of your forehead. This opposing circular motion is the 'I'm Sorry' sign.

The 'New Start' sign

The 'New Start' sign can best be described as the 'winding' action from the nursery rhyme 'Wind the bobbin up'. Repeatedly rotate your arms around each other in front of your body. It shows that we want a chance to 'start again' but it has been chosen to point us also to the rolling away of the stone on Easter Day that brings about that great 'new start' for the whole world. The 'New Start' sign appears and reappears in so many of the stories. It's the sign for:

- Mary's song about the 'topsy turvy God who turns things upside down' (which is sung in response to John's prophetic somersault)
- 'The first will be last and the last will be first' in God's revolutionary, 'topsy turvy' kingdom (that we touched on above)
- Jesus turning the tables 'topsy turvy' in the Temple – 'Look! Jesus is giving the Temple a new start!'
- Jesus washing the disciples feet, as the longed for king turns everything upside down to become the servant
- The prayer 'Holy Spirit, come!' as Jesus' friends wait for the Spirit who will turn their lives (and the world) topsy turvy at Pentecost
- Paul falling 'topsy turvy' off his horse when he meets Jesus and is given his 'new start'.

And more. Keep an eye out for the 'New Start' sign in the storytelling. It creates a golden thread of forgiveness and can appear in the most surprising of places!

Let's put our hands on our head.
I wonder if there's anything we've thought this week
that we wish we hadn't thought?

Lead the children in placing your hands on head, singing:
With my hands on my head,
I remember the things I've thought today,
I remember the things I wish I'd thought a different way.

I'm sorry, I'm sorry, *'I'm Sorry' sign twice*
I wish I could start again. *'New Start' sign*
I'm sorry, I'm sorry, *'I'm Sorry' sign twice*
I wish I could start again. *'New Start' sign*

Let's put our hands by our mouths.
I wonder if there's anything we've said this week
that we wish we hadn't said?

With hands by mouth, singing:
With my hands on my mouth,

I remember the things I've said today,
I remember the things I wish I'd said a different way.

I'm sorry, I'm sorry, *'I'm Sorry' sign twice*
I wish I could start again. *'New Start' sign*
I'm sorry, I'm sorry, *'I'm Sorry' sign twice*
I wish I could start again. *'New Start' sign*

Let's cross our hands on our chest.
I wonder if there's anything we've done this week
that we wish we hadn't done?

With hands crossed on chest, singing:
With my hands on my chest,
I remember the things I've done today,
I remember the things I wish I'd done a different way.

I'm sorry, I'm sorry, *'I'm Sorry' sign twice*
I wish I could start again. *'New Start' sign*
I'm sorry, I'm sorry, *'I'm Sorry' sign twice*
I wish I could start again. *'New Start' sign*

Continue with a Saying Sorry Action or move straight to 'God Gives Us a New Start', below.

Saying Sorry Action

You don't need to use a Saying Sorry Action. For some groups the song will be enough. However, if you would like to, choose from the following options according to which unit you're in.

Saying Sorry Action: any unit: Option 1

→ Psalm 103.12
→ Action: crumpling a piece of paper to show how you feel when you're cross or sad and placing it in a basket.

Invite two children to give out a piece of paper to everyone who would like one.
Name and Name are going to bring round some paper.
If you like, you can take a piece of paper
and hold it in the air
to show that there are things that you wish you hadn't done.

As the paper is given out, lead the group in singing the 'I'm Sorry' refrain.

Once all the children and adults who wish to take a piece of paper have done so:
When we do things that make God or other people sad,
it can make us feel sad and cross inside.
Let's crumple our paper up to show how we can feel
when we know we've made someone feel sad.
Let's put our feelings into the paper.

Lead the children in crumpling your paper to show your feelings: crossly, with frustration, sadly, etc. For example:
I'm feeling cross with myself for making my friend feel sad.
I'm going to put my crossness into this paper.
Crumple the paper crossly.
Whatever we're feeling, we can give our feelings to God.
Name is going to bring this basket around.
If you like, you can put your paper in the basket
and give it to God.

While all the children and adults who wish to place their paper in the basket do so, lead the group in singing the 'I'm Sorry' refrain.

Place the basket in the centre of the circle or on a focal table, if you use one (see p. 188).
Continue with one of the New Start Actions in the 'God Gives Us a New Start' Building Block on p. 168.

Saying Sorry Action: any unit: Option 2

→ **Action: crumpling a piece of paper with *other* people's feelings and placing it in a basket.**

Invite two children to give out a piece of paper to everyone who would like one.
Name and *Name* are going to bring round some paper.
If you like, you can take a piece of paper
and hold it in the air
to show that there are things that you wish you hadn't done.

As the paper is given out, lead the group in singing the 'I'm Sorry' refrain.

Once all the children and adults who wish to take a piece of paper have done so . . .
Sometimes we can do things that make OTHER people sad.
Let's crumple our paper up to show
how we can make other people feel when we hurt them.
Let's put their feelings into the paper.

Lead the children in crumpling your paper with feelings: e.g. crossly with frustration, or gently with sadness, etc.
We can do things that hurt other people.
The Good News is:
we can give the hurtful things we've done to God
and God will give us a new start.
Name is going to bring this basket around.
If you like, you can put your paper in the basket
and give it to God.
Let's ask God for a new start.

While all the children and adults who wish to place their paper in the basket do so, lead the group in singing the 'I'm Sorry' refrain.

Place the basket in the centre of the circle or on the focal table (see 'Setting Up' on the website).

We've said sorry to God.
I wonder if there's anyone else you need to say sorry to this week?

Continue with one of the New Start Actions in the 'God Gives Us a New Start' Building Block on p. 168.

Saying Sorry Action: any unit: Option 3

→ **Micah 7.19; Psalm 38.4; Hebrews 12.1; Matthew 11.28**
→ **Action: placing a pebble on a piece of fabric or in a bowl of water.**

Make sure the pebbles are large enough not to present a choking hazard and that this action is appropriate for your current group. For instance, assess whether they are likely to be thrown.

Invite two children to take around two baskets of pebbles to everyone who would like one.
Name and *Name* are going to bring round some pebbles.
If you like, you can take a pebble
and hold it in the air
to show there are things you wish you hadn't done.

As the pebbles are given out, lead the group in singing the 'I'm Sorry' refrain.

Once all the children and adults who wish to take a pebble have done so:
Let's hold our pebble in our hand.
Lead the children in weighing the pebble in their hand.

When we do things that make God or other people sad,
it can make us feel heavy and weighed down inside
like this pebble weighs our hand down.

When we're feeling sad and heavy,
we can give our feelings to God.

Place a basket, a piece of fabric, or a bowl of water in the centre of the circle and invite the children to place their pebble within it. Or ask two children to take baskets around the circle to collect the pebbles.

> *If your group is using water, make sure it's in a container that is deep and transparent, so the children can see their pebbles sinking:*
> The Bible says:
> God will sink all our wrong things
> to the bottom of the sea!
> Let's put our pebbles in gently
> and watch them sink to the bottom.
> Let's imagine God sinking the wrong things we've done
> to the bottom of the sea.

Let's give our sad and heavy feelings
to God now as we sing.

While all the children and adults who wish to place their pebbles do so, lead the group in singing the 'I'm Sorry' refrain.

The Good News is:
God always wants to give us a new start!
God doesn't want us to carry round
things that make us feel sad and heavy!
God takes them from us!
After three, let's jump up high
and shout 'God gives me a new start!'

1, 2, 3 . . . God gives me a new start!
Let's use our new start to share God's love this week!

Saying Sorry Action: The Journey to the Cross unit: Option 1

→ **Action: taking some 'rubbish' and giving it to God the Maker to be transformed into blossom.**

For small groups

You will need:

- a 'sorry tree'
  Either: a large tree branch held in a Christmas tree holder or in a bucket filled with stones and sticky tack;
  Or: one or more copies of the bare tree template (see p. 194 or website) printed on white or blue paper.

- a wastepaper basket/battered cardboard box or old container with white and/or pink crumpled tissue/crepe/coloured paper torn into pieces that will look like blossom when crumpled up into a ball (not too big). If you've printed your tree outline on white paper, pink tissue paper will help to create a contrast.

Show the group the box of rubbish.
Show the group the torn paper.

Here's some rubbish.
When we do things that make God or other people sad,
it can make US feel like rubbish:
If you like, you could tear a little piece of paper off this rubbish
and crumple it up.
Let's show how we feel when we're feeling rubbish!

While this is taking place, lead the group in singing the 'I'm Sorry' refrain.

When everyone who wishes to take some paper has done so:
The Good News is:
when we feel like rubbish . . . God LOVES rubbish!

It's time to give our rubbish to God the Maker.
Place your tree in the centre of the circle.

> *Either (real tree):* Let's take our rubbish paper
> and stick it on our sorry tree.
> *Or (printed tree):* Let's place our rubbish paper on our sorry tree.

While this takes place, lead the group in humming/singing again.
When the group is ready:
What looked like rubbish becomes beautiful blossom,
a sign of new life!
God can make amazing things with rubbish!
After 3, let's say, 'God gives us a new start!'
1, 2, 3 . . . God gives us a new start!

Expect some of the blossom to end up looking as if it's blown from the tree or fallen to the floor. This is what blossom does!

Saying Sorry Action: The Journey to the Cross unit: Option 2

➔ **Action: crumpling a piece of tissue/crepe paper to show how you feel when you're feeling 'rubbish' and giving it to God the Maker to be transformed into blossom.**

For large groups

You will need:

- a 'sorry tree'
  one or more copies of the bare tree template (see p. 194 or website) printed on white or blue paper.
- a wastepaper basket/battered cardboard box or old container with white and/or pink crumpled tissue/crepe/coloured paper torn into pieces that will look like blossom when crumpled up into a ball (not too big). If you've printed your tree outline on white paper, pink tissue paper will help to create a contrast.

Show the group the box of rubbish.

When we do things that make God or other people sad,
it can make us feel 'rubbish':
Like we've ruined everything!

Name and *Name* are going to bring some paper around now.
If you like, take a piece and crumple it up.
Let's make our paper into rubbish!
Let's show how we feel when we're feeling rubbish!

While this takes place, lead the group in singing the 'I'm Sorry' refrain.

When the group is ready:
The Good News is:
when we feel like rubbish . . . God LOVES rubbish!

It's time to give our rubbish to God the Maker.
Place your trees in the centre of the circle upside down to show the 'rubbish' back.
Here's another piece of rubbish!
Turn it over to show the trees.
But look, this rubbish has been made into saying sorry trees!

> *Either:*
> As we sing, let's give our rubbish to God.
> Let's put our crumpled-up paper on our sorry trees.
> *Or:*
> *Name* and *Name* are going to come around now
> and collect our rubbish to give to God.

While this takes place, lead the group in humming/singing again. If the paper has been collected by children, ask them to gently tip it out over the pictures of the bare trees so they look like blossom.

When the group is ready:

What looked like rubbish becomes beautiful blossom,
a sign of new life!
God can make amazing things with rubbish!
After 3, let's say, 'God gives us a new start!'

1, 2, 3 . . . God gives us a new start!

Expect some of the blossom to end up looking as if it's blown from the tree or fallen to the floor. This is what blossom does!

Saying Sorry Action: The Journey to the Cross unit: Option 3

→ **Action: dipping finger in water and drawing a cross on forehead.**

This option is particularly appropriate for churches that use sprinkling with water ('asperges') during Lent.
If relevant, it's particularly appropriate to use the same water that will be used in your main church service.
If there is an older child present who is unlikely to spill the water you could invite him or her to take the water around the circle.
You may wish to ask more than one child to take a bowl around the circle, going opposite ways or starting at different points in the circle. Alternatively take a bowl around yourself and/or ask adults to help.

One of the ways we get ready in Lent
is by making sure our hearts are clean and ready.
In Lent, we're sprinkled with water *Action like rain falling*
and we ask God to make us clean
Not just on the OUTside *Rub arm*
but on the Inside. *Trace circle around heart*

> *If appropriate (adapt accordingly):*
> Did you see the water being sprinkled in church?
> *Or:* Right now the adults are being sprinkled with water!

Name is going to bring this bowl of water around.
If you like, you can dip your finger into it *Show finger*
and draw a cross on your forehead. *Demonstrate*
Let's ask God to wash our hearts clean.

While this takes place, lead the group in singing the 'I'm Sorry' refrain.

When the group is ready:
The Good News is:
God always wants to give us a new start!
After 3, let's shout, 'God gives us a new start!'

1, 2, 3: God gives us a new start!

Saying Sorry Action: Jesus Is Alive! Alleluia! unit: Option 1

→ **Action: bursting out of a 'Dark Cave'.**

When we do things that make God or other people sad,
it can make us feel like we're in a Dark Cave.
Let's curl up in a ball as if we're inside a Dark Cave
feeling sad and lost.
Lead the children in curling up on the floor, or crouching.

Jesus' love is stronger than the dark!
Jesus burst out from the Dark Cave!
We can burst from OUR Dark Caves with Jesus.

After 3, let's get ready to burst out of our cave with Jesus.
Let's jump and shout, 'Alleluia! God gives me a new start!'

1, 2, 3 . . . *Lead the children in jumping up with hands in the air*
Alleluia! God gives me a new start!

Saying Sorry Action: Jesus Is Alive! Alleluia! unit: Option 2

→ **Action: dipping finger in water and drawing a cross on forehead.**

This option is particularly appropriate for churches that use sprinkling with water ('asperges') during Easter.
If relevant, it's particularly appropriate to use the same water that will be used in your main church service.
If there's an older child present who is unlikely to spill the water you could invite her or him to take the water around the circle. You may wish to ask more than one child to take bowls around the circle, going opposite ways or starting at different points in the circle. Alternatively take a bowl around yourself and/or ask adults to help.

At Easter, we remember our baptism!
The special moment when we promised to follow Jesus
and to love everyone as Jesus loves.

We sprinkle everyone with water
to help us remember when water was sprinkled on our head.
Mime sprinkling water.

> *If appropriate (adapt accordingly):*
> Did you see the water being sprinkled in church?
> *Or:* Right now the adults are being sprinkled with water!

Name is going to bring this bowl of water around.
If you like, you can dip your finger into it *Show finger*
and draw a cross on your forehead. *Demonstrate*

Let's remember our baptism
and our promise to follow Jesus.
If you haven't been baptized,
you could ask God
to help you get ready for baptism.

While this takes place, lead the group in singing the 'I'm Sorry' refrain.
When the group is ready:
The Good News is:
God always wants to give us a new start!
After 3, let's shout, 'God gives us a new start!'
1, 2, 3: God gives us a new start!

Let's use our new start to follow Jesus.

Saying Sorry Action: Jesus Is Alive! Alleluia! unit: Option 3

→ **Action: placing coloured tissue paper on a cross (on a tray if it will be carried around the group) or in an Easter Garden (see p. 60).**

Invite two children to give out pieces of coloured tissue paper.
Name and *Name* are going to bring around some paper.
If you like, you can take a piece and hold it in the air
to show that there are things that you wish you hadn't done.

As the paper is given out, lead the group in singing the 'I'm Sorry' refrain.

When the group is ready:
When we do things that make God or other people sad,
it can make us feel sad and cross inside.
Let's crumple our paper up to show how we can feel
when we know we've made someone feel sad.
Let's put our feelings into the paper.

Jesus' love was stronger than
> *Either:* the Dark Cave
> *Or:* the cross,

and stronger than every wrong thing.

Jesus' love is so strong that it can change
even dark things into beautiful things.

As we sing, let's give our paper and feelings to God.
Let's put it on
> *Either:* our empty cave
> *Or:* our cross.

As leader, place your paper on the garden/cross as an example.
Look! The paper looks like little flowers
springing up to new life.
Let's watch God's love changing
> *Either:* the Dark Cave
> *Or:* the cross

into something beautiful with our sorries.

Lead the group in singing again as the paper is placed. Some groups may like to ask two children to take the cross or garden around the group as you sing so the other children can stay in their places. Once the paper has been collected, the cross or garden can then be placed in the centre of the circle.

When the group is ready:
Look at our beautiful garden/cross!
After 3, let's shout, 'Alleluia! *Hands raised* God gives me a new start!
1, 2, 3 . . . Alleluia! *Hands raised* **God gives me a new start!**

Saying Sorry Action: Jesus Is Alive! Alleluia! unit: Option 4

→ Action: sunbathing in God's love.
→ Song: 'Alleluia! Jesus Christ, the Son, is ris'n!' Words: © Sharon Moughtin.
→ Tune: 'If you're happy and you know it, clap your hands' (traditional).

[Musical notation with lyrics: "Al-le-lu-ia! Jesus Christ, the Son, is ris'n! Al-le-lu-ia! Jesus Christ, the Son, is ris'n! And God's love will shine on us! God's love will shine on us! Al-le-lu-ia! Jesus Christ, the Son, is ris'n!"]

When we do things that make God or other people sad,
it can make us feel dark inside,
like the sun's stopped shining.

Let's close our eyes and feel the dark.
Lead the children in closing eyes for a moment.

> **Tip**
> There is a uniquely English traditional wordplay on the 'Son rising' and the 'sun rising' on Easter Day that's worth celebrating!

On Easter Day, Jesus 'rose',
like the sun 'rises' in the morning!

Let's open our eyes and show the light of God's love
rising like the sun.
Let's crouch down low . . .
Lead the children in crouching down.
Let's show the sun coming up and up and out . . .
in the morning:
Lead the children in showing the sun rising with your hands as you stand up, holding hands together in front of your chest then reaching up and out.
up, and up, and out!

Now let's hold our faces up to the sun
and imagine God's love,
warm and bright,
shining on our face and body,
and all over us like the warm sun!
Let's hold our arms out.
Lead the children in holding arms forwards with hands up.
Imagine sunbathing in the warm light of God!

> Optional:
> *Lead the children in singing:*
> **Alleluia! Jesus Christ, the Son, is ris'n!**
> **Alleluia! Jesus Christ, the Son, is ris'n!**
> **And God's love will shine on us!**
> **God's love will shine on us!**
> **Alleluia! Jesus Christ, the Son, is ris'n!**
>
> *When learning this song for the first time, you could teach it 'my turn' Point to self, 'your turn' Leader's hands out to group.*
> Let's learn a song about sunbathing in God's love!

> "There's something about sunbathing that tells us more about what prayer is like than any amount of religious jargon. When you're lying on the beach or under the lamp, something is happening, something that has nothing to do with how you feel or how hard you're trying. You're not going to get a better tan by screwing up your eyes and concentrating. You give the time, and that's it. All you have to do is turn up. And then things change, at their own pace. You simply have to be there where the light can get at you . . .
>
> [To pray] all you need to do is to be where the light can get at you – in this case, the light of God's love. Give the time and let go of trying hard (actually this is the difficult bit). God is there always. You don't need to fight for his attention or make yourself acceptable. He's glad to see you. And he'll make a difference while you're not watching, just by radiating who and what he is in your direction. All he asks is that you stay there with him for a while, in the light. For the rest, you just trust him to get on with it."
> ROWAN WILLIAMS[3]

Saying Sorry Action: Jesus Is Alive! Alleluia! unit: Option 5

→ **Action: placing small 'x' shapes on a cross or Easter Garden (see p. 60).**

For groups with school-aged children, who might be familiar with the idea of an 'x' and 'getting it wrong'.

Sometimes it can feel like we've got it wrong.

Name and *Name* are going to bring around a basket of 'x's as we sing.
If you like, you can take an 'x' shape
and hold it up to show
you know you've got some things wrong.
Model holding up the 'x' so it looks like an 'x' (and not Jesus' cross).

As the crosses are given out, lead the group holding up their 'x' and singing the 'I'm Sorry' refrain.

When the group is ready:
We all do things that are wrong.
When Jesus died,
he took all our wrong things onto HIS cross.
Jesus' cross is our cross as well.

Let's turn our 'x' shapes around . . .
Lead the children in turning the 'x' shape around to look like a † shape.
Look! They look like Jesus' cross!
Let's give our 'x's to Jesus
and make his cross into our cross too.

Lead the group in singing again as the crosses are placed on either your Easter Garden next to Jesus' cross, or onto a larger cross. Some groups may like to ask two children to carry the garden or cross around the circle on a tray to collect the little crosses. The garden/cross can then be placed in the centre of the circle.

When the group is ready:
If we give our cross to Jesus,
the Dark Cave becomes our Dark Cave too!

Let's curl up in the Dark Cave with Jesus.
Lead the children in curling up on the floor.

After 3, let's burst out of the cave with Jesus.
Let's shout, 'Alleluia! *Hands raised* God gives me a new start!'
1, 2, 3: Alleluia! God gives me a new start!

God Gives Us a New Start

Every time of Saying Sorry should end by assuring the children that God gives them a new start. Most Sowing Seeds Saying Sorry Actions already include this promise of a new start. If they don't – or if you've created your own Saying Sorry Action – you should choose from one of the following New Start options, or create your own assurance of forgiveness. You could also choose to move straight from the Sorry Song to God's promise of a new start, without any Saying Sorry Action.

New Start Action: any unit: Option 1

→ **Action: tracing a cross/smile on each other's forehead.**

The Good News is:
God always wants to give us a new start!

Let's turn to the person next to us
and show that God gives us a new start.
Let's take our thumb/finger *Show thumb/finger*
And draw a cross/smile on that person's forehead *Draw a cross/smile in the air*

If your group is drawing a smile, add:
to show that God is very happy with us!

Let's say, 'God gives you a new start!'
Then let the other person give you a new start, too!

When the group has finished showing each other God's new starts:
Let's use our new start to share God's love this week!

New Start Action: any unit: Option 2

→ **Action: standing up and hugging each other.**

The Good News is:
God always wants to give us a new start!

Let's help someone next to us stand up from the floor.
Then let that person help you stand up too!
Lead the children in helping each other stand up.

Then let's give each other a hug and say:
'God gives you a new start!'

When the group has finished showing each other God's new starts:
Let's use our new start to share God's love this week!

New Start Action: any unit: Option 3

→ **Song: 'God loves to give me a new start!' Words: © Sharon Moughtin.**
→ **Tune: 'Give me oil in my lamp' (traditional).**

The Good News is:
God always wants to give us a new start!
Let's sing our New Start song together.

God loves to give me a new start! *Trace a smile/cross on own forehead*
How amazing God's love for me! *Cross hands on chest*
God loves to give me a new start! *Trace a smile/cross on own forehead*
How amazing is God's love for me!

Sing hosanna! Sing hosanna! *Wave hands in the air*
Sing hosanna to the King of Kings!
Wave hands in the air followed by crown on head.

Sing hosanna! Sing hosanna! *Wave hands in the air*
Sing hosanna to the king!
Wave hands in the air followed by crown on head.

Prayers for Other People

Introduction to Prayers: The Journey to the Cross unit

It's time for us to take ourselves to a quiet place
to pray like Jesus.
Let's sit in a circle and have a moment of quiet.

Introduction to Prayers: Jesus Is Alive! Alleluia! unit

It's time for us to bring our prayers to the Risen Jesus,
who loves to meet with us.

Prayers for Other People: Option 1

→ Song: 'Jesus, hear our prayer!' Words: © Sharon Moughtin.
→ Tune: 'Brown girl in the ring' (traditional).

For the world: Jesus, hear our prayer. For the Church: Jesus, hear our prayer. For our place London: Jesus, hear our prayer. Lord Jesus, hear our prayer. A - men. For the sick and lonely: Jesus, hear our prayer. For our friends and family: Jesus, hear our prayer. For ourselves: Jesus, hear our prayer. Lord Jesus, hear our prayer. A - men. Take our prayers: Jesus, hear our prayer. Make them holy: Jesus, hear our prayer. Make them beautiful: Jesus, hear our prayer. Lord Jesus, hear our prayer. A - men.

Invite the children to sit in a circle in a moment of quiet.
Let's imagine holding our prayer gently,
Hands together gently in traditional prayer gesture, but cupped so you can imagine a prayer inside.
and then let it go up in prayer to God.
Hands opened upwards to God.

Jesus *Hands together, cupped*
hear our prayer. *Hands opened upwards to God*
Let's pray . . .

For the world:	**Jesus, hear our prayer!**
Make a circle shape.	*Open hands upwards to God.*
For the Church:	**Jesus, hear our prayer!**
Praying hands.	*Open hands upwards to God.*
For our place, London*	**Jesus, hear our prayer!**
Hands down moving out in a semi-circle to show the land around us.	*Open hands upwards to God.*

Lord Jesus, hear our prayer. Amen.
Open hands upwards to God.

* Insert local area/school/church/community/parish.

For the sick and lonely:	**Jesus, hear our prayer!**
Fingers showing tears falling down cheeks.	*Open hands upwards to God.*
For our friends and family:	**Jesus, hear our prayer!**
Arms around yourself.	*Open hands upwards to God.*
For ourselves:	**Jesus, hear our prayer!**
Both hands on heart.	*Open hands upwards to God.*

Lord Jesus, hear our prayer. Amen.
Open hands upwards to God.

Let's close our eyes for a moment.
I wonder if there's someone special
you'd like to pray for?
Let's imagine that person now.

Now, let's imagine Jesus coming to them.
Does Jesus say anything?
Does Jesus do anything?

Let's open our eyes.
Continue with one of the Prayer Action options outlined below. Once the Prayer Action has been completed, you may like to use the following verse to close this time of prayer.

Take our prayers:	**Jesus, hear our prayer!**
Hands together gently.	*Open hands upwards to God.*
Make them holy:	**Jesus, hear our prayer!**
Hands together gently.	*Open hands upwards to God.*
Make them beautiful:	**Jesus, hear our prayer!**
Hands together gently.	*Open hands upwards to God.*

Lord Jesus, hear our prayer! Amen.
Hands together gently, then open hands upwards to God.

Prayers for Other People: Option 2

→ Song: 'The Sowing Seeds little prayers song'. Words © Sharon Moughtin.
→ Tune: 'Frère Jacques' (traditional).

For our food, For our food, thank you, God. thank you, God. For our teach-ers, For our teach-ers, thank you, God. thank you, God. For Rach-el's Nan-ny, For Rach-el's Nan-ny, hear our prayer. hear our prayer. For peo-ple with no homes, for peo-ple with no homes, hear our prayer. hear our prayer.

These prayers are especially suited to churches that prefer less traditional prayer forms.
 Either: choose what you'd like the group to pray for before the session.
 Or: ask the children at this point if there is anything or anyone that they'd like to pray for. Ask them or others to suggest actions.

You will need two different 'thank you' suggestions and two different 'hear our prayer' suggestions. Try to encourage at least one prayer for other people outside the group.

Invite the children to sing after you, repeating your words and their actions. Sometimes it might be almost impossible to fit the child's own words in! It's really valuable to do this where possible, resisting the urge to try and 'neaten' their suggestions.

For *our foo-ood,*
For *our foo-ood,*
Thank you, God!
Thank you, God!

Fo-r *our teachers,*
Fo-r *our teachers,*
Thank you, God!
Thank you, God!

For *Rachel's Nanny,*
For *Rachel's Nanny,*
Hear our prayer!
Hear our prayer!

For *people with no homes,*
For *people with no homes,*
Hear our prayer!
Hear our prayer!

Having sung your prayers, you could insert a Prayer Action, repeat the process or move straight on to close with the following (or other words that remain the same each week).

For today,	Point hands down for 'now'
For today,	Point hands down for 'now'
Thank you, God!	Open hands upwards to God or hands together in prayer
Thank you, God!	Open hands upwards to God or hands together in prayer

Fo-r your love,	*Cross hands on chest*
Fo-r your love,	*Cross hands on chest*
Thank you, God!	*Open hands upwards to God or hands together in prayer*
Thank you, God!	*Open hands upwards to God or hands together in prayer*

Prayer Actions

You don't need to use a Prayer Action. For some groups the song will be enough. However, if you would like to, choose from the following options.

Prayer Action: The Journey to the Cross unit: Option 1

→ **Action: placing leaves on a prayer tree.**

For small groups

You will need:

- *a 'prayer tree': a large tree branch held in a Christmas tree holder or in a bucket filled with stones and sticky tack;*
- *little green leaves cut from green paper.*

Place your tree in the centre of the circle.
Lent means 'springtime'.

In the spring we see new life
and new beginnings starting all around us.
We see tiny leaves growing on the trees.
We can be part of bringing
God's new life to the world when we pray.

Place your baskets of leaves and sticky tack at the base of the tree.
If you like, you can take a leaf.
You can stick it on our prayer tree
and ask God to hear it as a prayer.

While this takes place, hum the tune together, singing the words 'Jesus, hear our prayer' or 'Hear our prayer' as a refrain. When the group is ready:
This Lent, let's watch new life grow
on our prayer tree and in our lives as we pray.

Prayer Action: The Journey to the Cross unit: Option 2

→ **Action: placing blossom on prayer trees.**
You will need:

- *'prayer trees': for instance one or more copies of the bare tree template (see p. 194 or website) printed on white or blue paper.*
- *'blossom': either real blossom, or white/pink tissue/crepe/coloured paper crumpled up into small balls. If you've printed your tree outline on white paper, pink tissue paper will help to create a contrast.*

Place your trees in the centre of the circle.
Lent means 'springtime'.
In the spring we see new life
and new beginnings starting all around us.
We see blossom growing on the trees.
We can be part of bringing
God's new life to the world when we pray.

Show baskets of 'blossom'.
In a moment, *Name* and *Name*

are going to bring around these baskets of 'blossom'.
If you like, you could take some and hold it up.
Let's ask God to hear our blossom as a prayer.

While this takes place, hum the tune together, singing the words 'Jesus, hear our prayer' or 'Hear our prayer' as a refrain. When the group is ready:

> *Either:* As we sing, let's give our blossom prayers to God.
> Let's sprinkle our blossom on our prayer trees!
>
> *Or: Name* and *Name* are going to come around
> with our trees.
> As we sing, let's give our blossom prayers to God.

While this takes place, lead the group in humming/singing again. When your group is ready, end this time of prayer with the final verse of the Prayer Song you've chosen.

This Lent, let's watch new life grow
on our prayer trees and in our lives as we pray.

Expect some of the blossom to end up looking as if it's blown from the tree or fallen to the floor. This is what blossom does!

Prayer Action: The Journey to the Cross unit: Option 3

→ **Action:** placing a small cross as a prayer on a large cross (Jesus' cross) placed on a cloth (purple, if your church uses liturgical colours).

If you're going to ask a child to carry the cross around the group, place the cloth and cross on a tray.
In Lent we follow Jesus on the way to the cross.
Invite two children to take around two baskets of small crosses.
Name and *Name* are going to bring around these baskets of crosses now.
If you like, you can take one of these crosses
and hold it high.
Let's ask God to hear our crosses as a prayer
for ourselves and a special person.

While the crosses are taken around, hum the tune together, singing the words 'Jesus, hear our prayer' or 'Hear our prayer' as a refrain. When your group is ready:
The way of the cross isn't always easy
but we know Jesus is there with us.

> *Either:* place your large cross in the centre.
> You can place your cross prayer with Jesus' cross here.
> Let's ask Jesus to be with us and our special person.
>
> *Or:* ask a child to take a large cross around on a tray.
> *Name* is going to bring Jesus' cross around.
> If you like you can give your cross prayer to Jesus.
> Let's ask Jesus to be with us and our special person.

While this takes place, hum the tune together, singing the words 'Jesus, hear our prayer' or 'Hear our prayer' as a refrain. When the group is ready, end this time of prayer with the final verse of the Prayer Song you've chosen.

Prayer Action: Jesus Is Alive! Alleluia! unit: Option 1

→ **Action:** placing flowers as prayers on an Easter Garden (p. 60). These could be real flowers, silk flowers, paper flowers, 'flowers' made from tissue/crepe paper, or pictures of flowers, etc.

Show the children the flowers you have chosen in one or more baskets or trays.
Name and *Name* are going to bring around these baskets of flowers.
If you like, you can take a flower.
Let's ask God to see these flowers as a prayer for a special person.

Hum the tune together, with the words 'Jesus, hear our prayer' or 'Hear our prayer' as a refrain, until all the children and adults who wish to take a flower have done so.
Place your Easter Garden in the centre of the circle.

> *If you have not already asked this question:*
> Can anyone tell me what this is?
> *Accept the child's response.*

The Easter Garden and empty cave
remind us that Jesus burst from the Dark Cave at Easter.
We all have new life!

If you like, you can place your flower in our garden as a prayer.
This Easter, let's watch new life and beautiful things
growing in our garden and our lives as we pray.

Hum the tune together again while everyone places their flowers. Some groups may like to invite two children to carry the 'garden' around the group to collect the flowers. The garden can then be placed in the centre.
End this time of prayer with the final verse of the Prayer Song you've chosen.

Prayer Action: Jesus Is Alive! Alleluia! unit: Option 2

→ **Action: placing flowers as prayers on a cross (if it will be taken around the group, on a tray). These could be real flowers, silk flowers, paper flowers, 'flowers' made from tissue/crepe paper, or pictures of flowers, etc.**

Show the children the flowers you have chosen in one or more baskets or trays.
Name and Name are going to bring around these baskets of flowers.
If you like, you can take a flower.
Let's ask God to see these flowers as a prayer for a special person.

Hum the tune together, with the words 'Jesus, hear our prayer' or 'Hear our prayer' as a refrain, until all the children and adults who wish to take a flower have done so.

When the group is ready, place the cross in the centre of the circle.
Jesus' love is stronger than every sad thing.
Stronger even than the cross!
If you like, you can place your flower on Jesus' cross as a prayer.
Jesus' love changes the cross into a beautiful thing.
When we pray, we can be part of sharing that love!

Hum the tune together again while everyone places their flowers. Some groups may like to invite two children to carry the cross (on a tray) around the group to collect the flowers. The cross can then be placed in the centre.
End this time of prayer with the final verse of the Prayer Song you've chosen.

Prayer Action: Jesus Is Alive! Alleluia! unit: Option 3

→ **Action: placing flowers as prayers on a 'garden': a tray filled with soil or with brown cloth/paper folded on it. The flowers could be real flowers, silk flowers, paper flowers, 'flowers' made from crumpled tissue/crepe paper, or pictures of flowers, etc.**

At Easter, we see new life starting all around us.
We see trees becoming green with leaves
and flowers beginning to 'blossom'.
We can be part of bringing GOD's new life and love
to the world when we pray!

Show the children the flowers you have chosen in one or more baskets or trays.
Name and Name are going to bring around these baskets of flowers.
If you like, you can take a flower.
Let's ask God to see these flowers as a prayer for a special person.

Hum the tune together, with the words 'Jesus, hear our prayer' or 'Hear our prayer' as a refrain, until all the children and adults who wish to take a flower have done so.

Place your 'garden' in the centre of the circle.

If you like, you can place your flower in our garden as a prayer.

This Easter, let's watch new life and beautiful things 'blossoming' in our garden and our lives as we pray.

Thank You, God

Thank You, God: Option 1

→ Song: 'My hands were made for love'. Words: © Sharon Moughtin.
→ Tune: 'Hickory, dickory, dock' (traditional).

Invite the children to sit in a circle for a moment of quiet.

It's time to remember all the things we've done this week.
It's time to say 'thank you' to God
for when we've been part of showing God's love.

Let's wiggle our fingers!
I wonder when you've shown love
with your hands this week?

Wiggle fingers as you sing.

My hands were made for love!
My hands were made for love!
Thank you for the love they've shown!
My hands were made for love!

Let's wiggle our feet!
I wonder when you've shown love
with your feet this week?

Wiggle feet as you sing.

My feet were made for love!
My feet were made for love!
Thank you for the love they've shown!
My feet were made for love!

Let's put our hands gently on our neck.
Let's sing 'Ahhh!'
Ahhhhh!
Can you feel your throat vibrating and dancing with your voice?
I wonder when you've shown love
with your voice this week?

Hold neck and feel your voice 'dancing' as you sing.

My voice was made for love!
My voice was made for love!

Thank you for the love it's shown!
My voice was made for love!

Thank You, God: Option 2

→ Song: 'For the love we've shown'. Words: © Sharon Moughtin.
→ Tune: 'All through the night' (traditional).

For the love we've shown with our hands, thank you, God! For the love we've shown with our feet, thank you, God! When we love all those around us, it's the same as loving Jesus. For the love we've shown with our voice, thank you, God!

Invite the children to sit in a circle for a moment of quiet.
It's time to remember all the things we've done this week.
It's time to say 'thank you'
for when we've been part of showing God's love.

> *Either:* Let's wiggle our fingers.
> *Or:* Let's hold up our hands.

I wonder when you've shown love
with your hands this week?

> *Either:* Let's wiggle our feet.
> *Or:* Let's show our feet.

I wonder when you've shown love
with your feet this week?

Let's put our hands gently on our neck.
Let's sing 'Ahhh!'
Ahhhhh!
Can you feel your neck vibrating and dancing with your voice?
I wonder when you've shown love
with your voice this week?

Let's sing our 'thank you' song to God
For the times we've been part of sharing God's love.

For the love we've shown with our hands,
Hold hands up or wiggle fingers.
thank you, God!
For the love we've shown with our feet,
Point to feet or wiggle feet.

thank you, God!
When we love all those around us,

Cross hands on chest.
it's the same as loving Jesus!
For the love we've shown with our voice,
Hands on neck or point to singing mouth.
thank you, God!

Thank You, God: Option 3

→ Song: 'We thank you, God, for all that's good'. Words: © Sharon Moughtin.
→ Tune: 'Greensleeves' (traditional).

We thank you God for all that's good that makes us feel alive today! We thank you God for all that's good that makes us want to sing! Thank you for love and life we praise your name for ever! Thank you for love and life we praise your name always!

This option has been created for use in contexts that include adults as well as children of different ages. Groups that only include children up to the age of 7 may prefer to use one of the other 'Thank You, God' options.

Invite the group to sit in a circle for a moment of quiet.

> *If your time together is held during a communion service, you might like to start with these words:*
> Our service today is called a 'Eucharist'.
> Eucharist means thank you!

It's time to remember all the things that we want to say thank you to God for.

> *Optional: Invite two children to give out a wooden or paper heart to everyone who would like one.*
> **Name** and **Name** are going to bring round some hearts.
> If you like, you can take a heart and hold it in the air to say thank you to God.

Lead the group in singing. If your group is not handing out hearts you might like to use the following actions.

We thank you God *Heart shape with fingers* **for all that's good**
that makes us feel alive today. *Jazz hands*
We thank you God *Heart shape with fingers* **for all that's good**
that makes us want to sing! *Twirl finger up from lips to show singing*

> *If your group is giving out wooden or paper hearts, repeat as necessary. Once all the children and adults who wish to take a heart have done so:*

Let's close our eyes for a moment.

Let's remember the times we felt most alive this week!
It might have been spending time with someone special
or doing something you love to do
or seeing something that made you think 'Wow!'

What made you feel most alive this week?
What made you want to sing?

> *Either: if your group has given out hearts:*
> Let's bring all our thank-yous into our circle.
> *Name* is going to bring this basket around.
> If you like, you can put your heart in the basket
> and give it to God as a thank you.
>
> *While all the children and adults who wish to place their hearts in the basket do so, lead the group in singing.*
>
> *Or: if your group has not given out hearts:*
> Let's remember those moments now and thank God for them.
> *Lead the group in singing:*

Thank you for love and life! *Heart shape with fingers*
We praise your name forever! *Jazz hands*
Thank you for love and life! *Heart shape with fingers*
We praise your name always! *Jazz hands*

Repeat the whole song or the second part as appropriate until all hearts that have been given out are gathered and given to the leader or placed on a focal table (see p. 188).

> **Tip**
>
> In whole church worship, this song can also be adapted to be used a prayer at the end of the service, including as a post-communion prayer as follows.

We thank you God for this time today, *Open hands upwards or heart shape with fingers*
for being here with us, *Place hands downwards*
for loving us. *Cross arms on chest*
We thank you God for this time today. *Open hands upwards or heart shape with fingers*
It makes us want to sing! *Twirl finger up from lips to show singing*

Thank you for love and life! *Open hands upwards or heart shape with fingers*
We praise your name forever! *Jazz hands*
Thank you for love and life! *Open hands upwards or heart shape with fingers*
We praise your name always! *Jazz hands*

Creative Response

See the Creative Response starter ideas in Part 3 of this book.

Sharing God's Peace

This Building Block is particularly designed for children's groups that join the adult congregation to share communion but can also be used to end any session or Service of the Word.

Sharing God's Peace: Option 1

→ Isaiah 66.12, NIV
→ Song: 'I've got peace like a river' (traditional).
→ Tune: traditional.

> **Tip: Peace cloth**
>
> Groups that choose to use a peace cloth for the 'Sharing God's Peace' Building Block will need a long piece of blue fabric. The fabric needs to be long enough for all the adults and children to stand around it, and to allow each child to hold a section of the fabric with both hands. It helps to have an adult or older and experienced child standing at each end.

Either: hold one end of the peace cloth and ask one of the older children or an adult to hold the other end. Start singing the Peace Song. As the children begin to gather, invite them to join in holding a small section of the cloth, raising and lowering it so it 'flows' like a river as you sing together.

Or: invite the children to sit in a circle in the worship space. Start singing the Peace Song. As the children begin to gather, invite them to join in raising and lowering their hands like the waters of a flowing river.

I've got peace like a river,
I've got peace like a river,
I've got peace like a river in my soul.
I've got peace like a river,
I've got peace like a river,
I've got peace like a river in my soul.

If your group is about to rejoin the adults for communion: when all the children are gathered, continue with the words of the Peace, below.

Sharing God's Peace: Option 2

→ Isaiah 66.12, NIV
→ Song: 'Peace is flowing like a river' (traditional).
→ Tune: traditional.

Either: hold one end of the peace cloth and ask one of the older children or an adult to hold the other end. Start singing the Peace Song. As the children begin to gather, invite them to join in holding a small section of the cloth, raising and lowering it so it 'flows' like a river as you sing together.

Or: invite the children to sit in a circle in the worship space. Start singing the Peace Song. As the children begin to gather, invite them to join in raising and lowering their hands like the waters of a flowing river.

Peace is flowing like a river,
flowing out through you and me.
Spreading out into the desert,
setting all the captives free.

If your group is about to rejoin the adults for communion: when all the children are gathered, continue with the words of the Peace, below.

Sharing God's Peace: Option 3

→ Song: 'I've got peace in my fingers'. Words: © 1995 Susan Salidor ASCAP.
→ Tune: © 1995 Susan Salidor ASCAP.
→ The words and music can be found on the album *Little Voices in My Head* by Susan Salidor © 2003 Peach Head. They can also be found on iTunes or YouTube, or at <www.susansalidor.com>.

If your group is about to rejoin the adults for communion: when all the children are gathered, continue with the words of the Peace, below.

The Peace

→ 2 Thessalonians 3.16; 1 Peter 5.14

Once you have finished singing . . .
The peace of the Lord be always with you.
Hold hands open to the children.
And also with you.

Invite the children to open their hands towards you.
Let's shake hands or hug each other
and say, 'Peace be with you'
> *Or whatever is said on sharing the Peace in your church*
as a sign of God's peace.

Lead the children in giving and receiving the Peace. If your group is meeting during a communion service, this is a good time to then lead the children back to join the rest of the congregation to continue worship with the Eucharistic Prayer. Or you might like first to sing the 'Around a Table' song with them (see below).

Around a Table

→ Song: 'Around a table'. Words © Sharon Moughtin.
→ Tune: 'On top of Old Smokey' (traditional).

This Building Block is particularly designed for groups that are held during a communion service, either when the children are present throughout, or when the children will be returning to join the rest of the congregation to receive communion.

Around a table *Hold arms out, palms up*
with God's gifts to share.
as sisters and brothers, *Hold hands, or stretch hands out wide towards each other*
we lift up our prayer. *Swing hands to and fro then lift them in prayer*
And bread is broken, *Mime breaking*
and wine is poured. *Mime pouring*
And Jesus is with us *Hold arms out, palms up*
and blesses us all. *Mime placing a hand on a row of heads*
The Spirit is poured out *Palms down above head, moving down*
again and again *Palms down above head, moving down*
and all of God's people *Point around group and beyond*
will shout 'AMEN!' *Cup hands around mouth to shout*

Taking God's Love into the World

→ Song: 'This little light of mine' (traditional).
→ Tune: traditional.

This Building Block is particularly designed for groups that are not held at the same time as a communion service. Alternatively, you could use one of the Peace Songs above to end your worship.

Our time together is coming to an end.
Invite the children to sit in a circle for a moment of quiet.

God has lit a little light of love inside all of us.
Trace a circle on your heart.
Let's make our finger into a candle.
Bring your finger from your heart and hold it out.
Let's be God and light our little light of love together, after 3.
Lead the children in lighting their finger candle by striking an imaginary match in the air on 3 and pretending to light your finger.
1, 2, 3 . . . Tssss!
Let's imagine God's love shining and dancing like light in us.

Wave your finger in front of you.
This little light of mine, I'm gonna let it shine!
This little light of mine, I'm gonna let it shine!
This little light of mine, I'm gonna let it shine!
Let it shine, let it shine, let it shine!

Blow on your finger as if blowing out a candle on 'puff'. Then hold it up high.
Won't let no one *Puff* **it out! I'm gonna let it shine!**
Won't let no one *Puff* **it out! I'm gonna let it shine!**
Won't let no one *Puff* **it out! I'm gonna let it shine!**
Let it shine, let it shine, let it shine!

Hold your finger behind a cupped hand, then take your cupped hand away to reveal the 'candle' and hold it high!
Hide it under a bushel? No! I'm gonna let it shine!
Hide it under a bushel? No! I'm gonna let it shine!
Hide it under a bushel? No! I'm gonna let it shine!
Let it shine, let it shine, let it shine!

Lead the children in placing your finger back on your heart.
Now let's put our little light of love
back in our hearts, where it belongs.
Let's remember to let our little light shine
in all our playing and working today . . .

If you're building a Service of the Word and this is your final Building Block, you may like to close with a familiar blessing, the Peace and/or one of the following.

    Either: Praise the Lord! *Both hands to self*
    Alleluia! *Both arms upwards in 'V' shape*

    Or: Let us bless the Lord. *Both hands to self*
    Thanks be to God. *Both arms upwards in 'V' shape*

    Or: And all the people said . . . *Both hands to self*
    Amen! *Both arms upwards in 'V' shape*

Go in Peace to Love and Serve!

→ Song: 'Go in peace to love and serve!' © Sharon Moughtin.
→ Tune: Bobby Shaftoe (traditional), the same tune as 'I am going to follow Jesus' (p. 11).

Go in peace to love and ser - ve! Go in peace to love and ser - ve!
Go in peace to love and serve! To serve God here! A - men!

This Building Block is particularly designed for groups that are held within a communion service. Alternatively, you could use one of the Peace Songs above to end your worship.

It's time for us to go out into the world!
Go *Point* in peace *Wiggle fingers to show a river*
to love *Cross arms* and serve! *Open hands out*

Let's sing that and point to each other to send each other out
to serve God here in our place!

Go *Point* **in peace** *Wiggle fingers*
to love *Cross arms* **and serve!** *Open hands out*
Go *Point* **in peace** *Wiggle fingers*
to love *Cross arms* **and serve!** *Open hands out*
Go *Point* **in peace** *Wiggle fingers*
to love *Cross arms* **and serve!** *Open hands out*
to serve God! *Open hands out* **here** *Point down*
Amen. *Clap softly twice*

Sowing Seeds resources

Introduction

Sowing Seeds is designed to be sustainable. We aim to use what's already around us rather than buying in lots of new resources. As a starting point, however, we've found the following helpful.

Imaginative aids

Sowing Seeds encourages the use of imaginative aids during the Gathering Song to send a strong signal that this is an environment where imagination is celebrated. Imaginative aids can be anything that the children can use to make shapes and show feelings.

Why use imaginative aids?

- to fire up imaginations
- to familiarize children with active participation
- to present opportunities for worshipping God in ways beyond words
- to give babies the opportunity to explore their bodies and bring them into worship
- to give toddlers and children the confidence to use their whole bodies in worship
- to open up opportunities for babies, toddlers and children to become lost in the moment
- to cut down on preparation time: imaginative aids can become whatever you want them to be!

We tend to use the following imaginative aids but your choice will depend on your space, numbers, imagination and budget. For instance, we've also used fallen autumn leaves to wave during the autumn season.

- hand scarves
- yellow ribbons threaded on to rings
- green streamers on sticks.

For examples of places to purchase these, see the Setting Up page on the website.

If your group is related to a church that uses liturgical colours, you may wish to use imaginative aids that correspond to the season's colour. If your church doesn't use liturgical colours, it may still be worth using only one colour at a time, to prevent upset about which colour each child is given. This will help to keep the emphasis on the children's imagination and how they use the aids rather than on the choice set before them.

The use of imaginative aids during the Gathering Song provides a wonderful opportunity to include any babies who are present and encourage them to take a leading role. Many babies when handed a streamer or dance scarf will instinctively shake it, hide behind it or make some really interesting shapes. We've found that the older children really enjoy copying a baby in her or his innovative actions. They seem to love to discover that babies are individuals, and it's always wonderful to see the reaction of small babies as they realize that everyone is looking to them and following their lead. It can also be a great time to encourage a newcomer or child who may be feeling a little shy to take a lead, where appropriate

Peace cloth

Your group might like to use a peace cloth for the 'Sharing God's Peace' Building Block. Either find a blue piece of fabric that's long and wide enough for all the adults and children to stand around, holding a section with both hands to wave 'the river' up and down as the group sings. (It helps to have an adult or older and experienced child standing at each end.) Alternatively, you could find a long and thin piece of blue fabric or ribbon and stand in a circle, each holding a section with both hands to wave 'the river' up and down as you sing.

Focal table

Your group might like to have a focal table to place objects on during your time together, as indicated in the material. If your church is one that follows liturgical colours, you could place a cloth matching the colour of the season on the table.

Creative Response resources

Sowing Seeds books provide a wide range of creative 'starter ideas' that aim to spark the children's imaginations as well as one or more 'print-and-go' options for each week.

This time of Creative Response is optional but for those groups who choose it, these materials will come in helpful on a weekly basis:

- white paper (different-coloured paper is a nice addition)
- coloured pencils (it's worth getting good-quality pencils that need sharpening less often)
- chunky crayons (for younger children)
- white card (not essential but useful)
- child-safe scissors
- PVA glue kept in small lidded pots with spatulas (for younger children)
- sticks from outside, wooden lollipop sticks or wooden coffee stirrers
- string or wool.

For further ideas for more creative resources, take a look below.

Collage materials

These aren't essential, but will always be useful. Many younger children will not spend long with crayons/pencils and are more likely to enjoy glueing and sticking to make a collage. Most units have suggestions for collaging, which requires little preparation if you have suitable materials to hand.

Gathering a range of textures and patterns as well as colours is ideal. Useful items include:

- scraps of coloured paper discarded by the children when cutting out in the sessions
- coloured envelopes from birthday cards
- felt (you can buy offcuts of felt from eBay)
- scrap material
- offcuts from people who sew
- ends of wool from people who knit
- paper napkins
- string bags used to hold courgettes or satsumas (depending on the type; some fall apart)
- ribbons snipped into small pieces (Christmas and birthdays are good times to keep an eye out for these)
- tinfoil and cotton wool
- newspapers
- broken gift bags or wrapping and tissue paper from presents
- sweet wrappers or gold chocolate-coin wrappers
- packaging from postal parcels
- leftovers from arts-and-crafts sets
- bark or leaves
- sandpaper.

Interesting media

While pencils and crayons are adequate for many Creative Responses, we've found that encouraging the children to explore using different media can be inspirational. When introducing a different medium, make it available during the whole unit to give the children the opportunity to develop their use of it, while also saving time on planning and preparation.

Ideas of the different media that might be useful include:

- pastels, including extra-soft pastels
- chalks
- watercolour paints
- ready mixed paints (using these with shaving brushes can work well for very young children)
- watercolour pencils (for older children, if you have time to show them how they work)
- charcoal
- dyed string or coloured wool soaked in PVA glue
- sticks and mud
- sponges or rollers and paint
- edible cornflour finger paints (see p. 191)
- dyed cooked spaghetti (see p. 190)
- dyed uncooked pasta (see p. 190).

We also encourage the children to draw or paint on different media as well as paper. These might include:

- thick brown or white card
- cardboard from recycling
- stones
- graph paper, lined paper
- pieces of wood (ensure these are free of splinters)
- shells
- fabric, especially pale fabric
- tracing paper or baking parchment
- coloured or textured paper
- patterned wallpaper
- newspaper or magazine cuttings (check these are appropriate before use)
- long rolls of paper taped to the floor with masking tape.

Exploring the possibilities of 'ephemeral' or 'transient' art can give children the opportunity to discover that beautiful things can be fleeting and last only a moment. We don't need to be afraid of the idea that things may not last: we can still celebrate their beauty. Suitable items include:

- things from the natural world, depending on the season: pressed flowers, leaves, grasses, blossom, bark, twigs, sand, berries, stones, shells (check all these for safety)
- buttons
- milk bottle tops of various colours
- dyed cooked spaghetti, or uncooked rice or pasta (see p. 190)
- salt dyed with paint or food colouring
- edible cornflour paint (see p. 191)
- coloured paper in different shapes: squares, circles, triangles, diamonds, rectangles, hexagons, octagons, etc.

Creative materials from home:

- wooden mosaic shapes
- Etch-a-Sketch
- 'Cordz' sets
- felt sets and boards
- magnetic boards and shapes
- ink pads and stamps
- Post-it pads
- Spirograph
- stencils to use with paint or pencils.

Recipes

How to make salt dough

Mix 2 cups of flour with 1 cup of salt and 1 cup of water. If you'd like coloured salt dough, add a few drops of food colouring to the water before mixing. If it's too sticky, add more flour; if it's too dry, add a drop more water. If you're making the dough in advance, it can become sticky when stored, so make sure you take extra flour with you and check the dough before use. The shapes that are made with the salt dough will air-dry in time (unless they're very thick). The dough can also be dried in an oven (on a low heat for around 3 hours) or in a microwave (check every few seconds).

How to dye cooked spaghetti

Cook the spaghetti according to the packet instructions with a little oil, drain it, then immediately run cold water over it in a colander or sieve to stop the cooking. Divide the cooked spaghetti up into bowls according to how many different colours you would like, add food colouring and mix well. Let the spaghetti dry (this takes an hour or so).

How to dye uncooked pasta

Place the uncooked pasta in a bowl. Mix food colouring with ½–1 teaspoon of vinegar. Pour the vinegar dye mix over the pasta and stir well. Once the pasta is fully coated, spread it out in a single layer on a baking tray to dry.

How to dye uncooked rice

Place the uncooked rice in a bowl. Mix food colouring with ½–1 teaspoon of vinegar. Pour the vinegar dye mix over the rice and stir well. Once the rice is fully coated, spread it out in a single layer on a baking tray to dry.

> **Tip**
>
> If you'd like to make dyed pasta or rice with children, you could use sealed food bags or plastic boxes for the mixing: invite a child to shake them until the pasta or rice is fully coated.

How to make bread

This is a simple bread recipe that has worked for us.

500g strong flour

7g (1 sachet) fast-action dried yeast

1 tsp salt

1 tsp sugar

350ml warm water
sunflower oil to grease

To make the dough, put the flour, salt and yeast in a large bowl and form a well in the centre. Pour most of the water into the well and mix to make a slightly wet dough. Add a little more water if needed. Tip the dough out onto a floury surface. Cover your hands with flour, then knead the sticky dough for at least 10 minutes until it's stretchy (you can also do this with a mixer that has a dough hook). Grease a bowl with oil, place the dough in the bowl, cover it and leave it until the dough has doubled in size. When handing the dough out to the children, make sure their table top and hands are floured first and that the dough isn't excessively sticky (add a small amount of flour if it's too wet).

To bake the bread: if possible, leave the dough to rise again once the children have shaped it. Place the dough shapes into a preheated oven (220°C/fan 200°C/gas 7) for around 10–15 minutes according to their size (a full loaf will take more like 30 minutes). Tap the bottom of the shapes to check whether they're cooked: they should sound hollow when they're ready.

How to make edible cornflour paint

This paint is completely edible, but its neutral taste means that babies and toddlers aren't encouraged to eat it.

Mix 4 tablespoons of cornflour in a pan with enough cold water to make a medium-thick paste. Pour in 1 cup of boiling water slowly and stir until there are no lumps. Heat the mixture gently on a hob, stirring continually. Once you see clear streaks in the mixture, turn off the heat but continue stirring as the mixture thickens. Divide the mixture up into separate pots according to how many different colours you're planning, add food colouring and mix well. If you place it in the fridge (where it will keep for a couple of weeks), make sure you take it out and let it reach room temperature before use. If the paint needs thinning to use, add boiling water a drop at a time.

Photocopiable templates

The templates on the following pages are for use with the Creative Response starter ideas.

They are listed here.

Angel (p. 193)

Bare tree (p. 194)

Bird (p. 195)

Bodies (p. 196)

Candle (p. 197)

Chalice (p. 198)

Crosses (p. 199)

Crown (p. 200)

Easter egg (p. 201)

Empty tomb (p. 202)

Face (p. 203)

Finger puppet (p. 204)

Fire (p. 205)

Fish (p. 206)

Hen and chicks (p. 207)

Keys (p. 208)

Large heart (p. 209)

Palm leaf (p. 210)

Picture frame (p. 211)

Postcard (p. 212)

Sheep (p. 213)

Wheel with arrow (p. 214)

Body (large) (p. 215)

Chick (p. 216)

Circle (p. 217)

Jesus (p. 218)

Stained-glass window (p. 219)

Instructions for finger-puppet template

1 Cut the finger puppets out along the thick lines.

2 Fold the flaps along the dotted lines, folding away from you.

3 Again folding away from you, fold the puppet in the middle where the arrow is.

4 Tape the flaps to the other half of the puppet.

Instructions for crown template

1 Cut along zigzag line.

2 Sellotape the two halves together with 1 cm overlap so that you have one long strip.

3 Put the strip round your head so that you can measure where to sellotape the ends.

4 Sellotape the ends together to make a crown.

Instructions for the hatband

1 Fold a sheet of A4 paper in half or thirds lengthways.

2 Open it out and then cut into strips along the folds.

3 Tape or glue the ends together to the required length.

Joy (8) drew this angel. What can you make from it? Or would you like to draw your own? *An alternative angel template is available in Book 1 (p. 213).*

Sowing Seeds actively encourages peer-led learning by children. All our templates are created by children or child-leaders. Copyright © Sharon Moughtin 2017, 2025. From Sharon Moughtin, *Sowing Seeds Book 2: Bible storytelling and worship with children, includes Lent and Easter.*

Joy (8) drew this tree. What can you do with it? Or would you like to draw your own?

Sowing Seeds actively encourages peer-led learning by children. All our templates are created by children or child-leaders. Copyright © Sharon Moughtin 2017, 2025. From Sharon Moughtin, *Sowing Seeds Book 2: Bible storytelling and worship with children, includes Lent and Easter.*

Joy (9) drew this bird. What can you make from it? Or would you like to draw your own?

Sowing Seeds actively encourages peer-led learning by children. All our templates are created by children or child-leaders. Copyright © Sharon Moughtin 2017, 2025. From Sharon Moughtin, *Sowing Seeds Book 2: Bible storytelling and worship with children, includes Lent and Easter.*

Julia (6) drew these bodies. What can you make from them? Or would you like to draw your own? *A larger body template is available on p. 215.*

Sowing Seeds actively encourages peer-led learning by children. All our templates are created by children or child-leaders. Copyright © Sharon Moughtin 2017, 2025. From Sharon Moughtin, *Sowing Seeds Book 2: Bible storytelling and worship with children, includes Lent and Easter.*

Julia (6) drew this candle. What can you make from it? Or would you like to draw your own? *Alternative tall candles are available in Book 1 (p. 219).*

Sowing Seeds actively encourages peer-led learning by children. All our templates are created by children or child-leaders. Copyright © Sharon Moughtin 2017, 2025. From Sharon Moughtin, *Sowing Seeds Book 2: Bible storytelling and worship with children, includes Lent and Easter.*

Sarah (7) drew this chalice. Would you like to decorate it? Or would you like to draw your own?

Sowing Seeds actively encourages peer-led learning by children. All our templates are created by children or child-leaders. Copyright © Sharon Moughtin 2017, 2025. From Sharon Moughtin, *Sowing Seeds Book 2: Bible storytelling and worship with children, includes Lent and Easter.*

Zayden (6) drew these crosses. What can you make from them? Or would you like to draw your own?

Sowing Seeds actively encourages peer-led learning by children. All our templates are created by children or child-leaders. Copyright © Sharon Moughtin, *Sowing Seeds Book 2: Bible storytelling and worship with children, includes Lent and Easter.*

Philip (6) drew this zigzag line. Can you cut down it to make a crown?

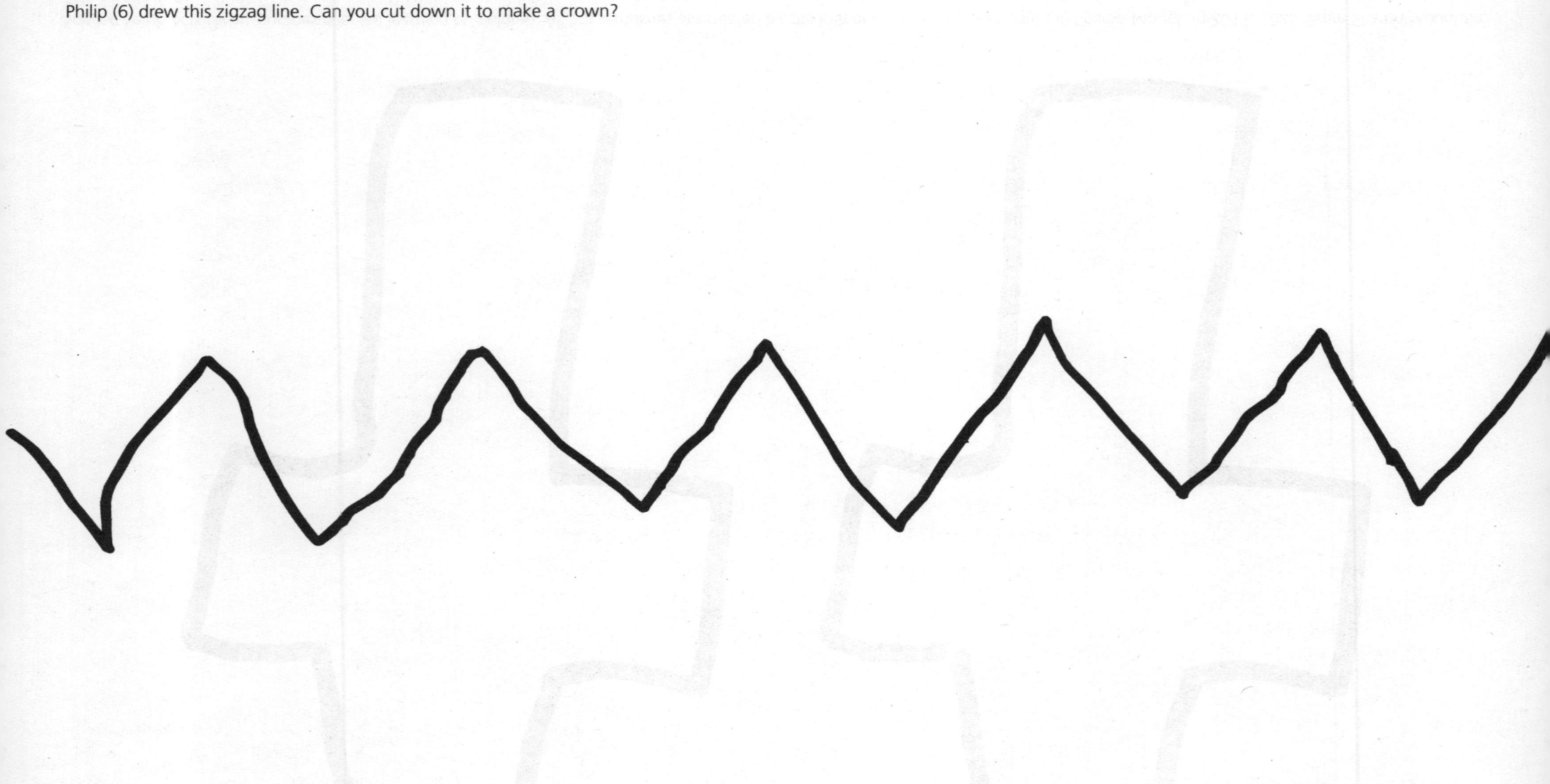

Sowing Seeds actively encourages peer-led learning by children. All our templates are created by children or child-leaders. Copyright © Sharon Moughtin, *Sowing Seeds Book 2: Bible storytelling and worship with children*, includes *Lent and Easter*.

Zayden (6) drew this egg shape. What can you make from it? Or would you like to draw your own?

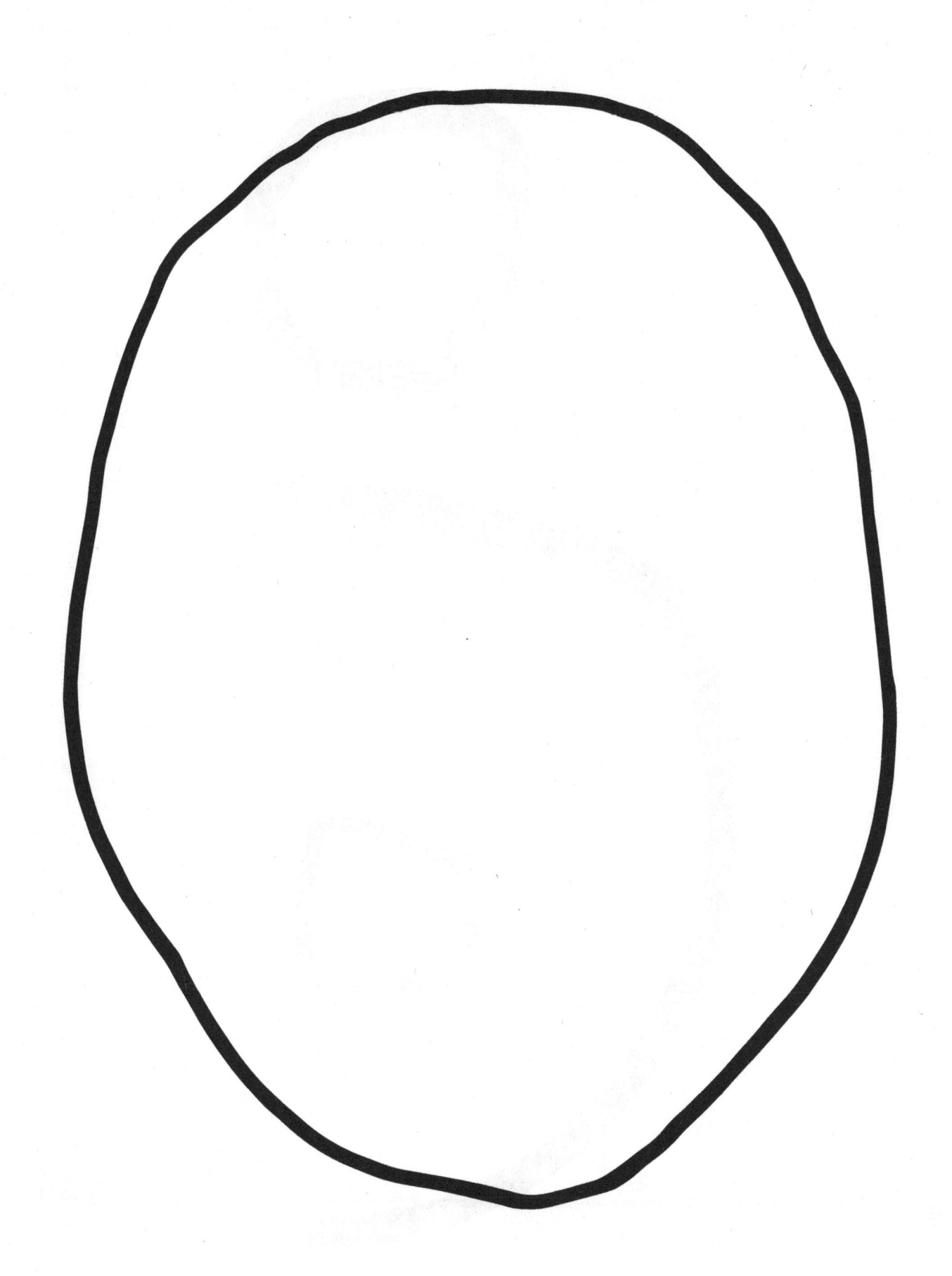

Sowing Seeds actively encourages peer-led learning by children. All our templates are created by children or child-leaders. Copyright © Sharon Moughtin 2017, 2025. From Sharon Moughtin, *Sowing Seeds Book 2: Bible storytelling and worship with children, includes Lent and Easter.*

Abigail (6) drew this Easter tomb. What will you do with it? Or would you like to draw your own?

Sowing Seeds actively encourages peer-led learning by children. All our templates are created by children or child-leaders. Copyright © Sharon Moughtin, *Sowing Seeds Book 2: Bible storytelling and worship with children*, includes *Lent and Easter*.

Kayleigh (7) drew this face. What can you make from it? Or would you like to draw your own? *Another face template is available in Book 1 (p. 222).*

Sowing Seeds actively encourages peer-led learning by children. All our templates are created by children or child-leaders. Copyright © Sharon Moughtin 2017, 2025. From Sharon Moughtin, *Sowing Seeds Book 2: Bible storytelling and worship with children, includes Lent and Easter.*

Isabella (7) drew these finger puppets. Would you like to make them into people? Or would you like to make your own?

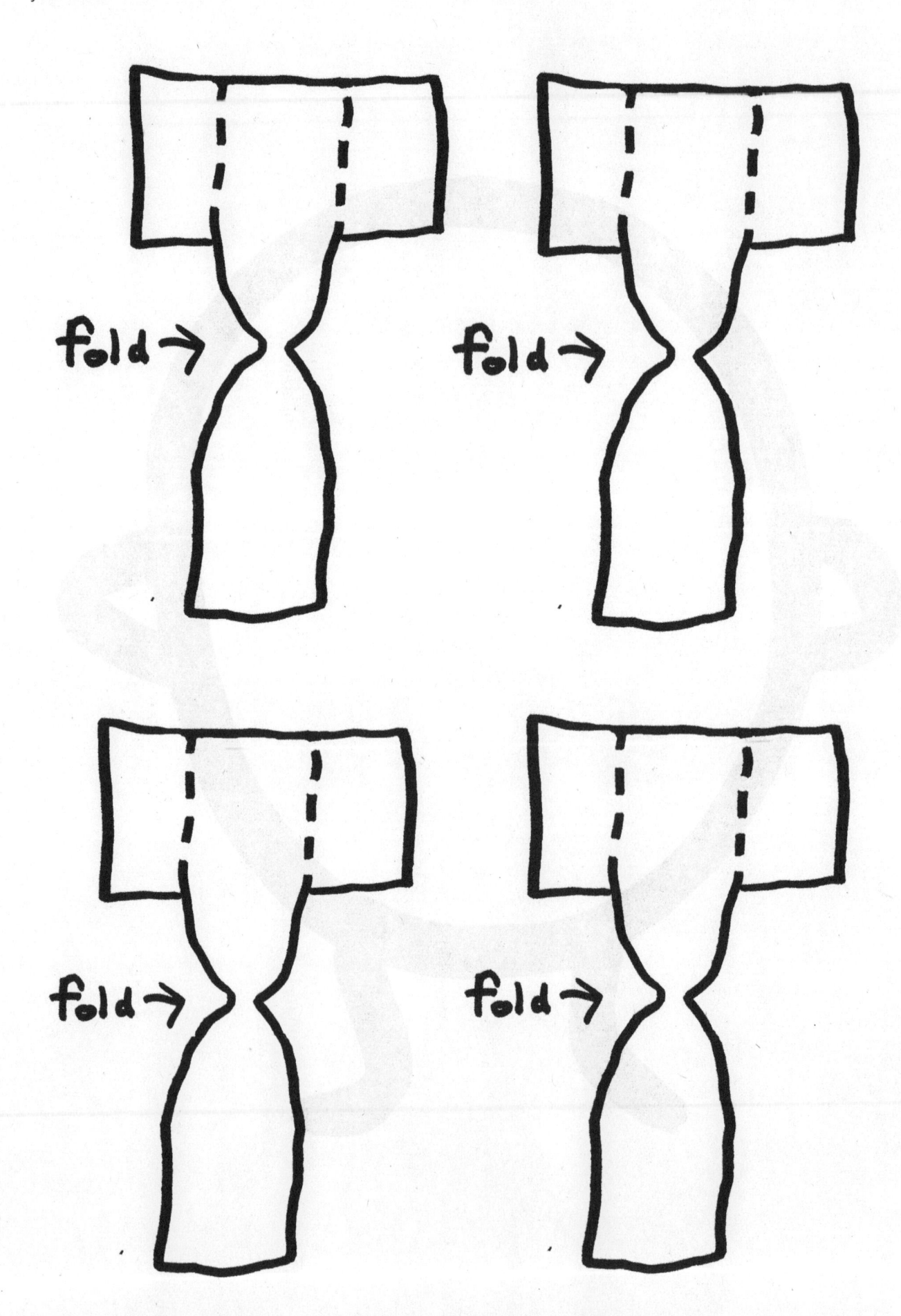

fold →

fold →

fold →

fold →

Sowing Seeds actively encourages peer-led learning by children. All our templates are created by children or child-leaders. Copyright © Sharon Moughtin 2017, 2025. From Sharon Moughtin, *Sowing Seeds Book 2: Bible storytelling and worship with children, includes Lent and Easter*.

Sultan (7) drew this fire. What can you make with it? Or would you like to draw your own?

Sowing Seeds actively encourages peer-led learning by children. All our templates are created by children or child-leaders. Copyright © Sharon Moughtin 2017, 2025. From Sharon Moughtin, *Sowing Seeds Book 2: Bible storytelling and worship with children, includes Lent and Easter.*

Lily (7) drew this fish. What can you make with it? Or would you like to draw your own?

Sowing Seeds actively encourages peer-led learning by children. All our templates are created by children or child-leaders. Copyright © Sharon Moughtin, 2017, 2025. From Sharon Moughtin, *Sowing Seeds Book 2: Bible storytelling and worship with children, includes Lent and Easter.*

Isla (6) drew this hen and chicks. What will you make from them? Or would you like to draw your own?

Sowing Seeds actively encourages peer-led learning by children. All our templates are created by children or child-leaders. Copyright © Sharon Moughtin 2017, 2025. From Sharon Moughtin, *Sowing Seeds Book 2: Bible storytelling and worship with children, includes Lent and Easter.*

Zoe G. (7) and Joy (8) drew these keys. What will you make from them? Or would you like to draw your own?

Sowing Seeds actively encourages peer-led learning by children. All our templates are created by children or child-leaders. Copyright © Sharon Moughtin 2017, 2025. From Sharon Moughtin, *Sowing Seeds Book 2: Bible storytelling and worship with children, includes Lent and Easter.*

Amy (6) drew this heart. What can you make from it? Or would you like to draw your own? *An alternative heart shape is available in Book 1 (p. 226)*.

Sowing Seeds actively encourages peer-led learning by children. All our templates are created by children or child-leaders. Copyright © Sharon Moughtin 2017, 2025. From Sharon Moughtin, *Sowing Seeds Book 2: Bible storytelling and worship with children, includes Lent and Easter.*

Michelle (7) drew this palm leaf. What will you make from it? Or would you like to draw your own?

Sowing Seeds actively encourages peer-led learning by children. All our templates are created by children or child-leaders. Copyright © Sharon Moughtin 2017, 2025. From Sharon Moughtin, *Sowing Seeds Book 2: Bible storytelling and worship with children, includes Lent and Easter.*

Amy (6) drew this picture frame. What can you draw in it? Or would you like to make your own?

Sowing Seeds actively encourages peer-led learning by children. All our templates are created by children or child-leaders. Copyright © Sharon Moughtin 2017, 2025. From Sharon Moughtin, *Sowing Seeds Book 2: Bible storytelling and worship with children*, includes *Lent and Easter*.

Anastasia (8) drew this postcard. What can you write or draw on it? Or would you like to draw your own?

Sowing Seeds actively encourages peer-led learning by children. All our templates are created by children or child-leaders. Copyright © Sharon Moughtin, *Sowing Seeds Book 2: Bible storytelling and worship with children*, includes *Lent and Easter*.

Anastasia (8) drew this sheep. What can you make from it? Or would you like to draw your own?

Sowing Seeds actively encourages peer-led learning by children. All our templates are created by children or child-leaders. Copyright © Sharon Moughtin 2017, 2025. From Sharon Moughtin, *Sowing Seeds Book 2: Bible storytelling and worship with children, includes Lent and Easter.*

Harry (7) drew around a circle shape to make this chart and Amelia (6) drew the arrow. What can you make with it? Or would you like to draw your own?

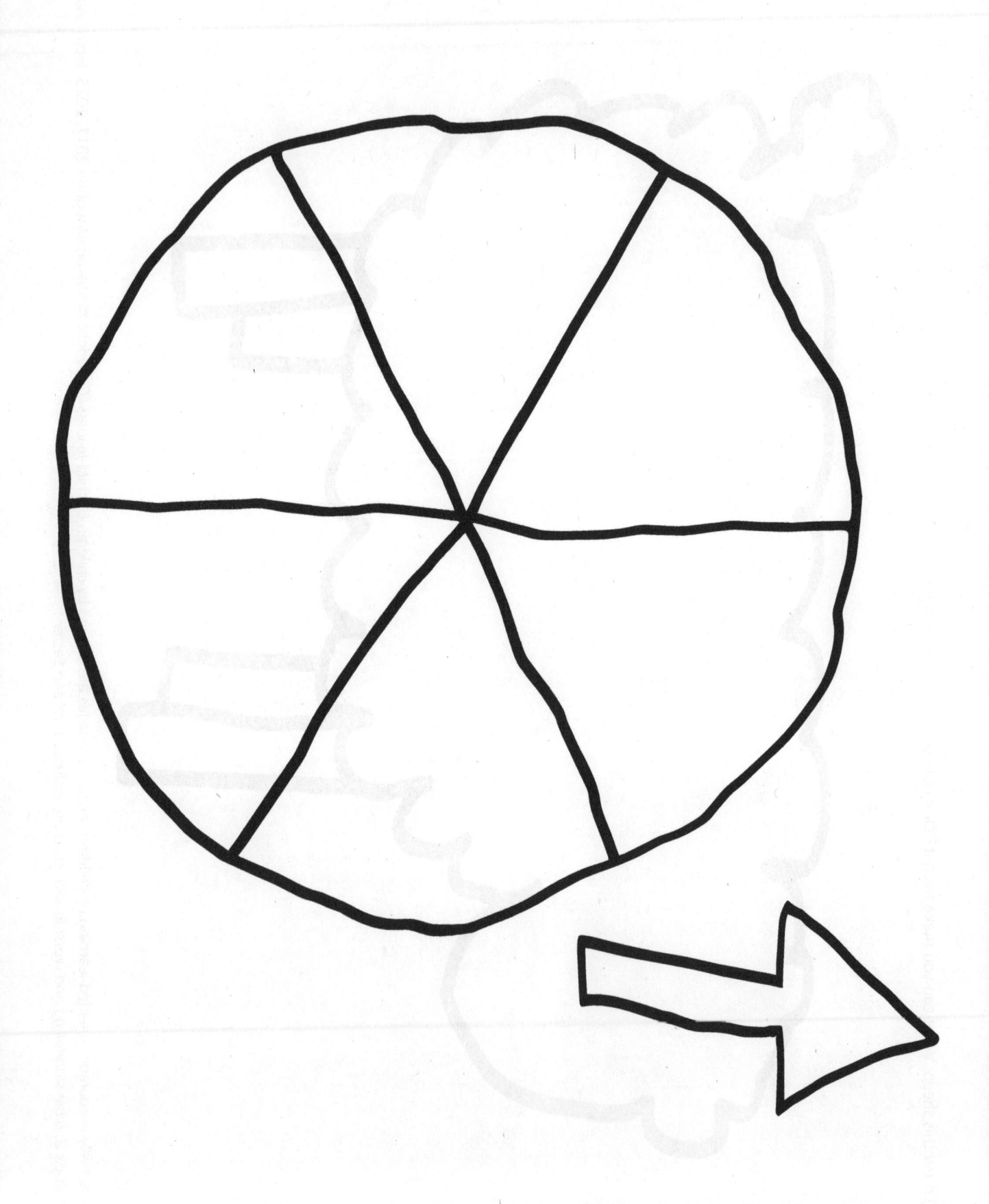

Sowing Seeds actively encourages peer-led learning by children. All our templates are created by children or child-leaders. Copyright © Sharon Moughtin 2017, 2025. *From Sharon Moughtin, Sowing Seeds Book 2: Bible storytelling and worship with children, includes Lent and Easter.*

Julia (6) drew this body. What can you make from it? Or would you like to draw your own?

Sowing Seeds actively encourages peer-led learning by children. All our templates are created by children or child-leaders.
Copyright © Sharon Moughtin 2017, 2025. From Sharon Moughtin, *Sowing Seeds Book 1: Bible storytelling and worship with children, includes Advent, Christmas and Epiphany*.

Nathaniel (3) drew this chick.

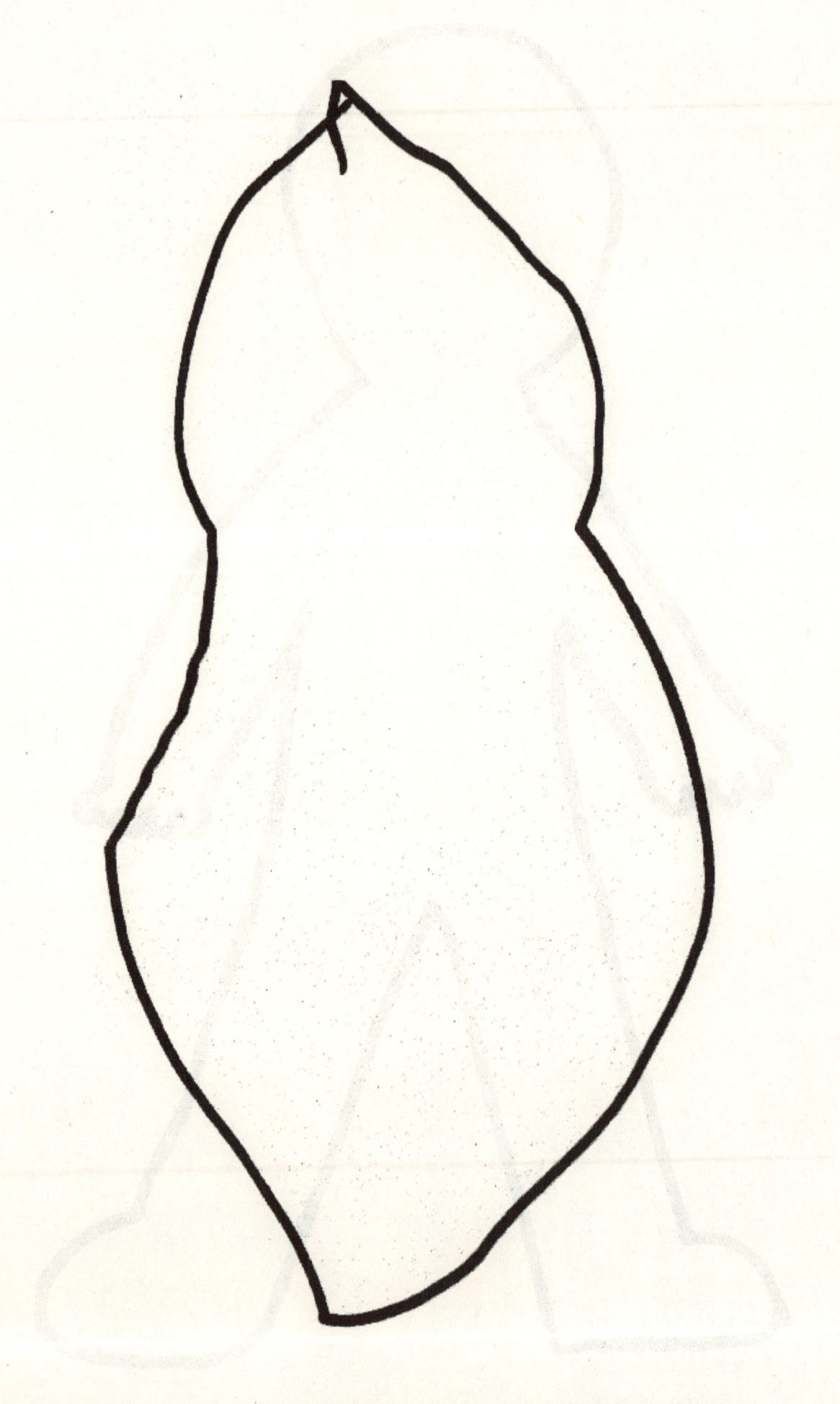

Sowing Seeds actively encourages peer-led learning by children. All our templates are created by children or child-leaders.
Copyright © Sharon Moughtin 2017, 2025. From Sharon Moughtin, *Sowing Seeds Book 1: Bible storytelling and worship with children, includes Advent, Christmas and Epiphany*.

Abigail (6) drew around a plate to make this circle. What can you make from it? Or would you like to draw your own?

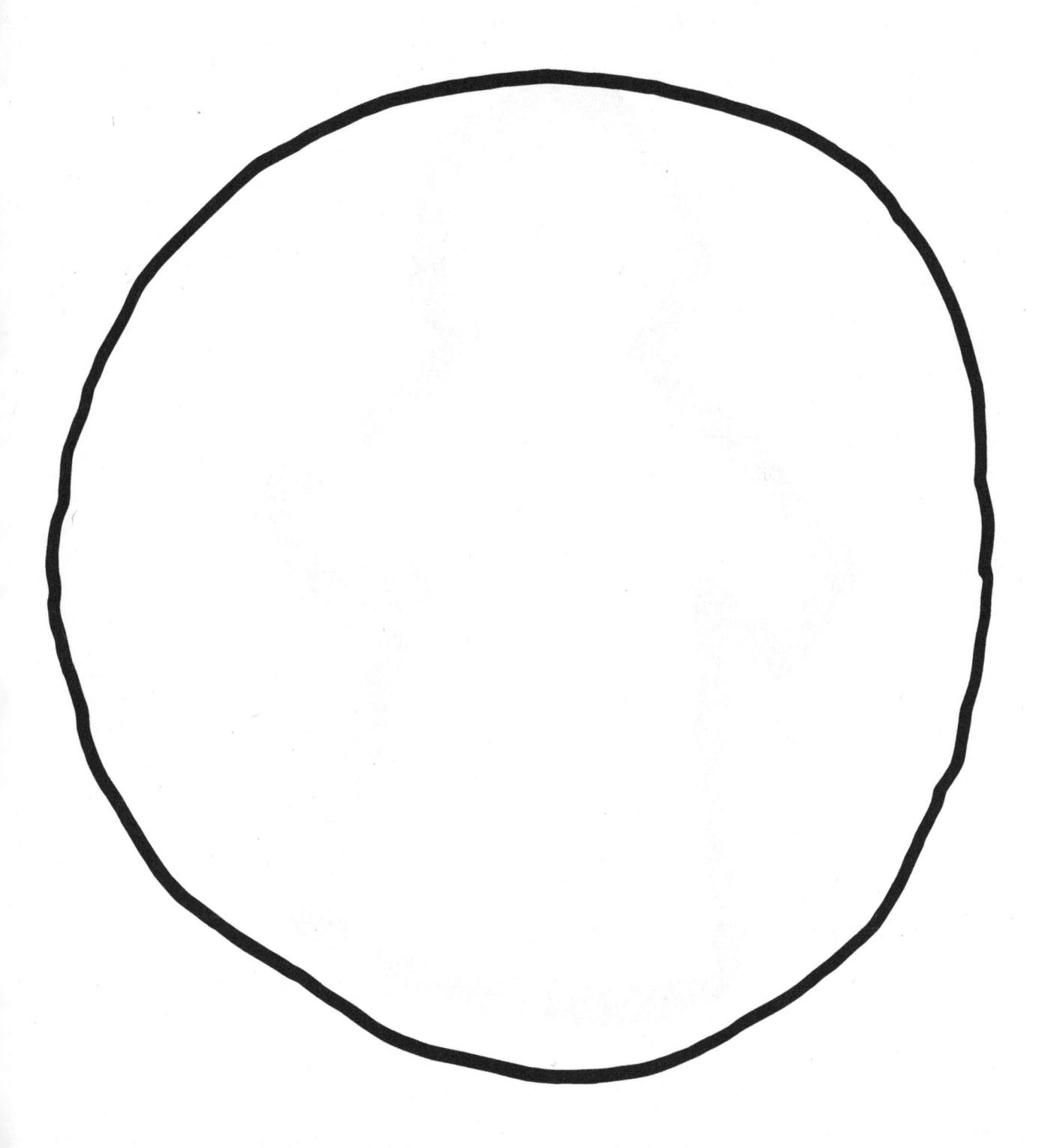

Sowing Seeds actively encourages peer-led learning by children. All our templates are created by children or child-leaders.
Copyright © Sharon Moughtin 2017, 2025. From Sharon Moughtin, *Sowing Seeds Book 1: Bible storytelling and worship with children, includes Advent, Christmas and Epiphany.*

Anastasia drew this figure of Jesus.

Sowing Seeds actively encourages peer-led learning by children. All our templates are created by children or child-leaders.
Copyright © Sharon Moughtin 2017, 2025. From Sharon Moughtin, *Sowing Seeds Book 1: Bible storytelling and worship with children, includes Advent, Christmas and Epiphany.*

Zoe drew this stained-glass window.

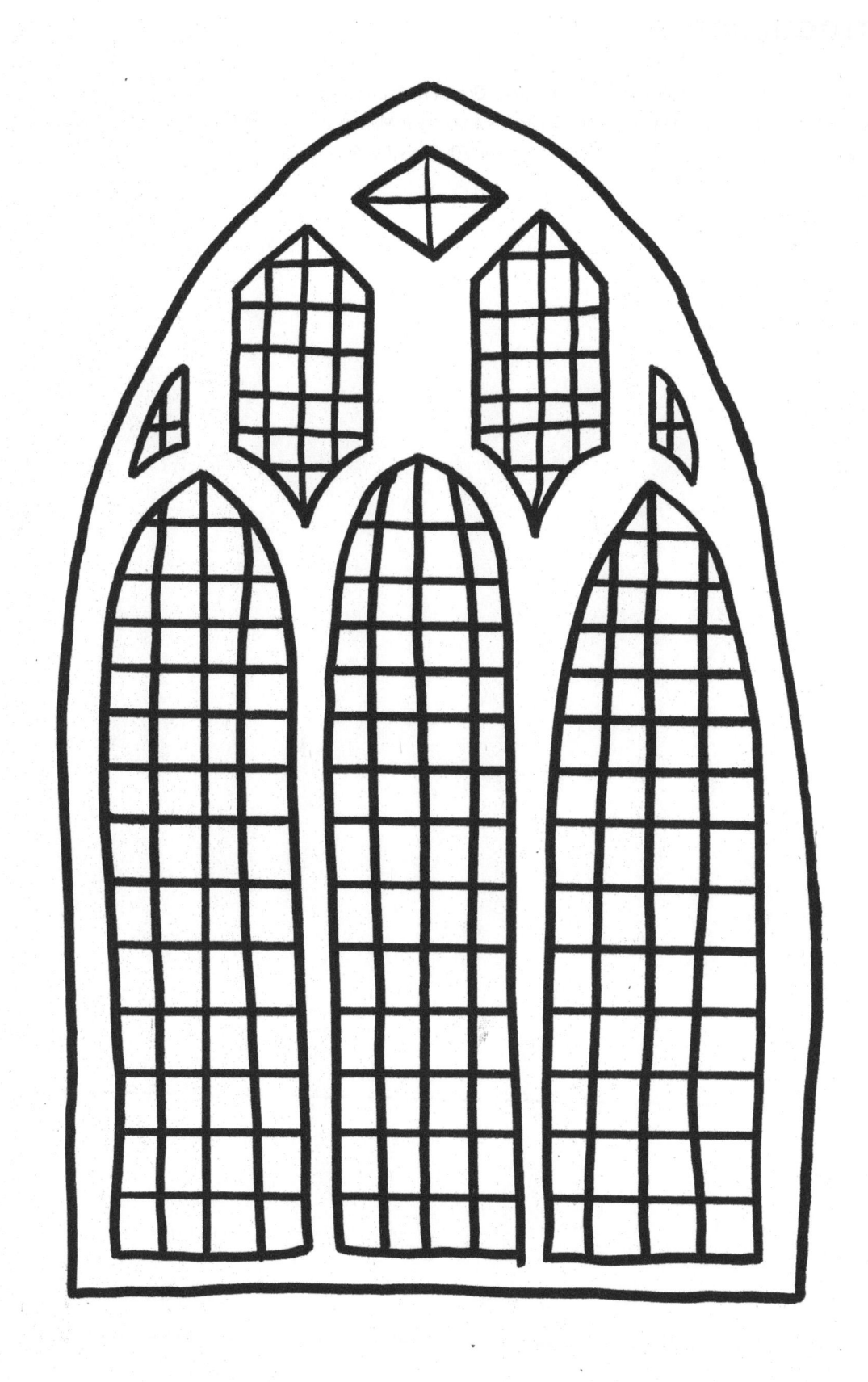

Sowing Seeds actively encourages peer-led learning by children. All our templates are created by children or child-leaders.
Copyright © Sharon Moughtin 2017, 2025. From Sharon Moughtin, *Sowing Seeds Book 1: Bible storytelling and worship with children, includes Advent, Christmas and Epiphany*.

NOTES

Introduction

1 Søren Kierkegaard, *Three Discourses on Imagined Occasions* (1845).
2 See Rebecca Nye, *Children's Spirituality: What It Is and Why It Matters* (London: Church House Publishing, 2009).
3 Rowan Williams, broadcast Tuesday 18 October 2005 on *The Terry Wogan Show*, BBC Radio 2.